BRESCIA COLLEGE
LONDON ONTARIO

Sods, Soil, and Spades

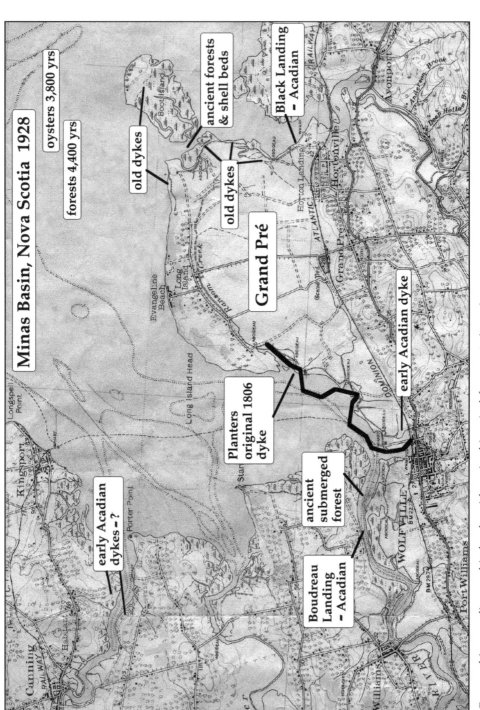

Minas Basin, Nova Scotia 1928

oysters 3,800 yrs

forests 4,400 yrs

old dykes

old dykes

ancient forests & shell beds

Black Landing – Acadian

Grand Pré

early Acadian dyke

Planters original 1806 dyke

ancient submerged forest

Boudreau Landing – Acadian

early Acadian dykes – ?

Geographic area discussed in book, with major historical features indicated.

Sods, Soil, and Spades

The Acadians at Grand Pré and Their Dykeland Legacy

J. SHERMAN BLEAKNEY

McGill-Queen's University Press
Montreal & Kingston · London · Ithaca

Legal deposit fourth quarter 2004
Bibliothèque nationale du Québec

Printed in Canada on acid-free paper

This book has been published with the help of a grant from the Canadian Federation for the Humanities and Social Sciences, through the Aid to Scholarly Publications Programme, using funds provided by the Social Sciences and Humanities Research Council of Canada. Funding has also been received from the Planter Studies Centre, Acadia University, made possible in part by a generous donation from Alex Colville.

McGill-Queen's University Press acknowledges the support of the Canada Council for the Arts for our publishing program. We also acknowledge the financial support of the Government of Canada through the Book Publishing Industry Development Program (BPIDP) for our publishing activities.

Figures were reproduced with permission of the following: Agriculture and Agri-Food Canada, Figure 8.3; Canadian Hydrographic Service, Fisheries and Oceans, Ottawa, Figure 3.4; Conrad Byers Collection, Nova Scotia, Figure 9.5.3; Jeff Wilson Collection, Nova Scotia, Figures 5.3, 9.6.2, 9.6.3; National Air Photo Library, Natural Resources Canada, Figures 5.5, 6.7–6.9, 7.2, 9.1.6, 9.2.3, 9.3.2–9.3.4, 9.4.1, 9.5.5, 9.6.4; National Library and Archives Canada, Fig 9.6.4-small insert; Nova Scotia Archives and Records Management, Figure 9.1.7; Nova Scotia Department of Agriculture and Marketing, Figures 5.2, 6.6, 9.2.2, 9.2.4; Nova Scotia Department of Natural Resources, Figures 2.1, 6.4, 9.1.2–9.1.4; Nova Scotia Registry of Deeds, Figure 9.6.5. Additional aerial photos, ground photos, and graphics by the author.

NATIONAL LIBRARY OF CANADA CATALOGUING IN PUBLICATION

Bleakney, J. Sherman (John Sherman)
Sods, soil, and spades: the Acadians at Grand Pré and their dykeland legacy / J. Sherman Bleakney.
Includes bibliographical references and index.
ISBN 0-7735-2816-4
1. Dykes (Engineering) – Nova Scotia – Grand Pré Region – History.   2. Acadians – Nova Scotia – Grand Pré Region – History.   3. Reclamation of land – Nova Scotia – Grand Pré Region – History.   4. Salt marshes – Nova Scotia – Grand Pré Region – History.   5. Grand Pré Region (N.S.) – History.   I. Title.
TC345.C3B53 2004   627'.549'0971634   C2004-902848-0

Typeset in 11/14 Sabon with Caflisch Script and Scala Sans.

DEDICATION

To *John Frederic Herbin, 1860–1923*, who accomplished his dream of preserving in perpetuity an original Acadian village site as a memorial to his mother's people. In doing so he inadvertently lent credence to Longfellow's mythical heroine Evangeline by providing an authentic physical setting for that Acadian epic tale.

In 1907 he purchased a few acres of the original Grand Pré Acadian village, providentially undisturbed since the Expulsion, and he unselfishly guided its promotion and protection as historic and hallowed ground. Physically the site is small and lacks original structures, but spiritually its dimensions are global, a symbolic shrine for millions of descendants of Acadian exiles, and a geographic site of pilgrimage.

John Herbin's father was a Huguenot, an exile from France, and his mother, Marie-Marguerite Robichaud, was a granddaughter of an original Acadian who had returned to Nova Scotia. It was at his mother's knee that he first heard the tragic tales of Acadian culture and history, tales that would direct his life and be the subject of his exceptional literary talents.

He was a remarkably accomplished person: superb athlete, coach, linguist, archaeologist, historian, archivist, author, goldsmith, jeweller, optometrist, town mayor, and a prolific poet of international stature. His poems can evoke a particular moment or event or emotion in such powerful detail that he was described by Archibald Lampman (in Davies, 1927) as a "landscape painter in verse."

From this wealth of verbal paintings, I have selected short excerpts to introduce some of the chapters in this book. The full poem that follows is presented here because these few descriptive lines, with their layering of contrasting emotions of joy and sorrow, encapsulate the entire Acadian saga.

Across the Dykes

The dykes half bare are lying in the bath
Of quivering sunlight on this Sunday morn;
And bobolinks aflock make sweet the worn
Old places, where two centuries of swath
Have fallen to earth before the mowers' path.
Across the dykes the bell's low sound is borne,
From green Grand-Pré, abundant with the corn,
With milk and honey which it always hath.
And now I hear the Matins o'er the plains,
See faith bow many a head that suffered wrong,
Near all these marshes taken from the tide.
The vision of their last great sorrow stains
The greenness of these meadows. In the song
Of birds I feel a tear that has not dried.

J.F. Herbin, 1909, 14

John Herbin died suddenly on 29 December 1923, while taking his accustomed contemplative evening stroll on his beloved Grand Pré dykelands, the wellspring of his literary creativity.

CONTENTS

APPENDICES

FIGURES AND TABLES

FIGURES

TABLES

Retirement opens up such wonderful opportunities. You can endlessly and uninterruptedly pursue any momentary interest. Such is the origin of this book. After some forty years of investigating marine biological aspects of the Minas Basin, famous as the site of the world's highest tides, I became interested in how the first Europeans, as opposed to fish and invertebrates and plants, had adapted to this dynamic macrotidal regime.

During my biological surveys I often noticed intriguing remnants of their construction efforts, but the available literature proved to be an inadequate source of answers for the questions I was asking myself.

This book is essentially a progress report on my continuing quest for answers, initially precipitated by finding an original Acadian aboiteau sluice log at Grand Pré. After much questing, accompanied by encouraging bouts of serendipity, I unearthed a considerable amount of new information, which raised many questions that I invite others to pursue. Undoubtedly much is yet to be discovered, both on the dykelands and in the private possession of the descendants of Acadians and New England Planters.

From 1994 to the present I have been digging for information in local muds, in local minds, in local museums and libraries, in maps, and at meetings, and I have gradually accumulated a treasure trove of artifacts, just plain facts, hypotheses, and scenarios. This book consolidates the data into a series of chapter topics, all of which are interrelated: geology, tides, soils, grasses, dyke construction, rising sea levels, old maps, and aerial photographs, ending with historical resumés of six different localities.

This book's underlying theme is the deciphering of how the first Europeans recognized and fulfilled the opportunities afforded by this unique marine environment, how the tidal marshes moulded them into a distinct society, and what happened at Grand Pré after the dismantling of that local Acadian culture.

An additional intent is to encourage others to apply similar archaeological methods and interpretations to other dykeland regions in Atlantic Canada, in the hope of similar revealing successes.

Be forewarned that this account of the effect of the local marine environment on local human history is unashamedly presented through the eyes of, and with the biases of, a marine biologist. The cultural history of the region has already been well documented and will not be repeated here.

ACKNOWLEDGMENTS

During this project I met dozens of persons with similar interests in local history, many of whom were active members of regional historical societies. Even the most casual encounters with such persons often provided precious gems of information. Most fascinating of all was the privileged experience of interviewing the "old timers" and discussing the finer points of dyking procedures. I am indebted to all these persons for generously sharing their knowledge and their scrapbooks.

Foremost amongst these are the fifty persons listed in appendix 8, in particular Avard Bishop, James Bremner, Fred Curry, James Eldridge, George Frail, Dean Gertridge, Ellis Gertridge, David Knowles, Gordon Knowles, and Jean Palmeter.

Glenda Bishop and David Wickwire provided me with the fruits of their genealogical labours at the Provincial Archives of Nova Scotia. Miles Russell, Manager of Collections, New Ross Farm Museum, expanded my understanding of soils, and of the history and importance of hay grasses in pioneer communities. In 1998–99 two photographic studio proprietors, Jeff Wilson in Lawrencetown and Conrad Byers in Parrsboro, helped me locate prints and negatives pertaining to Kings County dykelands. At that time they each had unique archival collections of original prints, negatives, and glass plates from the early twentieth century – photographs taken by A.L. Hardy, E. Graham, and R.T. McCully.

Jocelyne Marchand has been supportive since we first met during my discovery of an Acadian aboiteau at Grand Pré in 1994 and has shared her considerable knowledge and files. She was the first historian to examine the

J.F. Herbin archival donation at Acadia University and to inform me of its treasures.

Various organizations assisted in locating information, individuals, or artifacts: Old Kings Courthouse Heritage Museum (Bria Stokesbury); Acadia University Archives (Patricia Townsend); Grand Pré National Historic Site of Canada (Donna Doucet); Public Archives of Nova Scotia (Garry Shutlak); and the Centre of Geographic Sciences, Nova Scotia Community College (Ronald Robichaud, Ada Cheung, Tim Webster).

The enthusiastic Hank Kolstee, Supervisor of Land Protection, Agriculture and Marketing, Nova Scotia, provided much of the historical and recent quantitative data concerning dykelands. His department's archival survey maps, documents, and old photographs provided the factual basis that made this project worth pursuing. The interpretation of this information was made all the easier through consultations with two of Kolstee's staff members: Lindsay Carter, Aboiteau Superintendent; and Darryl Hingley, Chief Surveyor.

I was fortunate to have David Christianson, Chief Archaeologist, Nova Scotia Museum, take an interest in my project. He conducted field work with me, shared his insights, and encouraged me to write this book. Two other archaeologists, Jonathan Fowler and Steven Powell, astounded me with their ability to recognize a field that had been plowed for hundreds of years as an Acadian dwelling site, and to transform bits of gravel into fragments of dishes and clay pipes.

In May 2000 the Nova Scotia Museum awarded me a Cultural History Research Grant, which helped defray the expenses of field work, assembling material, and producing copies of a draft manuscript. As a historical aside, the first time the Nova Scotia Museum contracted me was precisely fifty years previously, in May 1950; at that time to conduct a survey of amphibians and reptiles.

The Scanning Electron Microscope (SEM) photographs were produced at the Acadia Centre for Microstructural Analysis at Acadia University through the skilled and patient assistance of Graham Cheeseman and Daniel MacDonald.

Finally, the Herbin clan must be acknowledged. The collective contributions of five generations of Herbins are scattered throughout this volume, some to the fore, some behind the scenes, but together they formed the framework on which I hung my observations.

Figure 3.4 Starr's Point area in 1978, with Cornwallis River channel in the foreground and the expanse of sandstone terraces of Boudreau Landing indicated by arrows. Many Acadians were deported from this site. A major shad fishery of 1880–1910 had nets attached to miles of poles set into the firm intertidal flats. (Fisheries and Oceans, Ottawa, adapted from Dohler, 1989)

Figure 4.3   The two species of intertidal grasses used for building dyke walls. Photo taken at the west end of Long Island, Grand Pré, 16 July 2000.

Figure 4.7   Layers of marsh grass turf accumulation, with a garden trowel for scale, at Little Island, Grand Pré. These layers represent hundreds of years of rising sea levels. The grey basal layer is ancient upland soil with well-preserved rhizomes of wild roses.

Pattern of Sod Cutting Procedures as Deduced from Interviews

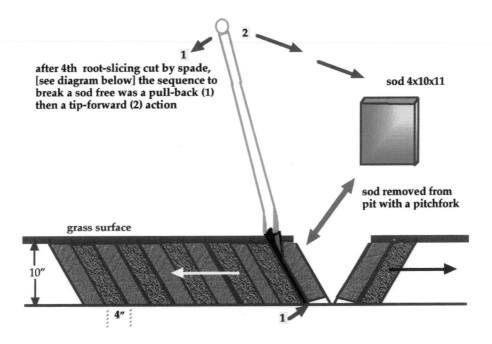

X-SECTION VIEW OF SOD PIT

2

1

after 4th root-slicing cut by spade, [see diagram below] the sequence to break a sod free was a pull-back (1) then a tip-forward (2) action

sod 4x10x11

sod removed from pit with a pitchfork

grass surface

10"

4"

1

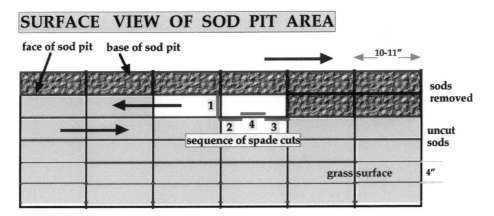

SURFACE VIEW OF SOD PIT AREA

face of sod pit   base of sod pit

10-11"

sods removed

1

uncut sods

2 4 3

sequence of spade cuts

grass surface   4"

Figure 4.11   Patterns of sod-cutting procedures as deduced from interviews and field observations.

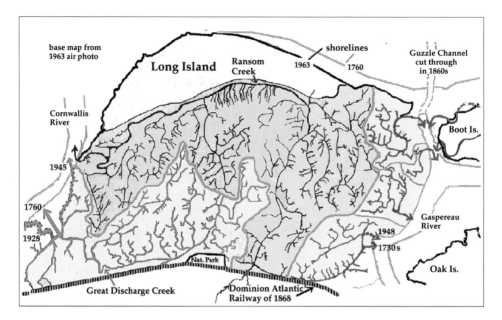

Figure 6.1 Most of the Grand Pré marshland drained to the west via two creeks, the green and the blue watersheds. The green creeks have periodically changed the location of their discharge outlet into the Cornwallis River. On the east side of the marsh (red), there were four small watersheds that, prior to the 1860s and the opening of a Guzzle channel to the north, discharged into the Gaspereau River channel. In 1947–48 the "Deportation Creek" outlet was moved to the north.

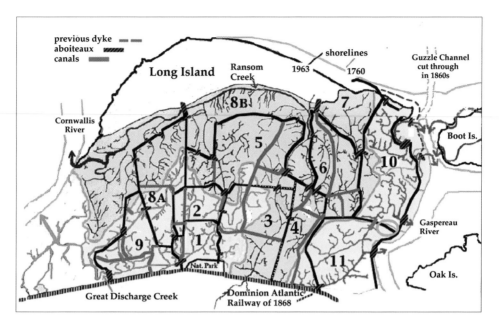

Figure 6.2   A plot of H. Cameron's stereo-photograph detected ridges at Grand Pré that he derived from 1945 and 1955 aerial photos. I consider the brown lines to be original roads and the black lines to be original dyke walls. The three white-speckled portions of walls bordering Enclosure 3 were not recorded by Cameron, but I believe they were there originally. By 2002, the only remnant of original Acadian dyke wall not flattened by bulldozers was within the green oval area bordering areas 10 and 11.

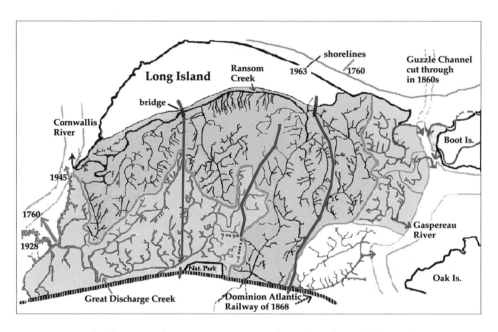

Figure 6.3   The three Acadian major access roads to their farm fields and to Long Island. The two original submerged bridges across Ransom Creek would later become aboiteau causeway dams. Note that the east and west roads cut across Grand Pré along the two most direct watershed tracts available. The central road accessed that immediate area, terminating at an east-west dyke wall parallel to a deeply dissected segment of Ransom Creek. Its south connection could not be determined.

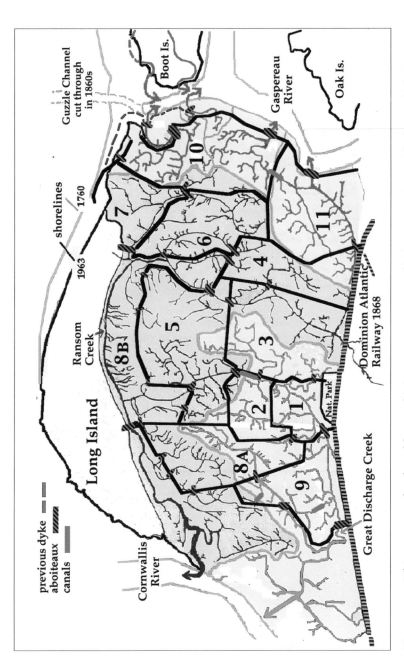

Figure 6.5   This map was developed by combining 1950s stereographic interpretations with the creek drainage patterns. Probable sites where over thirty aboiteau sluices may have been installed are indicated by the red/black bars. The pink bars indicate sites where canals connecting across watersheds may have been dug. Note the dashed line outside Enclosure 10, where an earlier Acadian wall was probably located.

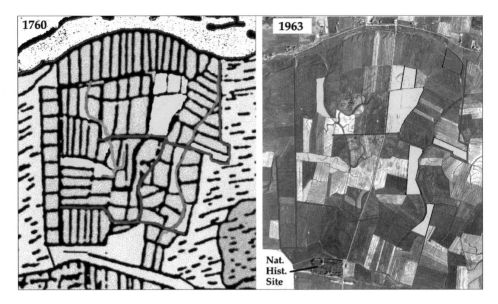

1760

1963

Nat.
Hist.
Site

Figure 6.8 *above*   Shapes of fields long established by the Acadians, surveyed and mapped by the Planters in 1760, and still used by farmers in 1963. The blue lines are the original survey of marsh creeks, easily located in the 1963 aerial photo. Recent colour-coded satellite images have the same patterns. An Acadian farmer of 1735 would still recognize his own fields. (National Air Photo Library A 18060-61)

Figure 6.10 *facing page above*   The area 8B had many wide, deep creeks and was therefore not prime farmland; note that the dyke walls skirted around that section. Its real value would have been as a hunting area, because seals, porpoises, sea bass, dogfish sharks, and many smaller species would have used this feeding area at high tide, and could have easily been trapped by various means. The installation of a large aboiteau across Ransom Creek would have deprived the community of this asset.

Figure 6.11 *facing page below*   The black lines are the final dyke walls, which made the grey walls and their ten aboiteaux redundant. The west dyke was 1.8 miles long with three large (and perhaps two small) aboiteaux. The east dyke was 2.2 miles long with three large aboiteaux. To achieve this, the Acadians had built at least 17.5 miles of dykes and thirty or more aboiteau sluices.

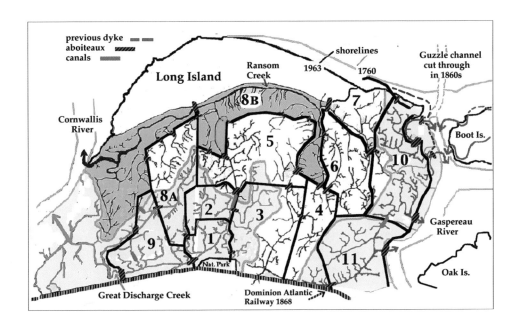

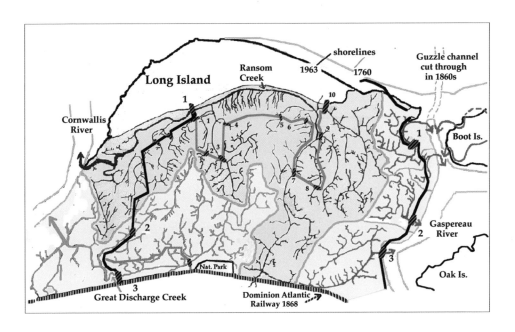

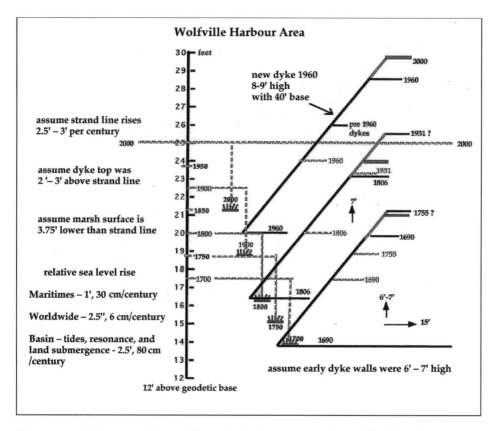

Figure 7.5   Diagrammatic – and hypothetical – representation of the historic sequence of three different dyke walls built on the marsh surface circa 1690, in 1805–06, and in 1960. Consult text for description and discussion of the rising strand line (high-tide line), additions to the height of walls, and current elevation of crests of these walls.

Figure 7.6   Storm-eroded dyke at northeast Grand Pré in 1999. In the 1940s, this wall and marsh continued beyond the far rock pile and then turned right, circling around Little Island. Note the rows of tightly fitted sods facing the sea, and the jumble of fill sods at the right.

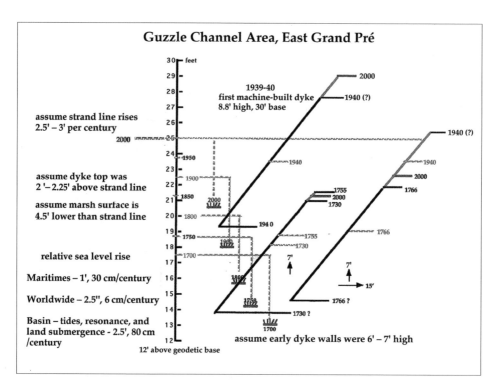

Figure 7.8   Diagrammatic representation of the historical sequence of three different dyke walls built on the marsh surface at east Grand Pré circa 1730, 1766, and 1940. These are the three dykes shown in Figure 7.7.

Figure 7.11　Storm-exposed shoreline between Long Island and Little Island, Grand Pré, illustrating sandy beach, centuries of accumulation of marsh-grass turf, and bands of preserved black roots of Salt Marsh Bulrush at different levels.

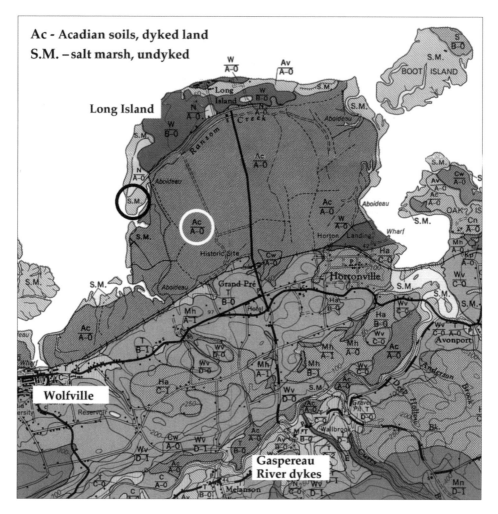

Figure 8.3   From a government soil map prepared in 1966, but showing shorelines and dykes from 1928 topographic maps. In addition, the Wickwire Dyke wall from Long Island to Wolfville lacks all its aboiteaux. Nevertheless, these province-wide maps, with their colour-coded grey S.M. and dark green Ac areas, provide the best visual representation of the extent of enclosed tidal marshes, including areas bordering rivers, such as the Gaspereau River at the bottom of this map. All of those areas were established by the Acadians, with the Planters contributing a few additions. (Courtesy of Agriculture and Agri-food Canada, Soil Survey, Kings Co., Report no.15, 1965)

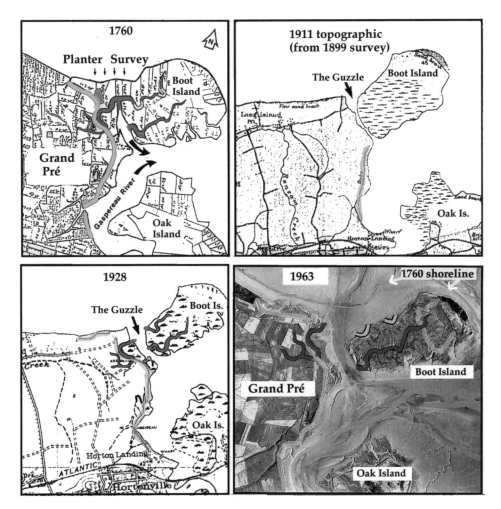

Figure 9.2.1 A history of development of the Guzzle channel using the shapes of the marsh drainage creeks as geographic reference points. Note the inaccurate representation of dyke walls on the 1911 topographic map. The two yellow remnants of a large creek in the 1963 photo had eroded away by 1992; now Boot Island is about half the size it was at the time of the Acadian occupation of these marshlands (see also Table 9.4.1).

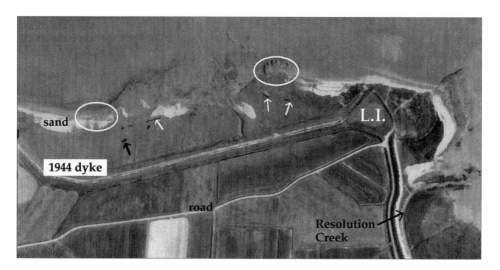

Figure 9.3.4 A 1987 aerial photo showing the Palmeter dyke and Little Island area. Note the many sand beaches on this storm shore. The white circles are sites of eroded old dykes. The white arrows indicate sod extraction trenches behind old walls, and the black arrow indicates a marsh pool that originally was a sod pit. (National Air Photo Library 87323-40)

Sods, Soil, and Spades

CHAPTER ONE

Introduction

The Dykes of Acadie

O marshes green, the dykes of Acadie,
I have been nursed upon your ancient breast,
And taught your patience and your hearts's calm rest,
Your large content and fine serenity!

J.F. Herbin, 1909, 22

The Dykeland People

In a mere seventy-five years, 1680–1755, the tidal meadows of Minas Basin in Nova Scotia created an unusual French subculture. These people became as unique as the tides that measured their days: an independent peasant French community that was democratic, highly cooperative, industrious, prosperous to the degree of trade alliances with New England, and devoid of the crushing bureaucracy of both church and state. They never bore arms with or against the French, British, or Mi'kmaq. After the Treaty of Utrecht in 1713, the Acadians officially declared themselves neutral in the ongoing French and British colonial wars. Living at Grand Pré was as near to a Utopian existence as any farming community of the eighteenth century could have imagined.

In 1755 the Acadians were suddenly and forcibly torn from their dykelands and widely dispersed. In the years following they were pursued, persecuted, and marginalized but, astoundingly, never culturally destroyed. That horrific experience has served to reaffirm their unique identity to such a degree that today they consider themselves a nation. Although they are highly fragmented geographically, this has not prevented the Acadians of Acadie from having their own flag and national anthem, their own recognizable language and literature, and their own heroes and famous sons and daughters. The tragic Evangeline in Longfellow's poignant epic is an internationally recognized icon.

These exiles are proud of their heritage. In 1994 a quarter million persons from all over the world arrived in New Brunswick for a two-week celebration through academic seminars, cultural events, and family-name reunions. Clive Doucet (1999) pointed out that the United Nations considered the reunion the cultural event of the twentieth century. Prime Minister Jean Chrétien and the UN Secretary-General Boutros Boutros-Ghali attended the opening ceremonies.

In 2004, 400 years after their ancestors first viewed the rich marine meadows and witnessed the unique Bay of Fundy tides that would transform them into "The Acadians," these exiles from the territory of Acadie plan to assemble in Nova Scotia from all points of their diaspora, to reaffirm and celebrate their unique heritage.

To fathom the reasons for that ethnic cleansing of 1755, which lasted until 1763, the reader may consult the extensive literature available on that subject. The core subject of this book is not what humans do to humans but rather what the environment does to humans. A fundamental reciprocity exists between peoples and their lands. Often, by necessity, they become master craftsmen of the medium on which they choose to live. Only those who work the land can truly know that depth of satisfaction derived from confidently extracting all the necessities of life directly from forest and field. It nurtures a depth of attachment that bonds across the centuries and a tribal cohesiveness that borders on fanaticism. Is it so strange that so many urban dwellers search their ancestry in the hope of identifying their "*land* of origin"? And how wonderfully appropriate that they term the quest "searching for their *roots*."

The Acadians became master craftsmen who used tidal marsh meadows, who could carve them and construct with them, and who could farm below sea level. They were the only North American pioneers to do so. Why they chose to do this, and precisely how, is the subject of this book. Their methods of dykeland management, well established by the early 1700s, were passed on to the New England Planters who were brought in to replace them in the 1760s, and did not change until the 1950s, when mechanical monsters replaced manual labour.

Appendix 1 provides an annotated chronology, an eclectic guide for the period covered in this book. It combines geology, tides, dyking, and historic human events.

The Marshland Environment

At the east side of the Bay of Fundy a deep narrow channel forms an entrance to the shallow Minas Basin. Every twelve hours and twenty-five minutes this basin fills and empties. About 4 cubic miles of water (14 cubic kilometres, some 14 billion tonnes) slosh in and out through that narrow channel at speeds of 7 to 8 knots. At mid-tide the flow is equivalent to the combined flow of all the rivers and streams on earth. From the sheer weight of that water, the land beneath the Minas Basin rhythmically sinks and rises with each tide. No other region on earth is quite like this one.

For six hours the incoming tides, rising at an average rate of 8 ft (2.44 m) per hour, sweep across miles of intertidal flats, quickly raising sea levels to 40 or 50 ft (12–15 m), finally flooding across thousands of acres of grassy tidal meadows. Over the next six hours the procedure is reversed.

Why did the pre-Acadians leave their Port Royal settlement (Annapolis Royal to the British) at the head of the Annapolis Basin, Nova Scotia, and move to the Minas Basin with its intimidating tidal geography? What attracted them to a seacoast with mile-wide tidal flats? Why is it that they soon considered themselves as unique as the tides that were creating their lifestyle? The Acadians are set apart from all other North American colonists and pioneer farmers because only they perfected methods that converted thousands of acres of salt-soaked seagrass meadows into rich arable farmland (Ross and Deveau, 1992). Their special craft was building high dyke walls, and their special tool was an unusual narrow sharp-edged spade that had no function other than to cut sod bricks for construction of sturdy waterproof seawalls.

In hindsight, it is understandable that some of the farmers at Port Royal would want to move to the Minas Basin. They undoubtedly had a European-based knowledge of marshland ecology, an understanding of fresh water marshes, through the farmers from the Poitou district in France and of salty seacoast marshes through the farmers from the Vendée and Saint Onge districts (Butzer, 2002). Techniques had been refined from the experience of generations of farmers who drained lands and built sea-water evaporation ponds for salt production. In the 1630s salt makers from France (with craft-based names like Saulnier and Saunier) were brought to Port Royal to create evaporative salt pans, in an attempt to eliminate the need to purchase the terribly expensive salt from government monopolies in France. The summer fogs of the Annapolis Basin undoubtedly put a damper on their efforts, but the potential of unusually thick deposits of marsh soil, a by-product of the macrotidal regime, must have impressed them. The large Belle Isle tidal marsh at Port Royal was the proving ground for their initial experiments in large-scale aboiteaux and dyke-wall construction (Butzer, 2002).

When they learned of the thousands of acres of marsh meadows at the other end of the Annapolis Valley on the shores of the Minas Basin, some of their company would certainly have investigated. They could see that the powerful tidal currents eroded the soft shorelines of the basin and transported the fine sediments onto the tidal meadows, silts that progressively buried and preserved the thick root entanglements in an airtight and waterproof clay. Such soils, when aerated by plowing and washed with rain, need no fertilizers, have neither stones nor trees to clear, are level, and have a rich and uniform distribution of nutrients throughout. The prominent laminated silt layers evident on the steep riverbanks would have indicated a deposition rate far exceeding any sites in Europe. I can imagine their glowing report upon returning to Port Royal.

Their most enticing challenge would be the dyking of the great meadow, le Grand Pré, a rectangular block of 3,000 acres of tidal meadows. In their favour, the meadow was protected from the sea by three connected islands (Long, Little, and Boot Islands) and was not dissected by any major river as were the marshes of the six adjacent river estuaries of Pereau, Habitant, Canard, Cornwallis, Gaspereau, and Avon. All these river estuaries were rich in migratory fish species, and the larger tidal creeks provided small-vessel access to the limits of the marshes during high tides.

With 50 ft (15 m) tides, and mile-wide (1.6 km) and firm intertidal flats, there would be no need to build or maintain small fishing vessels. Rather than taking the nets to the fish in the traditional way, they could simply set their nets at low tide and let the fish come to the nets during the high-tide phases. The fish could even be harvested from the nets at low water with the same wagons as used about their farms (Fig. 1.1).

The Acadians would have scouted about, asked around, or already known of the location of the few rocky landing sites on the banks of these otherwise slippery river slopes.

Thus began a partnership of sea and settler like no other, a relationship that the British would inadvertently forge into an attitude of cultural identity that proved to be indestructible.

I believe the Acadians knew exactly what to do with tidal marshlands, and how to do it, and knew why dyking tidal marshes would produce incompa-

Figure 1.1   Example of horse and wagon fishing in Minas Basin in early 1900s. Note birch poles and firmness of sandy ocean bottom at low tide.

rably better arable land than clearing forests and rocks from the thin, acidic, and leached upland soils.

Few, if any, of the British realized the agricultural sophistication of the Acadian efforts. They demeaned the Acadians' dyking prowess by declaring the French to be too lazy to clear stones and stumps from the adjacent rocky hillsides in the tried and true British pioneer axe-swinging tradition.

CHAPTER TWO

Geology, Geography, and Tides

Blomidon

Begotten of fire, quick was thy bringing forth,
Internal shudderings and thundering throes,
Rending the fiery depths whence thou arose
To lie all red and radiant o'er the earth.

J.F. Herbin, 1909, 107

Much has been written concerning the special nature of Acadian history and culture and its sociological origins. But none of that would have come to pass without those special tidal meadows of the Bay of Fundy region. Historically they are special because the marine soil to which the Acadians put their plows had its origins near the South Pole, about 500 million years ago. The story is worth telling for it adds to the mystique of the saga of those Bay of Fundy tidal-marsh farmers.

Near the South Pole, half a billion years ago, mountains in what is now northwest Africa were eroding into the sea, and the sedimentary rocks thus formed would one day contribute significantly to Acadian culture. A remnant of those original layered deposits can be viewed in Wolfville, at the top of Gaspereau Avenue beneath the Highway 101 overpass. However, half a billion years ago, the North American continental plate was far away, drifting about in equatorial latitudes. How did these rock formations get to North America and to Grand Pré?

If such an interminably long journey could be summarized in a few paragraphs, it might run like this: The African continental plate drifted northward as the North American plate drifted toward the future Europe and Africa, and then they collided. Thus the original Atlantic Ocean was obliterated and the African sedimentary layers pushed upwards to form new mountain ranges. These would eventually be ground down to form Minas Basin sandstone particles, from which our tidal meadow silts would be derived.

Back to proto-Nova Scotia circa 400 million BCE (Before Current Era), which was now located in the middle of Pangea, the world's largest-ever land mass (Donohue and Grantham, 1989; Atlantic Geoscience Society, 2001). The future Atlantic Canada was about to suffer through 200 million years of geological and climatological processes and alterations. It was at different times beneath the sea, a desert, a jungle, eroded by monsoons, and crushed and folded.

Then, about 180 million years ago, that conglomerate Pangea land mass broke up into the drifting continental plates that we recognize today. One of the split lines, the one that would create the present Atlantic Ocean, ran just to the east of the edge of North Africa and Europe. When the old North American plate broke away, it tore off sections of Africa and Europe, and two of those pieces eventually came together, forming a contact line along the north shore of Minas Basin, the Minas Geofracture. This geological dichotomy is strikingly evident on Nova Scotia geological maps: the rocks of northern mainland Nova Scotia, Cape Breton Island, and Newfoundland have geological ties to Europe, whereas Nova Scotia south of the Minas Basin juncture line has roots in African Morocco (Fig. 2.1).

Nova Scotia obtained its ocean-side location with the formation of the fledging Atlantic Ocean, and began travelling west with the rest of North America, non-stop towards Japan. By now much of the original mountain ranges had eroded, forming deposits of thousands of metres of sediments, the future farming soil of the Bay of Fundy and Minas Basin, officially known as the Wolfville Sandstones and Blomidon Shales. During that Triassic time travel from 180 to 65 million years ago, stresses fractured the floor of the Bay of Fundy and as many as seventeen sheets of lava flowed out over the top of the Bay of Fundy sandstones forming that long, high, and wide ridge of black basalt locally known as The North Mountain (Roland, 1982). It shelters the agricultural Annapolis Valley from the cold air of the Bay of Fundy and makes this valley the banana belt of Atlantic Canada.

The final geological act that formed the Minas Basin landscape was a downward tilting of the land towards the northwest into the Bay of Fundy

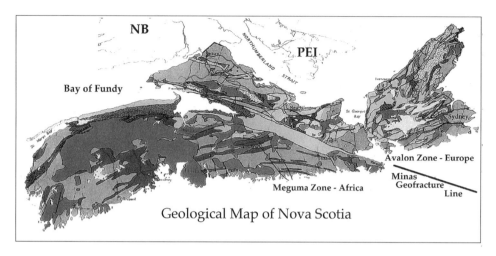

NB

PEI

Bay of Fundy

Avalon Zone - Europe

Minas Geofracture Line

Meguma Zone - Africa

Geological Map of Nova Scotia

Figure 2.1 Geological map of Nova Scotia showing the complex of units, and the Minas Geofracture Line between the northern Avalon Zone and the southern Meguma Zone. (Nova Scotia Department of Natural Resources)

and towards the Gulf of Maine. This created a Bay of Fundy trough that gradually filled with sea water as Pleistocene glaciers melted and sea levels rose worldwide. By 65 million years ago, when dinosaurs were fading and mammals first flourishing, the Atlantic Ocean had probably achieved 90 per cent of its present width.

Inadvertently, but crucial to our Acadian narrative, that final tilting of the land created a basin configuration that, when filled with water millions of years later, would resonate with the pulse of the moon's passage and generate the world's highest tides. Every basin has a theoretical natural resonance period that results in a rhythmic back and forth sloshing of its water mass when a synchronous force is applied. Considering all the many tidal basins, this special Bay of Fundy case of macro-amplification of tides is rare, and nowhere else has it transgressed the land to such an extent and laid down such deep marine soils. These soils are technically referred to as Acadia Soils, and belong to the Regosol Order of soil types.

The designation of maritime Canada by the early French as "Acadie" has become the accepted title not only for their decendants; it is also the official name for tidal marsh soils and for the forest formations of the Atlantic region of Canada.

CHAPTER THREE

Tidal Aspects and Effects

Ebb and Flow

Curling through creeks deep and crooked,
Gliding o'er levels of green,
Hiding the rounded red rush banks
That sing to the currents and lean ...
Flooding in power and silence,
Thrusting strong arms through the land,
Whirling the ships into harbor,
Lifting the keels from the sand ...
As swiftly the waters enter
So the tide shall return to the sea,
Ebbing again to the northward,
Southward again to the sea.

J.F. Herbin, 1909, 90

Nearly every basin of water, whether bathtub or Bay of Fundy, has a natural resonance period, and if acted upon by an external force of the same rhythm, its water mass will slosh back and forth synchronously. About 6–7,000 years ago, as glaciers melted and the Bay of Fundy began filling, a resonance period eventually developed that coincided with the twice daily tidal movements induced by the moon, it being the nearest celestial body and the major gravitational force affecting the earth.

The period of greatest acceleration in tidal amplitude was 3–4,000 years ago (Dalrymple, Amos, and Yeo, 1992). This time frame agrees with biological evidence of C^{14} dates of trees and oysters near Grand Pré (Fig. 3.1), which were buried at that time by heavy sediment loads from turbid waters (Bleakney and Davis, 1983; Bleakney, 1986).

The gradual increase in macrotidal amplitudes since then, combined with rising sea levels worldwide and with land submergence in Nova Scotia (Grant, 1975; Dalrymple, Amos, and Yeo, 1992), is responsible for the unusual depth of local marsh soils, soils that became the economic base of

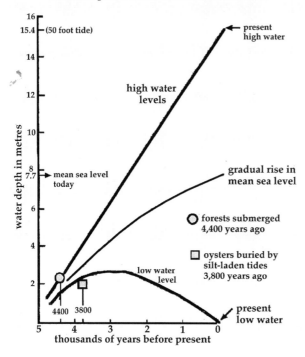

Model of present macrotides in Minas Basin

Figure 3.1
Diagram of basic changes in tidal amplitudes in Minas Basin over past 5,000 years. Note that increasing amplitudes have lowered low-tide levels, thereby exposing ancient forests and shell beds previously submerged.

Acadian society. Acadian prosperity depended on exports (Wynn, 1979), which required shipping, and that required sailing in turbulent Fundy waters as well as coping with the world's highest tides. To reach Grand Pré, mariners had to enter Minas Basin riding one of the fastest ocean currents, the 7 to 8 knot (8 to 9.2 mph) riptides of the Minas Channel; then once inside the basin, they had to avoid a grounding on the 1 to 2 mile (1.6 to 3.2 km)-wide intertidal shoals.

Consequently, the Acadian lifestyle would have focused on tidal phenomena, which exerted a subtle but pervasive control over their actions on shore and at sea. Our general populace today, in striking contrast, does not appreciate how widely the configuration of tides varies from one locality to another, from one year to another, and from decade to decade. These are recurring and thus predictable patterns and, for the benefit of mariners, the federal government annually publishes prediction tables of tides and currents for the coming year. A basic understanding of local tides is particularly pertinent to a more appreciative understanding of Acadian society. This knowledge became even more relevant in the post-diaspora period, because many displaced Acadians were forced to become fishermen on their return to Nova Scotia, New Brunswick, or Prince Edward Island.

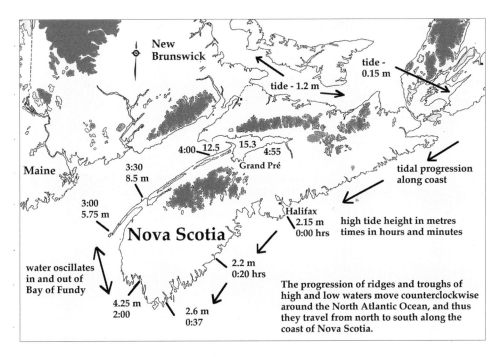

Figure 3.2   Time sequence of high tides with their heights, along the Atlantic coast and Bay of Fundy shores of Nova Scotia. There is a five-hour difference from the high tide crest at Halifax and the crest at Grand Pré. The oscillation of the Bay of Fundy water mass generates the world's highest tidal amplitudes, often exceeding 15 m.

To discuss the Acadian phenomenon from a marine perspective, a digression is in order. It begins with Fig. 3.2, a diagrammatic summary of general tidal aspects of Atlantic Canada. Those early French explorers and settlers would soon have gained knowledge of local tides and would have carried with them a mental map similar to this figure.

Note that tidal amplitudes vary from 50 ft (15 m) in Minas Basin, to 6 ft (1.8 m) on the Atlantic coast, to 4 ft (1.2 m) at PEI, and finally to as little as 3 to 6 inches (0.07 to 0.15 m) in the Bras d'Or Lakes, Cape Breton Island. Although Cape Breton's inland bodies of water have the appearance of freshwater lakes, they are fully marine and constitute an inland sea, as evidenced by their oyster and fish aquaculture industries, and by the summer swarms of large and stinging Lion's Mane Jellyfish (*Cyanea capillata*).

High tide is an oceanic wave crest that progresses counterclockwise from Europe and sweeps down the North American coast from Greenland and Newfoundland, on to Florida, and back to Europe in just twelve hours – but that is another story. As it passes the Gulf of Maine and Bay of Fundy, it forcibly nudges the waters of that basin and perpetuates a resonance sloshing that had its small beginnings about 5,000 years ago.

Fig. 3.1 may help readers visualize what is meant by a 50 ft (15 m) tide: water levels rise 25 ft (7.5 m) *above* Mean Sea Level (MSL), and then fall to 25 ft *below* MSL. A 6 ft (1.8 m) tide rises 3 ft (0.9 m) above then sinks 3 ft below MSL. It takes only six hours for the waters to rise from the low to high tide levels, which in Minas Basin is about 8 ft (2.4 m) per hour. In contrast, on the Atlantic coast of Nova Scotia the tide rises a mere 6 ft in six hours. Because marsh levels keep pace with rising sea levels, the depth of tidal marsh soils bordering the shores of Minas Basin is exceptional.

Four types of daily tides are recognized worldwide:

semidiurnal – twice daily; with two high and two low tides
diurnal – once a day; with one high and one low tide
strongly semidiurnal – mostly twice a day
strongly diurnal – mostly once a day

Atlantic Canada is unusual in possessing all four types (Fig. 3.3). The relatively narrow Chignecto Isthmus, with its dyked Tantramar marshes, connects Nova Scotia and New Brunswick. Uniquely, it has the world's highest semidiurnal tides on its Fundy side, but on its Gulf of Saint Lawrence shores the tides are only 4 ft (1.2 m) or less in amplitude. Near the Magdalen Islands in that gulf there are even lesser tides, and these are strongly diurnal. It all depends on the natural resonance period of each particular basin.

Tides constitute a vast and fascinating subject, and when we delve into the long-term tidal patterns of the Bay of Fundy region, we discover their relevance to dyke construction and maintenance. To begin with, the bimonthly spring and neap tides can shut down or encourage dyke construction, but few persons understand the meaning of these terms. Spring tides "spring up" as very high tides twice monthly, when the sun, moon, and earth are nearly in line and thus their gravitational forces are cooperating to maximum effect. Neap tides are "not-to-worry" tides, a consequence of the moon's location at right angles to the sun-earth axis, causing it to conflict laterally with solar forces, thus damping down tidal amplitudes. Spring tides occur at full and new moons, and flood the tidal meadows. Neap tides are also bimonthly, but usually do not reach the upper-level meadows. Because dyke walls were built on the higher marsh levels, and because the two spring tides in any one month may not be equal, it was often possible for the Acadians to proceed with construction for three successive weeks without any tidal inundation of their new wall or their sod pits.

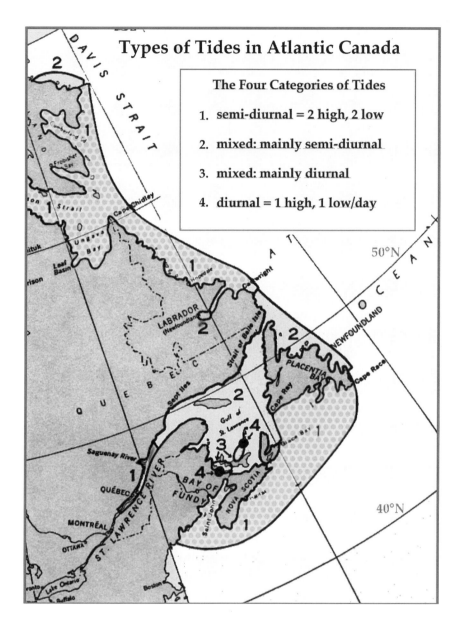

Types of Tides in Atlantic Canada

The Four Categories of Tides

1. semi-diurnal = 2 high, 2 low
2. mixed: mainly semi-diurnal
3. mixed: mainly diurnal
4. diurnal = 1 high, 1 low/day

Figure 3.3   The marine environment of the land Acadians knew as Acadie uniquely encompassed all four categories of the world's tidal regimes. (Adapted from Dohler, 1989, Fisheries and Oceans Canada)

The strongest tidal effect is from the Perigean Cycle (or Anomalistic Cycle) of 27.554 solar days, when the moon is nearest the earth. The second strongest effect occurs at full or new moon phases, every 14.765 solar days or, if calculating from new moon to new moon, it is the Synodic Cycle of 29.530 solar days. A third but relatively weak effect involves the declinations of the moon (how high or low in the sky) every 13.66 days. A fourth influence is related to the revolution of the Moon's Nodal Cycle and its alignment with the sun and moon at maximum declination every 18.61 years. In the Bay of Fundy tidal system the combined influences of the first two forces, Perigean and Synodic, have the greatest influence and are referred to collectively as a soli-lunar cycle, or Seros Cycle of 18.03 solar years. Dyke walls become especially vulnerable when the extreme spring tides of a Seros peak year are accompanied by storms. In this cycle (well known to ancient astronomers) solar and lunar eclipses recur (Desplanque, 1977; Desplanque and Mossman, 2000; Macmillan, 1966).

On days, weeks, or years when several of these cyclic influences coincide, the tides are higher and lower than usual. What all this adds up to is that high water peaks of tidal cycles occur in the Bay of Fundy every 12.4 hours, 24.8 hours, 14.8 days, 207 days, 4.52 years, and 18.03 years. As well, the 207 day peaks are advanced by 48 days each year. Because of this, Fundy tidal marsh meadows will experience extreme high tides in every month of the year. For Acadian dyke builders, the tidal effects of some summers would have been ideal for dyke construction, while others were truly a washout.

The Acadians presumably learned of these cycles the hard way. Table 3.1 summarizes the times when reported breaching of dykes coincided with peaks in the 18.03 year Seros Cycle. One can conclude that these breachings were in company with a storm, for many Seros maxima did not destroy dykes. After losses in 1687 and 1705, the Acadians probably recognized the cyclic aspect and raised the average level of their dykes, particularly those most exposed to the open sea. No further breachings were reported during their tenure of the dykelands, which ended in 1755.

The next recorded major Seros breaching was on 3 November 1759. This was after four years of abandonment, no annual maintenance or repairs, and four years of muskrats tunnelling and denning in the dyke walls. It is not surprising that some sections of walls gave way to pounding waves. Thus, the New England Planters arrived in June 1760 to a partially flooded Grand Pré, but probably did not realize they had nearly eighteen years to learn how to repair and rebuild, and to prepare for the next Seros peak. They either built higher dykes or were storm-lucky, for not until 1828 did they experi-

TABLE 3.1   HISTORICAL EVENTS LINKED TO 300 YEARS OF SEROS CYCLES OF
EXTREME TIDAL AMPLITUDES

1669	
1682	Acadians settle Grand Pré
1687	Breaching of dykes, March 1688
1704	Massachusetts army unit pillages Grand Pré and cuts the dyke walls
1705	Breaching of dykes, November 1705
1723	
1741	
1755	Expulsion of Acadians
1759	Breaching of dykes, 3 November
1760	Arrival of Planters in summer
1778	
1796	
1805–06	Construction of first Wickwire Dyke from Wolfville to Long Island
1814	
1828	Tides over dyke walls, 1,000 acres flooded (1832 less 4.5 years)
1832	
1850	
1868	Saxby Gale of 5 October 1869; entire 3,000 acres flooded (end of original 1806 dyke)
1886	Dykes damaged in February
1888	7 December storm and high tides; Beckwith Dyke damaged, less damage to Wickwire and Grand Pré
1901	Dykes breached in November during the 4.5 year peak
1904	
1913	Wickwire Dyke breached by severe storm of 30 October
1922	
1928	Wickwire Dyke breached in late December
1931	Remainder of Wickwire Dyke destroyed by 4 March storm
1940	Breached dykes, Bay of Fundy
1940	23 April, dyke breaks between Long Island and Little Island
1944	Habitant aboiteau (Canning) washed out, 4 September (another 4.5 year peak?)
1958	Aerial photos, 6 April, east Grand Pré breaching of walls, Fig. 9.2.4
1976	Shore erosion pronounced at Fort Ann, Annapolis Royal, in this period
1994	Shore erosion pronounced at Fort Ann, Annapolis Royal, near this time period

Years of extreme tidal amplitudes are in bold. Seros cycles peak every eighteen years and 11.5 days, with lesser peaks every 4.5 years. These peaks are closely correlated with the recorded tidal destruction of dyke walls.

ence a major breaching of dykes, one that coincided with one of the 4.5 year mini-peak phases of a Seros Cycle.

In early October 1869 the famous Saxby Gale struck the Bay of Fundy with unprecedented ferocity, with tidal levels topping dyke walls by an unimaginable 3 to 6 ft (0.9 to 1.8 m). "It was three years before the devastated area was reclaimed and brought back to condition for cropping" according to an article in *The Acadian* of 22 September 1932. That article also summarized the degree of destruction of major storms of 1869, 1893, 1923, 1927, and 1931.

The annually published *Tide and Current Tables* are astronomical predictions for all coastal regions, but they cannot predict the weather for any particular day, and that is the wild-card factor that can raise or lower the prediction figure substantially. Nevertheless, the margin of error is insignificant much of the time. Because tidal cycles and heights can be calculated years into the future and years into the past, biologists use them to plan research projects and to compare results with past tidal regimes. This is probably a neglected research tool that historians could use to correlate accounts in diaries and other documents with the recounting of severe coastal storms, loss of ships, breaching of dykes, loss of bridges, and similar historical events. For an example of historical information that can be revealed by using government tide tables, consult the addendum in Locality 5 in chapter 9, concerning Robert Palmeter's Record Book of dyke wall repairs in 1931.

Geology and tides were generous to the Acadians, creating the rich soil, a climate-sheltering North Mountain, the perpetual tidal mixing of nutrients that attracted countless migratory fish and birds, the mile-wide intertidal fishing grounds accessible by horse and wagon, and even a solution for docking ships at those slippery riverbanks, namely a few strategic bedrock outcroppings.

The Acadians took advantage of two marvellous natural landing sites – riverbank sites where the daily scouring of tidal ebb and flow prevented silts from accumulating on intertidal bedrock outcrops. These sites became two major focal points for settlements. Fig. 3.4 (p. xvii) shows Boudreau Landing (Boudreau's Bank) on the riverbank at Town Plot (near Starr's Point), which is a stepped series of Wolfville Sandstone terraces. Another site is Black Landing, now Horton Landing. This is a sloping outcrop of blue-black Horton Group carboniferous shales, its existence unrecognized until June 2000 (Fig. 3.5). The Starr's Point outcrop is plotted on a recently published geological map of the Wolfville-Windsor area (OFM ME 2000-3). Other

Figure 3.5   Horton Landing, called Black Landing in nineteenth-century dykeland ledgers, with Hortonville in the background. This intertidal outcrop of shale, providing the only firm landing site for ships in this area, extends up the slope to the grasses.

similar inconspicuous landing sites may lie along the shores of Minas Basin and its rivers, as yet undocumented.

These two landing sites are conveniently up rivers and around protective corners, sheltered from the open waters of the Minas Basin, and they provide a firm, rough surface for shore access at any tidal level. In each case, original roads, now over 300 years old, can be traced running directly from the landing sites to the adjacent upland: they account for the spreading outward of settlements from these geographic locations. Boudreau's Landing opened up the land to the north of the Cornwallis River, and from Black Landing roads developed west towards New Minas and south into the Gaspereau Valley.

CHAPTER FOUR

Sods, Soil, and Spades:
The Botanical Contribution

Haying

From the soft dyke-road, crooked and waggon-worn,
Comes the great load of rustling, scented hay.
Slow-drawn with heavy swing and creaky sway
Through the cool freshness of the windless morn.

J.F. Herbin, 1909, 26

Without some basic knowledge of marshland botany, one cannot fully appreciate how the Acadians accomplished what they did at Grand Pré in just seventy-five years. We have explored the contributions of geology and tidal evolution to marshland soil formation. Now we examine the crucial botanical aspects: how sea walls could be constructed from wet grassy sods, and why the enclosed dykeland fields did not require fertilizers.

Accounts emphasize that, where feasible, the Acadians preferred to farm tidal marshes rather than to clear large tracts of the forested uplands. But why go to all the trouble of building walls that may wash away in storms, walls that enclose fields that cannot be planted with crops for nearly three years? We know that dykes were built from tidal marsh sods, but how can a mere sod hold back a pounding sea? Was their decision founded on pure laziness, as stated by early chroniclers, or was it motivated by their knowledge of tidal marsh fertility and sod structure, gleaned from thousands of years of agricultural efforts in Europe and passed down from the ancients? I believe the latter, and in July 2001, Karl W. Butzer (University of Texas, Austin) sent me a copy of his manuscript "French Wetland Agriculture in Atlantic Canada and Its European Roots," which substantiates my beliefs.

The Acadians must have understood a great deal about the high fertility of marine-generated soils to have chosen that agricultural direction. They certainly knew how to release the agricultural potential of salt-soaked marshland, and within a few decades had dyked most of the Minas Basin's estuaries. The wisdom of their decision has been confirmed by knowledge gained from research in our lifetime. Recent archaeological investigations in England (Rippon, 2000) have revealed the surprising extent of utilization of coastal wetlands by the Romans. Two thousand years later, the Acadians were using those same Roman construction techniques to build their own dyke walls and sluice boxes.

Consider the following information, which, while it may seem obvious, is rarely articulated in a historical context:

- Local upland soils have been leaching for thousands of post-glacial years and consequently are tremendously variable in structure, nutrients, mineral content, and pH. This is the most fundamental difference between upland and tidal-marsh soils.
- Fundy marshland soils are not being leached annually, they are being formed annually and have organic and inorganic nutrients added to them monthly.
- Although particles eroded from the local sea cliffs are mostly of old leached upland subsoil, when transported in the strong currents of Bay of Fundy and Minas Basin tides, these particles attract ions to their surfaces, ions such as calcium, magnesium, potassium, and sodium, as well as trace elements and certain organic molecules (Hilchey, J.D., 1956; Hilchey and Cann, Report, 1950–51). Thus, when later deposited amongst the stems of the marsh grasses, they are coated with those basic plant nutrients. Accompanying silt particles in Minas Basin tidal waters are pieces of dead plants and animals, cast skins, eggs, larvae, shells, and waste products in general. All that nutritious mixture, with the further assistance of bacteria and fungi, is available to the growing grasses of marine meadows.
- Because of the thorough mixing of waters in the Fundy area, the nutrient contribution is rather uniform throughout the marshes. The tidal contributions reflect the natural concentrations that occur in sea water, which tend not to vary appreciably, and therefore the components of marsh soils do not become concentrated to excessive levels or drastically depleted.
- In sharp contrast, leached upland soils are extremely variable as to their total spectrum of nutrients, as well as their relative concentrations, which

can range from excessive to minuscule. Upland soils typically need to be fertilized and chemically adjusted, usually annually, even for pH.

The following paragraphs from Milligan's *Maritime Dykelands: The 350 Year Struggle* are pertinent:

The Bay of Fundy marshlands soils are technically known as Acadian Soils. The mixture of silt, sand, clay and water presented by these soils, after the salt has been leached out, is very productive for the growth of crops, particularly grass crops. Consequently some dykeland areas, utilizing the vast store of nutrients available, have produced good yields of hay continuously for more than two hundred years without the aid of fertilizer.

Tillable, upland soils around the Bay of Fundy contain significant quantities of plant nutrients only in the top 15 to 30 cm. Below that level practically all of the plant food has been leached out due to the extensive precipitation in the region. A recent comparison of nutrients in the top 75 cm of dykeland and upland soil showed dykeland with 6 times as much potassium, 2.5 times as much phosphorous, 3.5 times as much calcium and 4 times as much magnesium as the upland sample.

From these soils, the Acadians supplied themselves and others not only with hay but also with grains such as wheat, oats, and barley; with peas, chives, onions, cabbage, and other greens; and with corn, parsnips, turnips, carrots, beets, and herbs. Their flax and hemp crops were fed to spinning wheels and weavers' looms (Clark, 1968; Wynn, 1979; and appendix 12).

- With the advent of a post-glacial rise in sea levels, the past few thousand years on the tidal marshes have seen nutrient accretion and not leaching. Those nutrients and grass roots simply accumulate layer upon layer and become hermetically sealed in clay.
- Finally, we must acknowledge the root systems of marine marsh grasses. They are the structures that figuratively and literally tie all this cultural and natural history of dykelands firmly together. Roots spread through this nutritious soil in every direction, forming a tightly tangled root matrix that resists being pulled apart. When all the clay is washed from a marsh sod, which I discovered is not easily accomplished even with a garden hose at full pressure, a very firm replica of the original sod, consisting entirely of roots, remains (Figs 4.1 and 4.2).

These firm resilient blocks of roots would readily be recognized by gardeners as something root-bound from a flower pot. This compact entan-

Salt Meadow Hay – *Spartina patens*
washed sod   dried sod

Black Grass – *Juncus gerardi*
dried sod   washed sod

Figure 4.1   Freshly cut sods of the two grass species used in dyke construction. The central pair were air dried and have a shiny clay surface. The outer two were hosed to remove most of the fine clay silts, thus exposing the compact root matrix. It is this unusual feature that made it possible to pitchfork these "clay bricks" about without destroying them.

glement is why hand-cut dyke sods must be cut with a special spade, one with a sharp edge that can slice through the barrier of fine roots. It is also why such a sod can be speared with a pitchfork, tossed about, and then pounded into place to become part of the waterproof brickwork of a dyke wall. This unfamiliar, even rather startling, concept, that a grass sod could accept all this abuse without any appreciable alteration of its original tensile integrity, is the first step towards understanding Acadian agriculture. For comparison, try to imagine building a dyke wall, or a high wall of any kind, with soaking-wet sods from your lawn.

The general literature is no help in advancing one's understanding of dyke-land sods, for it perpetuates the myth of the "mud" sod. Even Milligan uses the word "mud" eight times on page 33 in a discussion of dyke construction, despite being a dykeland engineer who wrote his book to preserve all the historic dyke building information of which he was aware. He wrote that "marsh mud" was dug from the borrow pits (long ditches parallel to the base of dyke walls); that Acadians dug the compact wet "marsh mud" using a

Figure 4.2 In all cases, the darker root material and the darker clay bricks were from the Black Grass samples. Note that the general make-up of the matrix is of very fine rootlets supported by a coarser network of slightly larger roots.

dyking spade; that the key trench locked the dyke into the "marsh mud;" and so on. He does, however, cite another dykeland engineer, George Frail, as saying that Black Grass made particularly good sods "because its wiry roots bonded so well with marsh mud," as if it were the mud that held the roots together. It would be more accurate to say that the roots bond well with themselves and that the marsh mud becomes trapped in that firm, wiry, entangled matrix. If one simply substitutes "sod" for each "mud" on Milligan's page 33, his text would fit our new paradigm. To express this discussion more succinctly: on uplands, the roots spread through the soil matrix; on tidal marshes, the soil spreads through the root matrix.

When did the French realize the peculiarities and potential of tidal marsh sods? The answer, and we have it in writing, is 1606. Marc Lescarbot (1911 ed.) spent only 1606–07 at Port Royal, but his detailed accounts attest to his insatiable curiosity and attentive observations. He noted that during the production of charcoal, needed for their blacksmith's forge, they used sods from the tidal marsh to cover their smouldering piles of timber, sods that he considered unusual. "We found in the meadows (tidal marshes) more than 2 feet of *soil which was not earth*, but *mud and vegetable matter mixed* one with the other year after year since the beginning of the world, without having been cut." (The italics are mine.)

Over one hundred years later, another itinerant observer was also intrigued by these sods. In his description of Acadian agriculture and dyke construction Isaac Deschamps recognized that it was an unusual root matrix that made enclosure of tidal marshes a viable endeavour: "There grew a kind of grass whose roots were so sewn as to keep the Sods almost Solid. They took of these and set up Banks against the Rivers, and by degrees, Enclosed in this manner, large tracts."

Of the five local species of salt-tolerant grasses, only two were suitable for use as construction "bricks": Salt Meadow Hay, *Spartina patens*, a true grass; and Black Grass, *Juncus gerardi*, a member of the rush family (Fig 4.3, p. xviii). These were ideal because both occur on the upper flat marsh and are readily accessible between times of high tides. Each species spreads, forming large continuous mats that can be efficiently mined for sods by cutting methods to be described shortly.

On the eroding shore at the northeast corner of Grand Pré, the bases of several old sod pits have recently been exposed. In the small inset picture in Fig. 4.4 you can see where the spade sliced and where the sods broke off, creating a checkered pattern on the marsh. This same texture is evident in much of the foreground of the larger A.L. Hardy photo (circa 1913) of dyke repairs at Davidson Aboiteau at the west end of Long Island, Grand Pré.

Remnants of the many pits from which sods were excavated are still evident today in the guise of deep, square-sided marsh pools scattered about on our local marshes. Tidal marsh pools are of two types, by my interpretation. The rare ones are shallow with a gradual slope to the centre and could be termed natural evaporative salt pans, for during very dry summers combined with a series of low high tides, they can develop a white, salt-encrusted margin. The majority of tidal marsh pools are steep sided and 1 or 2 ft deep (0.3 to 0.6 m) and have persisted unchanged for the nearly forty years that I and my students have studied them. They have a well-developed and unusual flora and fauna, forming distinct marsh-pool communities. Their persistence is due to a combination of factors. After originally being dug to a depth of one or two spade depths, they were soon filled by tidal waters, but as one ingredient of marsh soil is a water-impermeable clay, the marsh grasses cannot colonize these pools of standing water. Only marine algae and the aquatic flowering plant, Widgeon Grass, *Ruppia maritima*, flourish under these conditions. In winter, the pools freeze and the pressure of expanding ice keeps pressing back the sides of the pools. However, if the pools are provided

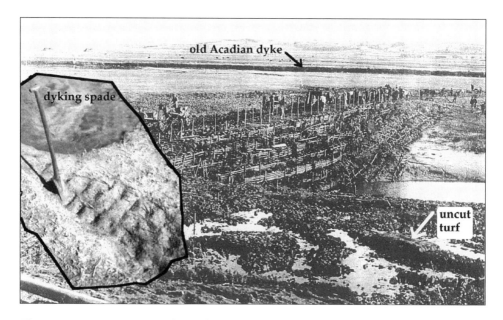

Figure 4.4 Repairing Davidson Aboiteau, Ransom Creek outlet, Grand Pré, circa 1913. Slumping of dyke structure is evident towards upper right. The marsh surface in the foreground and in the field behind the dyke has been mined for sods, except for one uncut block of turf at the white arrow. Inset photo is a 1930s sod-pit surface exposed by storm erosion in 2001. It had been buried beneath some seventy years of new marsh layers.

with a drainage connection to a tidal creek, they will accumulate silts, fill in, and become marsh meadows once again.

Another grass, Cord Grass, *Spartina alterniflora*, of the lower shore slopes, has a different, coarser root arrangement. It has to cope with currents and storms in a softer substrate and has developed long roots and large sub-surface horizontal stems (rhizomes or tillers) that spread and help anchor the plants and expedite colonization of soft new areas. These coarse stems and roots, concentrated near the surface, make it impossible to cut a sod brick that is smooth faced, symmetrical, and homogeneous.

Patches of other grasses and sedges grow along the shore (appendix 2). I have cut and examined sods of each and in my opinion they are all unsuitable as potential building material. Often they are on too shallow a root base, and they may contain a mixture of storm-driven strand-line items such as sand, ice-rafted stones, and tree trunks or branches. Several plant species, Salt Marsh Bulrush, *Scirpus maritimus*, Common Bulrush, *Scirpus americanus*, and Marsh Sedge, *Carex paleacea*, can form continuous mats on sandy slopes, but sand is definitely not dyke-wall material.

Thus, the Acadians had but two species with which to build dykes. Without those grasses, would they have had the motivation to build dykes by hauling rocks, driving pilings, or adding board facing to piles of mud? Would they have opted for clearing forests from upland rocks? Or would they have sensibly gone back to Europe in disgust?

Although Salt Meadow Hay and Black Grass belong to different plant families, structurally their root systems are similar, consisting of many small diameter roots and innumerable fine rootlets (Fig. 4.1). The diameter of the larger roots of Salt Meadow Hay near the surface is 2 mm, but below that it is 1.0 to 1.5 mm. Black Grass has maximum diameter roots of 1.5 mm, and most are 1 mm or less, creating a wool-like matrix. When I attempted to air-dry sods of both species, Black Grass retained its moisture longer than Salt Meadow Hay. It took twenty-five days of outdoor sun and shade drying before weight loss stabilized. The larger roots serve as little reinforcement rods, keeping everything to shape, and their interstices are in-filled with clay, water, and even finer woolly rootlets (Fig. 4.2).

After being told so often by the elderly dykers of how terribly heavy the cut sods were (in the order of 40 lb.) I decided to find out directly by cutting some. With the able and enthusiastic assistance of David Herbin (the great-grandson of J.F. Herbin, the poet and historian whose concept and initiative eventually established the Grand Pré National Historic Site), I cut three sizes of sods from patches of both species of grasses at the west end of Long Island, Grand Pré, and weighed them. Table 4.1 and Table 4.2 are a summary of their weights and their water and clay content.

First attempts at washing the roots by blasting away with a garden hose were quite satisfactory for Salt Meadow Hay, but the woolly rootlets of Black Grass were much more tenacious. Finally, I cut a set of smaller, more manageable sods, 4″ x 4″ and 10.5″ deep, and after weighing, sliced them into small units. These pieces were washed and squeezed in a bucket of water to completely remove the silts. After several days, most of the suspended sediments had settled, and after that I decanted the water on successive days until a thick clay was obtained. This was poured into bread pans, sundried to a solid clay brick, and weighed (Fig. 4.5 and Tables 4.1 and 4.2). Peculiarly, although the silts in the sods of the two species of marsh grass have the same origins, after their association with the root matrix, one dries a darker colour than the other.

The greater amount of clay in Black Grass (see Table 4.3) may be a reflection of the additional surface area and interstices provided by the finer woolly rootlets. The lesser amount of water may be due to space taken up by these numerous roots and their silts. Extracting information from all the sod

TABLE 4.1   SIZES AND WEIGHTS (LB.) OF BLACK GRASS SODS AND THEIR
WATER AND CLAY CONTENT

Black Grass	Sod No.	Field Weight	Air Dried		
4″ width	1	8.75 lb.	5 $^{11}/_{16}$ lb.		
4″ width	2	9 lb.	wet clay:	8 lb.	dried fibres: 7 oz.
			dried clay:	-4 lb.	dried clay: + 4 lb.
			water content:	4 lb.	dry matter: 4 $^{7}/_{16}$ lb.
			air dried 3 wks		air dried 9 wks
7.5″ width	1	20 lb.	11.75 lb.		11 $^{9}/_{16}$ lb.
			average weight about 2.4 to 2.5 lb. per inch of width		

Sods cut from Long Island marsh, Grand Pré, June and July 2000. All sods 4″ thick and
10.5″ long; 2 widths: 1 spade 4″; 2 spade 7.5″

TABLE 4.2   SIZES AND WEIGHTS (LB.) OF SALT MEADOW HAY SODS AND THEIR
WATER AND CLAY CONTENT

Salt Meadow Hay	Sod No.	Field Weight	Air Dried		Wash/Dried
4″ width	1	9 $^{2}/_{16}$ lb.	4 2/16 lb.		x
4″ width	2	9 $^{4}/_{16}$ lb.	wet clay:	6.5 lb.	dried fibers: 6 oz.
			dried clay:	-2.5 lb.	dried clay: + 2 $^{8}/_{16}$ lb.
			water content:	4 lb.	dry matter: 2 $^{14}/_{16}$ lb.
			air dried 3 wks		air dried 9 wks
7.5″ width	1	18 $^{6}/_{16}$ lb.	7 $^{8}/_{16}$ lb.		7 $^{4}/_{16}$ lb.
			sods average weight about 2.5 lb. per inch of width		

Sods cut from Long Island marsh, Grand Pré, June and July 2000.

TABLE 4.3   GRASS SPECIES WEIGHT COMPARISONS
(4 X 4 X 10.5 INCH SODS WEIGHING 9 LB.)

Salt Meadow Hay	4 lb. water	2.5 lb. clay	6 oz. roots
Black Grass	4 lb. water	4 lb. clay	7 oz. roots

Figure 4.5   The two bags contain sliced up sods of Black Grass and Salt Meadow Hay. All clay was washed from the sods, and subsequently they were dried in bread pans to a brick-like consistency (see Table 4.1).

data, one can roughly calculate the weight per each inch of width of sod, assuming the sods to be 4″ thick and 10–11″ deep. The weight is about 2.5 lb. (1.1 kg) per inch of width. Therefore, approximate weights would be: 4 inch-wide sod (one spade width) = 10 lb. or 4.54 kg; 7.5 inch-wide sod (two spade widths) = 18.75 lb. or 8.5 kg; 10.5 inch-wide sod (three spade widths) = 26.25 lb. or 11.9 kg; 12 inch-wide sod (three spade widths) = 30 lb. or 13.6 kg. This analysis should be considered exploratory, and the figures are only estimates. Nevertheless, they are illuminating and deserve further study.

I have been told by Ellis Gertridge, an elderly local historian, farmer, and experienced dyker (consult appendix 3 for a listing of all persons interviewed during this project), that when patching a dyke or covering an excavated area of muskrat burrows, an extra-wide sod might be cut to bridge a gap with one piece. Such sods were called "two-man sods" because it required two simultaneously applied pitchforks to transport and place them.

The standard research procedure for suspended sediment studies has been to sample under conditions of strong unrestricted tidal flow from the water column in the Minas Basin and in the Cornwallis River. No information is

Figure 4.6   Area A is of flocculent clay particles and skeletal fragments of organisms washed from sods. B is an enlargement of a skeletal fragment. C shows the typical size and shape of mineral particles washed from sods – particles suspended in the water column and transported across tidal meadows during high tides.

available on what selectively happens to those sediments when the high-energy river water floods onto the meadows and begins to slowly work its way through that grassy barrier. Obviously, the total profile of river water suspended sediments is not what reaches the high tidal meadows, but it is this unstudied component that forms the inorganic elements of those unique Acadian soils (and provides the grit that polishes steel implements used on dykeland soils).

Because tide-transported silt is so fine (Fig. 4.6 C) it fills every marsh surface cavity and, as more sediment accumulates above it, becomes compressed into an airtight and watertight soil. Therefore, there is no natural air or water circulation in local marsh turf, as opposed to upland turf aerated by earthworms. To bring oxygen to those tissues, the grasses and rushes have responded by developing a system of air transport tubes from their leaves down into their roots. Peculiarly, the anaerobic bacterial action in this anaerobic soil seems to be negligible, even where the marsh turf has accumulated to depths of several metres after hundreds of years (Fig. 4.7, p. xviii). Could the living roots of these highly specialized grasses produce an antibiotic to prevent the bacterial production of toxic hydrogen sulphide? Whereas there is strong anaerobic activity in the black sulphurous oozes at the bottom of the marsh pools, there was none in the adjacent marsh root entanglements where we cut out our sod samples. This merits a focused investigation.

This nil-decomposition feature favoured the Acadians, for they could strip off live sods to a depth of 10 to 12 inches (0.25 to 0.3 m), and then take another root layer, to be used as wall fill, from beneath. With their slightly increased ratio of wet clay to root, these subsurface sods from the second and third layers in a sod pit were more malleable and could be packed tightly together, no matter what their shape. These softer sods were also useful for filling in gaps created by the trunks and branches of the brush layers at the aboiteaux.

All this was possible because those entanglements of live and dead roots remain intact. At the eroding Wolfville riverbank, one can see live roots from the marsh turf above, hanging exposed beneath the undercut banks. They are, on average, one metre long, but they are incomplete because the tidal battering that undermines the bank also removes the finer terminal portions of the roots. Unless one dyed an individual plant system, it would be a near hopeless challenge to trace an entire root complex simply by turf dissection.

After the Acadians had enclosed a section of marsh, and rain had washed away the surface salts, their plowing exposed these dead entombed roots to rain and air, and then they quickly decomposed. This is the other reason that there was no need for fertilizers; the enclosed marine fields had a built-in compost component. So why would anyone want to clear rocky, forested, and leached uplands? Only mad dogs and Englishmen, of course.

The old roots are so well preserved in their clay shroud that I have been able to identify both species from sods taken from the 1806 dyke at Wolfville. Salt Meadow Hay was used as core fill and Black Grass, as expected, was on the outer face of the dyke wall. When viewing cross-sections of the 1 to 2 mm roots under a binocular dissecting microscope, the arrangement of the air tubes (aerenchymal tissue) is distinct for each species. In cross-section, the roots of Salt Meadow Hay have a large central cavity surrounded by an outer cortex of equally large rounded tubes (Fig. 4.8). Black Grass is considerably different, with a core cluster of small tubes and a cortex region with large narrow tubes radiating from the central vascular tissue (Fig. 4.9 A). The most distinctive feature of this species, however, is a ring of thick-walled cells (possibly lignified cellulose endodermis) forming a tough cylinder around the central vascular bundle (Fig. 4.9 B). This small-diameter cylinder resists decay, and its distinctive fluted surface can be used to identify Black Grass in 200-year-old dyke-wall sods (Fig. 4.9 C, D).

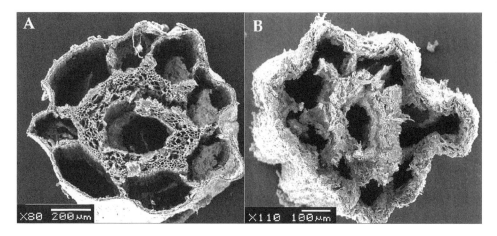

Figure 4.8   Cross-section of Salt Meadow Hay (*Spartina patens*) roots. A is a dried fresh root and B is from the core of the 1805–06 Planter dyke wall at Wolfville.

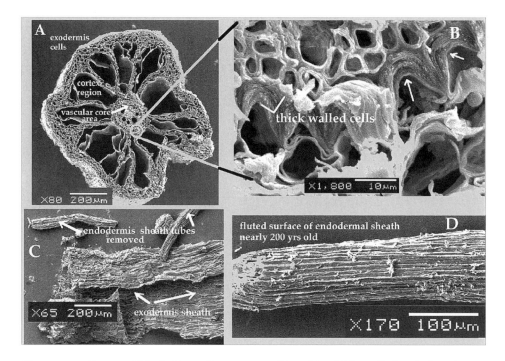

Figure 4.9   Roots of Black Grass (*Juncus gerardi*) and its thick-walled endodermis cells. A and B are freshly dried roots. C and D are from the face sods of an 1806 dyke wall. The roots of Salt Meadow Hay (*Spartina patens*) have no similar decay-resistant cellular cylinder.

Amos (1978) reported marsh-plant rootlets in a core sample from the bottom of the Minas Basin, and those roots were determined to be 8,665 years old. The deposition pattern of their clay surround indicated a quiet Minas Basin at that time, with a low tidal range.

Black Grass was preferred for facing the dykes because its rootlets form an almost wool-like mesh that, combined with the clay, tenaciously traps moisture. This is part of its strategy of survival, for it lives at the higher tidal levels and may not be inundated by sea water for weeks at a time. It was, therefore, naturally more tolerant than other marsh grasses of the non-submergence habitat on the face of a dyke wall. But no one really knows for how many years the marine grasses would continue to grow on a dyke wall. The Black Grass would be inundated periodically by high spring tides, but this possibility varies year by year and month by month as outlined in chapter 3. The salt-tolerant species are eventually replaced by more competitive upland grasses, which seed in very quickly. Competition is an important limiting factor, for if Salt Meadow Hay or Black Grass are transplanted to a greenhouse or garden setting, they thrive without sea water as long as they are kept thoroughly weeded. Four summers ago (June 2000), I transplanted a sod of Salt Meadow Hay and one of Black Grass to my flower garden. They have thrived without a daily sea inundation, and have tolerated hot dry summers and soil-freezing winters. It would be informative to build a replica section of dyke wall faced with hand-cut sods and to record the sequence of replacement of grass species over time.

Black Grass has another feature appreciated by dykers: it starts spring growth six weeks before other grasses. By mid-June at Grand Pré, Black Grass is already in flower, whereas the adjacent patches of Salt Meadow Hay are only evident as short new green shoots. Thus, Black Grass is conveniently available as a vigorously growing turf in time for spring dyking repairs and new construction.

Dyking Spades

The dyking spade seems to have been considered as unworthy of study, in spite of its cultural significance. Little is known or published about its origin and evolution in Europe, the templates used by blacksmiths, commercial production by blacksmiths and by factories, those blacksmiths who signed their works, or the possibility of regional differences in spade design. An article by Boutin and Guiteny (1987) includes several interesting diagrams of varieties of spades used by the salt makers in France, long ago. I can easily imagine dyking spades becoming a collectible item of historical significance and worthy of study.

Grassy sods for facing a dyke wall had to be cut consistently at a predetermined slope and predetermined size, so that when transferred to the wall they would fit tightly with sides flush, in the manner of bricklaying. This was essential, as any water or air pockets between sods were potential sites for tidal and storm erosion. Imagine the skill required to step onto a grassy marsh, lean on your spade and produce hundreds of identical sods, each cut at a 60° slope and each square-sided with dimensions in the order of 4″ x 8″ (0.1 x 0.2 m) at the grassy surface and 11″ (0.28 m) in depth. This was done at the rate of one sod every ten to fifteen seconds. Such were the capabilities of the master cutters, those senior, experienced dyke builders so crucial to transforming the tidal marsh into tillable farmland.

The cutting instrument they employed, the dyking spade, was a design they brought from Europe, a design possibly thousands of years old when one considers how long ago men may have begun cutting sods from peat bogs and tidal marshes.

The designation of "cutters" and not "diggers" is a significant distinction. Dyking spades were designed as knives that would slice through those root mats. Their narrowness, 4 to 5 inches, is a delicate compromise between too wide a blade, which cannot be forced through the roots, and too narrow a blade, which requires too many slices per sod. The cutters could turn out a variety of sod widths by slicing laterally once, twice, or three times. The old dyking measurement term for a sod that was cut the width of a spade was "a spitten wide," two contiguous cuts was "two spittens wide," and so on. Spitten is an Old English term for a spade. According to the Oxford English Dictionary, the term "spitting" was first used in 1595 and referred to the action of digging to a spade's depth, and a spittle was a small spade.

The unusual shape of this spade reflects its unique function, yet it appears deceptively simple for such a highly sophisticated instrument (Fig. 4.10). When pressed into marsh turf, all resistance is concentrated at the sharp straight edge, which is also the widest part. The sides angle in from the cutting blade and so do not adhere as the spade penetrates further. The bulging metal socket that receives the wooden shaft is on the front of the blade and it, with the two adjacent and forward curving shoulders of the blade, serves to separate a sod from the spade surface as it is being cut. By this means the strong adhesion potential of the wet clay is kept to a minimum. This is also an important feature when a forward thrust of the spade levers the sod away from the pit wall and breaks it off at its base (Fig. 4.11, p. xix). I had been told that with this spade it was easy to fling a seemingly wet sticky sod

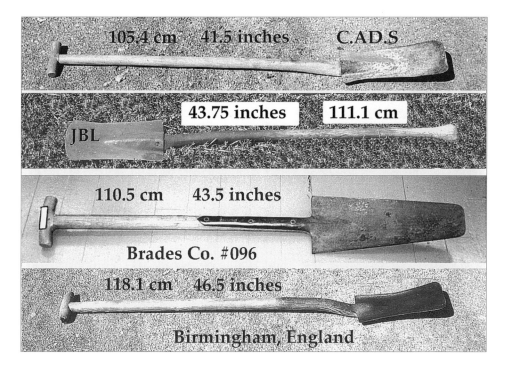

Figure 4.10   A selection of dykeland spades. The upper two were used for cutting marsh grass turf into square-sided sods for construction of dyke walls. The lower two are believed to be ditch-clearing spades because of their heavy construction and the metal tangs extending up the shaft.

Often a blacksmith's initials or the name of a foundry are stamped into the metal. For example: L.E. – Leonard Estabrooks, Sackville, NB; C.AD.S – Charles A.D. Siddall, Sackville, NB; J.B.L – John B. Lyon, Falmouth, NS; A&R Parkes & Co, Birmingham, England; Brades Co. #096 (production city unknown).

because the sod was perched above the blade on the two shoulders and the handle socket, and it shot off the lip of the spade as if it were greased. I was somewhat skeptical until Jean Palmeter provided the photographic proof (Fig. 4.12) with Robert Palmeter in his retirement demonstrating this technique. He kept his spade oiled and polished to his dying day, and it is now in the MacDonald Museum, Middleton, Nova Scotia (Fig. 4.13).

The traditional metal blade and wooden shaft and handle were made as light as possible to minimize the effort involved in the rapid in and out and right angle repositioning of the spade as the sods were cut. The tempering of the blade at the forge was an artful balancing act to achieve both lightness and strength.

Figure 4.12 Robert H. Palmeter of Grand Pré demonstrating sod cutting and tossing. (Courtesy of Jean Palmeter)

The spade shaft is short, with a small T-bar handle attached, or simply a terminal round knob slightly larger than the shaft, but part of it (Fig. 4.10). The spade was pushed into the marsh either by hand or by holding the T-bar against the stomach and hip area, and then bending the knees and leaning on it to exert the necessary pressure. The other hand was on the shaft, aiming and guiding the root cutting edge (Fig. 4.14). Feet were not used because the spade's shoulders were too narrow and sharp, and would have cut into bare feet, leather boots, and even rubber boots. More importantly, a sod cutter's feet would soon become clay laden and would slip off the shoulders of any type of spade or shovel. As well, it could be exhausting lifting a clay-encrusted foot up and down every few seconds.

These lightweight spades were not used in the typical fashion of digging, prying, and lifting sods as one does in the garden. The sods were cut and then levered forward and, because of their weight and rigidity, they broke off at their base. They were then removed by another person equipped with a pitchfork. These forks were also atypical, having two or sometimes three short tines that penetrated the sods enough to grip them but presented a

Figure 4.13   Robert H. Palmeter in the 1970s, standing with his cherished spade in front of plank facing installed in 1929–1930 over an original Acadian dyke wall at west Grand Pré. This was done following storm destruction of the Wickwire Dyke built by the Planters. (Courtesy of Jean Palmeter)

minimum of adhesion surface. In more recent times, these were often standard hay forks with their tines cut short. There is some evidence that the earliest sod forks were made just for that purpose, with short sturdy tines. Although the sods are heavy, they are not going to fall apart, and small tine holes are not going to pry apart that entanglement of roots.

Local elderly dykers remembered the vital importance of keeping that blade sharp, and they sharpened it bevelled from one side only. The spade was never used for anything else for fear of dulling or nicking its edge. It always hung at a special place on the farm, on a special rack that kept its edge off the ground, and it was not to be touched by anyone other than the sod cutters. Children must have been in awe of this peculiar instrument with all its restrictions and taboos. Most farms had dyking spades always at the ready. When a dyke needed emergency repairs, that was not the time to wonder where someone had last tossed the spade and whether it needed sharpening.

An early twentieth-century photo by A.L. Hardy of dyking repairs taking place at west Grand Pré (Fig. 4.15) shows many of the men holding spades, but not all would be master sod cutters. Only the sods on the face of the

Figure 4.14 Ellis Gertridge demonstrating the classic push method used for cutting tidal marsh turf. To the right, a selection of spade hand grips, including the knob handle of J.B. Lyon of Falmouth, NS.

walls were pressed together like bricks. The many blocks used as fill in the core of the wall need not be symmetrical and could be cut by amateurs and apprentices.

The minute mineral particles (Fig. 4.6 C) in the marsh soil are notoriously abrasive. Modern plow blades obtain a mirror finish after use on dykelands, and backhoes have their steel teeth worn down. Understandably, any dyking spade in regular use gradually became shorter, had its corners rounded, and had its general thickness reduced. Consequently, it had to be replaced regularly. For this reason, it is highly unlikely that any original eighteenth-century Acadian or Planter spades have survived. I have recently managed to locate, photograph, and measure forty-seven old dyking spades; many are cracked across the blade or broken off entirely and even the wooden shaft may be broken. What usually happens is that a spade is retired to a barn and years later, or even a generation later, is discovered by someone looking for a small spade to use in a flower bed or vegetable garden. At the

Figure 4.15   A.L. Hardy photo circa 1913 of repairs to Davidson Aboiteau and dyke wall, at the west end of Long Island. Over forty men are in the area, using hand barrows, dyking spades, pitchforks, ox carts and horse carts. Note the smooth grassy dyke face and rough sod pieces in the wall fill.

first attempt to pry upland soil, either the thinly worn blade or the slender shaft will fracture. (Appendix 4 is a sample of the dyking spade data sheet that I have been using.)

James Eldridge of Falmouth had three blades at his forge, one of which was never used because of several air bubbles in the steel. When compared with a similar blade, made by the same blacksmith, but well used and well worn, the unused blade at its cutting edge was $^1/2''$ (1.3 cm) wider, and $^{15}/16''$ (2.3 cm) longer (Fig. 4.16). Note also the well-rounded, worn corners of the used blade.

The first spades undoubtedly came from France with the salt makers, which is why these dykers were brought to Port Royal (Leonard, 1991). Additional spades could have been imported from France regularly, but I would guess that the original salt makers arrived with the skills and tools necessary to repair and make their marsh-cutting spades. The original design has not been improved upon; I have a 1965 photograph of a blacksmith, Leonard Estabrooks of Sackville, New Brunswick, working at his anvil making a typical seven-rivet dyking blade. Although the government was using heavy equipment on dykelands after 1950, the small patching jobs were still being contracted out to dyking spade crews well into the 1960s.

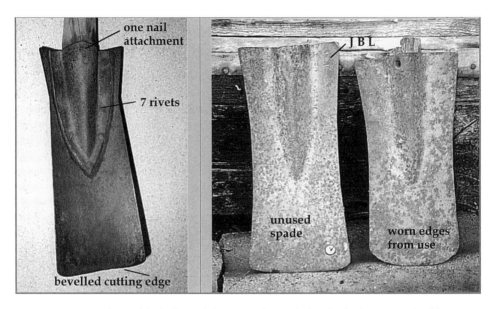

Figure 4.16 A classic blade for a dyking spade, with the shaft sleeve attached by seven rivets and one central hole for a nail to anchor the wooden handle. On the right, two of J.B. Lyon's non-classic blades produced by splitting the metal sheet to form the shaft socket and having an off-centre nail hole.

Not only professional blacksmiths made dyking spades. I have heard several tales concerning farmers who could turn out spades at their own home forges from the steel of large discarded blades from saw mills. I have found that the latter blades are coarser and heavier than the preferred lighter spades.

Some blacksmiths signed their creations by stamping their initials into the metal. I have thus far found three recurring signatures and there may be others. Two are from blacksmiths who lived near Sackville, New Brunswick, but whose spades were sold widely. The Sackville Historical Society has assembled a great deal of material on local dykeland history, including spades. Leonard Estabrooks and his son Lionel stamped their initials L.E. on the back of their blades near the wooden shaft. The other Sackville black-smith was Charles A.D. Siddall, whose stamp was C.AD.S, also on the back at the top. The third blacksmith worked at Falmouth, Nova Scotia, and his initials J.B.L. are embossed high on the face of the blade on one of the shoulder wings. He was John Benjamin Lyon and he is reported to have made hundreds of spades, assisted by his son, in preparation for the commu-nity installation of the Grand Dyke Aboiteau at Windsor, Nova Scotia, in 1908. Their spades had a round knob handle. Many photographic postcards

County	Spades	C.AD.S	L.E.	J.B.L.	Parkes Co.	Brades Co.
Kings County	19	3	2		1	
Hants	10			3		1
Annapolis	2		2			
Lunenburg	3				1	
Halifax	1				1	
Colchester	1					
Cumberland	1					
Sackville, NB	6		2			
	43					

See also Fig. 4.10

were produced from this event, depicting the hundreds of men and horse-carts involved. When these old photos are highly magnified, the knob-handled Lyon spades are easily recognizable.

I have found two other types of somewhat similar spades that were assumed by museum personnel to be sod-cutting spades because they were donated in that context (Fig. 4.10). I believe they may be ditching spades used to clean out the dale ditches that ran between the long strips of fields on dykeland. They are more heavily constructed and the blade's steel is extended up the shaft on both front and back sides (these extensions are known as tangs); the tang bears an embossed stamp. Both types were factory made. One was made by A & R Parkes & Co of Birmingham, England, and may have been brought to Nova Scotia by Yorkshire farmer immigrants in the early 1770s. The other is stamped simply Brades Co #096, which presumably is a company catalogue number, but preliminary research at the Ross Farm Museum library and Internet sites has so far drawn a blank. Table 4.4 summarizes in which county the forty-three measured spades were located and the distribution of the stamped ones.

Spade Construction

The blade is one piece of metal, usually 11 inches (27.9 cm) long and 4.5 inches (11.5 cm) at the cutting edge. To form the socket for insertion of the wooden shaft several methods were used:

- A half-sleeve socket with skirt was attached to the blade, using seven rivets that are nearly impossible to distinguish on the back of the blade, as they are usually flush.
- The socket skirt was welded to the blade plate, something only a master blacksmith could do, as the temperature had to melt the surfaces to be welded but not the rest of the spade blade. A special flux mixture (their own secret formula, passed down from father to son) was used.
- The heated steel blade was split along its top edge grain and a template driven in to form the shaft socket. I have been shown such spade sockets, and they do not appear to have been welded.

The wooden shaft was wedged into the socket and held in place with only one nail or screw. To ensure an absolutely tight fit, as a wobbly spade would hardly do for the surgical precision of sod cutting, the shaft was inserted into a heated metal socket, scorched, and removed; the blackened area was rasped away. The entire wood surface would soon fit the metal socket like a glove, and it only required a short nail to anchor it.

The wood used in some cases was ash, but it is not known how many other woods may also have been used.

The shaft was not only unusually short for a spade but also slender and often oval in cross-section. The oval shape made it easier to firmly grip the shaft halfway down with a wet slippery hand.

The upper ends of the shafts present an interesting variety of handle styles:

- The basic one is a small T-bar that would just fit in the hand. It was curved downwards so that slippery fingers did not slide off the short ends of the bar. To identify their own spade amongst the dozens in use at a construction site, many owners carved their names or initials into the butt end of the T-bar.
- The T-bars were attached several ways:
  - by mortise and tenon, with the tenon piercing the bar but finished flush. It was then drilled through at the neck and a wooden pin hammered in to anchor the bar. Often the drill hole was round but the pin square, as this produced a tight fit when driven in.
  - by mortise and tenon, but with the tenon not visible.
  - by mortise with a narrow slit sawed into the tenon into which a tiny wedge was inserted. When this was hammered into the mortise, the wedge spread open the tenon, essentially locking the two pieces together. No pin is required, and the means of attachment is not at all obvious.

- A different type of shaft is typical of the Lyon spade of Falmouth, Hants County. Instead of a T-bar, there is only a large round knob, a natural extension of the wood of the shaft and not an attachment.

During this survey, I became convinced that a mystique is attached to these unusual spades, something that makes persons want to retain them in the family, no matter how rusty or broken. These decrepit objects are treasured family heirlooms of horse and buggy and blacksmith days. Of the forty-seven spades I located, not one could be pried loose from an owner. I did have two, but one was on temporary loan and the other was a tool trade with a tool collector who had two spades picked up at auctions. Dyking spades occasionally do surface at country auctions, so be alert for these archaic European root cutters, and then please donate your purchase to some deserving museum.

CHAPTER FIVE

The Art and Science of Dyke Construction

Their dykes are made of large Sods of Marsh cut up in
square Pieces and raised about five feet higher than the
common Surface, of a competent Thickness to withstand
the Forces of the Tides, and soon grow very firm and
durable, being overspread with Grass, and have com-
monly Foot-paths on their Summit.

Otis Little, 1748

Envisage the first group of Acadians to arrive at the Grand Pré meadows,
watching as tidal waters slowly flooded into the creeks, realizing that here
were 3,000 acres (2,010 arpents) of flat land, soil with entombed nutrients
uniformly distributed throughout, neither trees nor rocks to remove, and a
drainage ditch system thousands of years old. All that was needed was a sea-
excluding wall, easily constructed from an on-site sod quarry, the marsh
itself. Add a plowing pattern that would crown long field strips, leave the
rains to leach salts into the ditches, and in a mere two to three years upland
grasses would produce lush hay and then bountiful crops. This was a dyke-
lander's heaven on earth.

Thus, after 350 million years of preparation, the Great Meadow (Grand
Pré) was visited by the French, and there began a labour and love affair with
that land that has only intensified over time. They arrived with basic knowledge and skills long practised in Europe, and they proceeded to release this
bountiful soil from its saline constraints. The very grasses of the marsh that
built up these soils were enlisted as walls to keep the sea from those selfsame

meadows. Their unique European dyking spade was the key to their success (Boutin and Guiteny, 1987). Construction of dyke walls and sluice boxes was merely a matter of assembling the pieces of sod or wood, but the production of properly and uniformly shaped sods required the special combination of a precise tool in the hands of a master craftsman sod cutter. As tide and time wait for no man, especially on marshlands, so it was that the production of the greatest number of uniform sod bricks in the shortest time was the ultimate key to quickly transforming saline tidal marshes into farmland.

In this and the following chapter, we examine how the Acadians organized their construction teams, what these teams could accomplish, and how they applied themselves to the challenge of enclosing the entire Grand Pré tidal meadows.

The general perception is that with the burning of their homes and their records at the time of the deportation in 1755, the cultural details of the daily life of the Acadians were lost forever. Therefore, to attempt a detailed discussion of how the Acadians built their dykes may seem presumptuous. However, many Acadians managed to avoid deportation and, after the arrival of the New England Planters in 1760, they were soon conscripted or coerced to instruct the English in methods of construction and repair of dykes. These early dyking proceedings were closely watched by a young man, Jonathan Crane of Windsor, Nova Scotia. Shortly afterwards, in 1774, he became Commissioner of Sewers (read: supervisor of dykeland maintenance) and applied those methods for the forty-one years of his career. In 1819 he wrote a comprehensive and invaluable newspaper article detailing these techniques (appendix 5). This appendix contains a copy of his text that I have interpreted, edited, and annotated, as well as a condensed version with diagrams.

After comparing information derived from my interviews of dykers (list of persons in appendix 3) with that in Crane's article, I have concluded that the dyking methods practised by the Acadians were the most efficient and were adopted essentially unchanged by the Planters and the Loyalists, and their descendants. A few men living today, now in their eighties, have cut sods with that distinctive Acadian dyking spade to repair dyke walls, and others have had opportunities to observe these repair methods as late as the 1950s. From these human sources and items in the literature, I have assembled a detailed scenario for dyke-wall construction, accompanied by diagrams based on my interpretations. The latter were examined by several elderly dykers for verification.

My conclusion is that dyke building was a relatively easy undertaking; my specific points of argument follow. Argument is an appropriate term, for most of the dykers in their mid-seventies that I recently interviewed emphasized what terribly hard work it was and how heavy the sods were. However, as teenagers in the 1930s, they had neither skills nor experience nor natural work rhythm, and had not the strength or the stamina of the older men. Several complained that the older men with whom they worked would never stop their working rhythms, except for lunch breaks.

The younger men, too inexperienced and inept to do anything else, were assigned the task of driving the horse drags that hauled sods from the cutting pits to the new wall. They often walked in heavy clay, but were forbidden to ride on the drags. If strong enough, some pitched sods onto or off the drags, or they drove stakes using heavy mallets. All of which was understandably distasteful to teenagers. In contrast, the oldest dykers I interviewed told a different story, one of efficient work rhythms that went on all day, lunch breaks that involved contests of throwing a sod the greatest distance, and wall builders who could catch a tossed sod in mid-air on their fork, redirect it, and slam it into position in one continuous motion, with the precision of a bricklayer and the pride of a master craftsman.

We can confidently assume that the Acadians were not at all intimidated by the task of dyking the 3,000 acres of Grand Pré and Wolfville tidal marshes, because they knew how feasible it was. Until recently, I, too, could not imagine the source of the Acadians' conviction that equipped only with an ox, a tiny spade and a pitchfork, they could exclude the world's highest tides from the Grand Pré meadows. However, now I do understand and hope that I may convince others, for once you appreciate how quickly dykes can literally be thrown up, then certain cultural and historical events can be reassessed from that new vantage point. It also makes my next chapter more understandable and acceptable.

The construction of dyke walls, and the blockage of large creeks with aboiteaux sluices, was a highly organized endeavour with workers divided into teams (Cormier, 1990). The minimal team was five or six men and an ox team, or horse with cart. Their duties were divided as follows:

- the sods were cut at a pit
- the sods were forked onto a drag
- the drag was driven to the wall
- the sods were pitched off the drag
- the dyke wall facing sods were placed in position, like bricks
- the loose centre-fill sods were packed down

From the elderly persons interviewed, I learned that this was a flexible system, with interesting variations. Two men could be cutting sods at the same pit, but working in opposite directions; or even three cutters could follow one another laterally, along tandem rows. In these cases, more horse drags were added to match the rate of sod production. If the pits were far from the wall, then more drags were used to keep a steady flow of loading at the pits and unloading at the wall. At the other extreme, if the pits were very close to the wall, some of the cutters were capable of pitching their own sods onto the wall. Such an accomplished display was possible because the shape of the spade elevated much of the sod off the blade and, instead of adhering, as on a flat garden spade or shovel, the sod slid off the dyking spade with ease. If this were truly a "mud sod," it would sag into the spade, but as a semi-rigid root mat it remains elevated and does not adhere to the blade.

If the marsh were wet and greasy, or otherwise too soft for oxen or a horse and drag, the sods were moved by being tossed along a line from man to man, or simply skidded along the wet surface from man to man. These abusive transport methods were possible only because the tidal marsh sod root matrix was nearly indestructible.

Walter "Ding" Kelly, of Grand Pré, eighty-eight years of age in 2000, was a hired farmhand at the Roy Woodman farm in Grand Pré for most of his life. As a young man, he became fascinated by sod cutting; he soon mastered the art and science of it and was greatly respected for his skills. When I handed him a dyking spade, his face lit up and his hands automatically grasped the shaft and twisted and turned it as he showed me the cutting motions; then he said "I've spent many an hour with one of these in my hands!" He proudly claimed he could cut sods fast enough to occupy a rotation of five horse drags. Sometimes the foreman would ask him to stop cutting and come to the wall to help lay bricks and reduce the backlog of his sods.

There is no reason to doubt his statements, particularly in light of George Frail's observations. Frail was an engineer hired by the government after it assumed responsibility for dyke-wall management around 1950 (Maritime Marshland Rehabilitation Administration). By then dykers were experimenting with a variety of heavy equipment for major repairs and new wall construction (drag lines, bulldozers, and conveyor-belt machines), but for minor patching jobs the old manual method was more efficient. As a supervisor, George Frail was in the unique position of hiring the last of the professional dyke builders and of being able to stand aside and carefully and objectively watch them perform. His fascinating accounts of their knowledge and skills verifies one's intuitive suspicions of their mastery of the craft. For example, he would request sods be cut at a specific angle to create the correct slope on the face of a dyke wall, and without hesitation or measuring, the cutters would tilt their spades accordingly and proceed to cut row upon row of sods at exactly that angle. They could even produce sods while talking face to face with someone, not looking where they were cutting, somehow sensing what their spades were doing.

When several cutters were supplying the same section of dyke under construction, precision fitting of sods at the wall was further enhanced by matching up spades of the same blade dimensions. As spades were made by different persons and at different localities, they did differ slightly. If the sods were not similar, then the possibility arose that when laid as required in brick-wall construction, eventually the edges of several would coincide, creating a long seam on the dyke face that could be vulnerable to storm erosion.

In the Avondale area, near Windsor, Hants County, David and Gordon Knowles recounted how some local cutters would parallel bevel their two side cuts so that when the facing sods were slapped together on the wall their edges overlapped from above, providing a better seal, with gravity squeezing out water and air pockets. Another Avondale construction variation was not having those typical borrow-pit trenches paralleling the inside of the dyke wall. They wanted to use all the reclaimed land for hay production as soon as possible. The interesting consequence of having dry margins around the fields was having woodchucks (ground hogs, *Marmota monax*) denning in the dyke walls. The usual bane of dykers are muskrats (*Ondatra zibethica*), which travel and feed in the pools of the borrow trenches and den in the dry dyke walls. The Knowles brothers were country raised and definitely know a woodchuck from a muskrat. At the uppermost marshes of the Avon River, near Castle Frederick, farmers had the same problem with woodchucks for the same reason, according to James Bremner. Woodchucks could tunnel into and actually through dyke walls during those periods of neap tides.

The basic Acadian construction scenario seems to have been laying a rope along the centre line of a future wall and removing a sod layer 6 ft (1.8 m) to either side (Cormier, 1990; Milligan, 1987). A shallow trench, termed a key trench, was dug along that centre line and at intervals of 6 to 10 ft (3 m) posts were driven in. Sod fill was packed into the trench and around the posts and, when the wall was finished, this combination functioned as an anchor, for until the wall settled and the grass roots spread into adjacent turf, there was the possibility of a high tide pushing the wall across its new slippery base and splitting it open.

In special instances, this sliding hazard could be put to positive use during wall repairs. Ellis Gertridge recalls his father rebuilding a section of dyke wall along the bank of the Gaspereau River and giving the wall a slight bulge towards the tidal river. After several high tides, the sods in the new wall had been pushed back and firmly compressed, and it was then in line with the

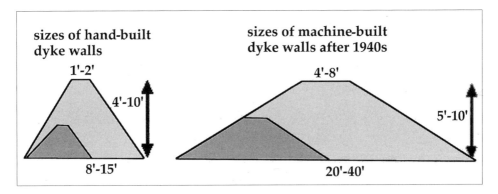

Figure 5.1   Diagrams of sizes of dyke walls adapted from dykeland engineer W.W. Baird, 1954. Variation in size has to do with location: the largest were those facing the open sea and the smallest were along the banks of the upper reaches of tidal rivers.

adjacent old sections. During spring runoff, when the volume of the Gaspereau River was greater than normal, the river water backed up where it met the flood tide, thereby creating a bulge in the river level. To compensate for this, the dyke wall was constructed higher along that section of the river.

Wall construction itself involved gradually building up the sloping seaward and landward dyke walls with precisely cut sods, and at the same time filling in and compacting the central space with any other sod material. The facing sods were laid lengthwise into the wall to their full depth, with their narrow grassy side facing outwards. Their roots would soon grow downwards and their rhizomes laterally, binding the sods together. Again, in keeping with efficiency of effort, dyke walls varied in size. The largest faced the open Minas Basin and the smallest lined the banks of the upper reaches of tidal rivers (Fig. 5.1).

I have several old photographs showing a different technique applied to repairing a breach in a dyke wall. To fill the breach with a tall solid wall as quickly as possible, they piled up the core sods first and then, at the next tidal opportunity and probably after compacting the sods with large flat mallets, they faced the rough wall with live green sods.

When full wall height was achieved, a bare flat crest remained, a footpath in width, upon which sods need not be wasted because wind-blown grass seeds accumulated there and soon formed a turf. Some of the rough fill came from the adjacent borrow trenches that paralleled the dyke wall, but these pits had to be at least six feet away from the wall base so as not to weaken it and risk slumping. They could also serve an important drainage function

Figure 5.2   A typical hand-built dyke with walls only slightly higher than the highest of normal tides, demonstrating that those seemingly insubstantial piles of sods had great strength, as long as sea water could not find a way through via muskrat burrows, or over the top via exceptional storm-generated tides. (Nova Scotia Department of Agriculture and Marketing)

if they were contoured towards adjacent natural creek drainage systems. Fig. 5.2 is a photo of a manually built dyke at Aulac, New Brunswick (Milligan, 1987). A borrow-sod trench runs along the inside of the wall, hay storage barns are in the background, and the high tide is challenging that narrow margin of safety on which dykers gambled. Fig. 5.3 is an unusual and dramatic photo of breaching in action at a similar type of dyke at Wolfville on 30 October 1913. A livestock fence and a footpath run along the crest of the wall.

The general construction of an aboiteau across a wide creek, and the incorporation of a one-way flow sluice box within that wall, is difficult simply because of the extreme variation in the sizes of these units. At the smallest of dyked areas, which would consist of a simple loop of dyke wall extending out from the upland and encircling a section of tidal marsh, all that was required was a small sluice box or log with the simple one-way clapper valve (clappet) to permit the escape of accumulated rainwater from behind the new wall (Fig. 5.4, not to scale). These small aboiteau sluices can still be discovered along tidal rivers, and I even found one in a seawall at Grand Pré in 1994. It was made from an 8 inch (20.3 cm) diameter tree, 17 ft long (5.2 m), with an adzed square-sided trough only 5 inches (12.7 cm) wide. Since then I have located five others, all slightly larger, in the Canning area. Larger creeks require larger trees, often 45 ft (13.7 m) in length and

Figure 5.3   A typical minor breaching of a dyke near Wolfville harbour in October 1913. According to newspaper reports at that time, it was easily repaired before the next set of high tides. The crest has a footpath as well as a livestock restraining fence. (Jeff Wilson Collection, Lawrencetown, NS; E. Graham photo)

over 3 ft (0.9 m) in diameter. At major creeks two or three such hollowed out sluice logs could be placed side by side. Once sawmills became well established, sluices could have been made of planking, but the total labour involved in building a sturdy plank sluice must have greatly exceeded that required for a more durable tree trunk. The latter had only to be burnt and adzed out, and then capped with short cross pieces of wood or by a single long piece of slabwood, all being attached with doweling pins.

One interesting feature of the wall construction immediately over the sluice log is the steepness of the structure. This is evident in the old aboiteau dams that are still extant. To hold down the sluice log (or logs) and prevent the force of water or winter ice blocks from shifting it, the wall in the area of the sluice was built nearly straight up and only toward the upper level was it sloped in to conform to the running dyke wall. The trees used as brush layers in this area were larger than usual, as they had to extend well into the wall. If they were not anchored in this manner, ice blocks could freeze against them in winter and pull them out as the tide receded. These butt ends are conspicuously exposed on remnants of old aboiteaux, as if their sod covering had eroded away. The sods trapped within the branches of the brush layers

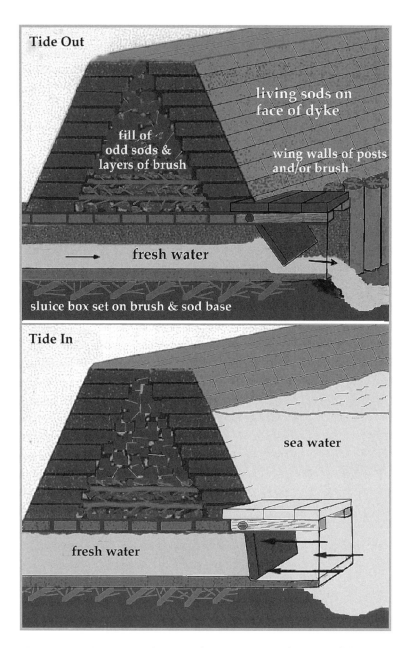

Figure 5.4   Composite diagram showing various features of dyke wall and aboiteau construction. Note the action of the clapper valve relative to direction of flow of water. The clapper recesses into an upper pocket to allow solid items to flow through the sluice unobstructed.

are the only ones remaining, but it may be that sods could not cling to this steep and regularly submerged wall face anyway and what we see today is the original configuration.

My recently acquired knowledge of dyke construction was derived from the general literature, some of which can be confusing, conflicting, and even accompanied by inaccurate diagrams; from that superbly detailed 1819 article by J. Crane; and from interviews with retired dykers, especially James Eldridge of Falmouth, Hants County. The latter remarkable person, aged eighty-five in 2001, is a truly accomplished "Renaissance Dyker," who followed in his father's footsteps and thus can draw upon the accumulated experience of two generations. His knowledge spans every aspect of tidal engineering: from tiny dykes to the Windsor Causeway; all sizes of aboiteaux; riverbank erosion control; sawmills; types of wood; types of tools; explosives; forges; horses; drag lines and bulldozers; spades and forks; seemingly everything. He first met dykeland engineer George Frail in the 1950s while working at Grand Pré. His endless talents were recognized and soon he was called upon to help construct and problem-solve all over Atlantic Canada, including Newfoundland. He installed small sluices at Grand Pré and a huge one at the Great Discharge Creek of the Wickwire Dyke in 1960, and he cured the problem of the new but leaking Windsor Causeway. He has kept diaries and photos, and has a set of photographic postcards of the 1908 installation of the Grand Dyke Aboiteau at Windsor, Nova Scotia, in which the various activities of hundreds of men and horse carts are recorded. The detail in these photos is such that when they are enlarged it is possible to identify the unusual knob handles of the dyking spades that are the trademark of blacksmith J.B. Lyon.

Several photographers in this area of Nova Scotia near the turn of the last century (1900) often recorded dyking events, and the detail on their glass plate negatives lends itself to exciting enlargements. They included Ruben Boyd in Windsor, Edson Graham (1869–1956) of Windsor and Wolfville, and Amos Lawson Hardy (1860–1935) in Kentville. On one occasion, circa 1913, Hardy took photographs, from several angles and at different times of the tidal day, of major dyke repairs taking place at Davidson Aboiteau at northwest Grand Pré, where Ransom Creek empties into the Cornwallis River. The complex construction is evident in the photos (Figs 4.4 and 4.15). In brief, the dam consists of posts driven in vertically, logs stacked behind them parallel to the dam, and a backfill of sods and layers of brush laid at right angles to the logs in staggered patterns that minimize any chance of a water channel forming from front to back or top to bottom of the structure.

During the layering and stepwise construction stages, clay sods are packed onto and between every layer to form a waterproof clay seal. Brush serves to prevent the sods from sliding across one another. Too much brush and water seeps through; too little brush and the entire dam slumps, slides, and collapses from its own weight. Such were the woes of the New England Planters and the Loyalists when they attempted to surpass the Acadians at dyking accomplishments. In 1806 they built a three-mile-long dyke with six aboiteaux extending from Long Island to Wolfville. In 1825 they completed the mile-long Wellington Dyke at Canard, but not until 1898 did the Planters attempt an aboiteau across that deepest part of Ransom Creek. By circa 1913 they already had slumping problems at that site (Fig. 4.4).

The Acadians avoided doing battle with those wide, deep creeks at the western discharge sites of Ransom Creek and Great Discharge Creek. They had the time and the ability to do it but, in my estimation, the foresight not to. The two approaches to dyking broad deep creeks involve contrasting trade-offs. The Acadians expended a minimum of labour and materials by building miles of small dykes that meandered along the high ground to each side of the creeks. The trade-off was that these miles of walls had to be patrolled and maintained, but that was easily accomplished. The Planters and Loyalists seem to have had that Yankee attitude of ingenuity, of "there must be a better way," for they opted for one huge aboiteau dam whenever possible, one that would protect a vast area and eliminate the traditional tedious maintenance patrolling of miles of dykes. However, even a cursory examination of that photo of repairs to the slumping 1898 Davidson Aboiteau on Ransom Creek (Fig. 4.4) reveals the magnitude of the materials required for the original construction and for its repair only fifteen years later. It has never been destroyed by storms since, but has had to be both repaired and relocated. In this 1913 situation any catastrophic risk to the rest of Grand Pré was mitigated by the fortuitous presence of an original Acadian dyke, the one casting a shadow across the background in Fig 4.4, a fail-safe backup dyke skirting the creek on higher ground.

Obviously, the farther out from the upland, the deeper were the creeks, for they had to carry away water from both the marsh watershed and the upland watershed. Setting a sluice log (or timber box) in these deep creeks was a science as well as a fine art. An aboiteau dam across a creek was an intricate construction. The basic concept was to pile up a wall of clay-infused waterproof sods, to keep them from sliding about by interspersing layers of trees with their branches, and at the same time to prevent water from seeping along the tree trunks and penetrating the wall, thus lubricating its sods and causing the whole thing to slump and collapse. The scientific principle was simple; putting it into practice was the art.

Setting the sluice in a creek bed involved preparing a long brush-sod-pole sluice bed, but one that bowed upwards towards the centre. The sluice was thereby installed curving downward towards each end, but after the full weight of the dyke dam was added above, everything compacted and the sluice became level. Ignoring this procedure creates a sluice box with a long pool of water in its bowed-down mid section, where sediment could accumulate and the water could freeze in winter.

The ideal material from which to construct an aboiteau sluice, be it 20 ft or 100 ft in length, is a tree trunk. When hollowed out it becomes a single unit of great strength, yet it is flexible enough to adjust to any settling of the dyke wall. Sluices made of timbers have to be fitted and joined with mortise and tenon and bolted, but they are still vulnerable to water penetration, warping, and popping, and they require layers of lumber to approximate the natural strength of a tree trunk. In the 1820s the walls of the Wellington Dyke sluices were, from the inside to outside, 12 inch timbers covered by 2 inch plank and then sheathed in 6 inch timber.

Tree trunks have other advantages. When hollowed, their inside diameter can be tapered from narrow upper end to the wider base diameter, if the wall thickness is kept nearly the same. This enhances water flow, and ensures that objects, such as ice, branches, or dead animals, that are small enough to enter the sluice will probably not get stuck once inside.

At the discharge end of a log sluice, the builder can carve the wood to accomplish several important features. The diameter can be increased by thinning the inside wall, and a broader spill-way sill can be formed by cutting back the side walls. These modifications attenuate the force of the water entering the spill pool by fanning it out right and left. The bottom of the spill pool was often lined with a brush mat, and that in turn was capped with an erosion-resistant layer of rocks.

A slight backward sloping of the ends of the sluice log side walls encouraged ice blocks to slide up and off the sluice, not to jam against it. The terminal cap of boards or plank pieces that cover the sluice also had to be set back from the end of the sluice so that it would not be pried off by floating ice, trees, or timbers.

The installation of the simple, flat, wooden, one-way valve was constrained by the principle that it should not project into the sluice when elevated by water flow, because items could become jammed and contribute to a blockage (J. Crane, 1819). For these reasons, the valve plate had a recess pocket and was flush with the rest of the sluice's ceiling when a full flow of water was draining the enclosed marshland. As well, when sea water pressed against it from the opposite direction, the valve needed a supporting ledge around its periphery, at the sides and bottom.

The advantage of working with a log is that a valve chamber can be custom carved. This carving method is even evident in old sluices whose walls were made of squared timbers. In the case of the large assembled timber sluice boxes built by the government in the 1950s, this larger valve-casement chamber had to be built on. However, when using tree trunks, the basic technique was to continue the wall thickness up to the valve-seat area, which was then formed by cutting back the walls and the floor, thereby forming a ledge on three sides, the side ones sloping back somewhat. To lessen sea water leakage inland, the sides and bottom lip should fit flush, and the rounded edge of the upper hinge side be as close fitting as possible.

The short cylindrical wooden extensions that form the hanging hinges are part of the wooden door itself. Precisely how they are hung is where so many diagrams are incorrect. The hinges do not project into holes in the walls of a log sluice (as they could not be installed or serviced) and they do not sit in a deep trough cut out of the top edge of the wall. If they did, they would form an obstruction of their own thickness in the sluice passage. An object could lodge against the valve, form a catch trap and a blockage, and then pressures would be exerted at right angles to the hinge pins, which are attached only through the grain of the wood.

The hinges, in fact, sit on the side walls and are held in place from above by a deep notch cut into a short length of planking attached parallel to and along the top of each side wall at the valve site. To these two pieces are attached the short cross planks that cap the sluice. With this configuration, the capping planks can be lifted and the valve repaired or replaced. This access feature also makes possible, during the aboiteau construction phase (Crane, 1819), the easy insertion and removal of a temporary reverse facing valve, whose purpose was to create and retain a pond of sea water behind the developing dam.

Where the two projecting hinge pins rest on either side wall of the sluice, a broad but shallow trough is often evident. These troughs are obviously not deep enough to accommodate an entire hinge cylinder, further evidence that the valves were hung at the same level as the roof of the sluice, such that they swung up out of the way. These troughs may have been carved simply to provide a positioning seat for the hinge, but there is another possibility. I was told they were pockets for slabs of pigskin on which the hinge pin sat. These slabs served as self-lubricating "grease cups" that lasted for many, many years.

A further consideration when dyking discharge areas of large creeks is the amount of non-arable acreage enclosed. For example, the first Wickwire Dyke of 1806 enclosed about 780 acres between west Grand Pré and Wolfville, but the farmers had to discount some 100 acres because of the steep muddy creeks and the many necessary access roads. The Acadians' decision to go with low-tech meandering walls has proven to be a wise one, for in 1931 the ambitious Wickwire Dyke, after repeated retreats and reconstructions, was finally destroyed by a storm. Fortunately, the original 1755 Acadian dyke walls at west Grand Pré (maintained by the English from the 1760s to 1806) prevented a disastrous inundation of all of Grand Pré. After an upgrading and facing with planks in 1929–32, that wall once again became the functional west Grand Pré sea barrier, and remained so for the next twenty-nine years.

However, at the east side of Grand Pré, the Acadians finally did dyke those four large creeks. But these creeks were smaller and narrower than those at the west side of Grand Pré because their watershed discharge was small in comparison with the amount of upland runoff carried by Ransom Creek and Great Discharge Creek.

Jonathan Crane had observed the Acadians teaching the Planters dyking methods, and he later used these construction methods himself for forty-one years, from 1777 to 1818. We can, therefore, assume that his 1819 detailed account of dyking principles and practices was derived directly from traditional Acadian methods. His article is too detailed to discuss here at any length, but is included as appendix 5. However, several aspects of dyking outlined in his article are relevant to generating a better sense of how Acadians viewed dyking and how they accomplished so much in so few years.

Although at first it seems counterintuitive, the Acadians built the aboiteaux dams and sluices first, and then built the running dyke walls to join creek to creek. As Crane pointed out in 1819, this is most sensible because the highest tides then had broad access to the marshes and were not forced by dyke wall barriers to concentrate and funnel through the gap where new construction was taking place.

In addition, the Acadians propped open the clapper valve in a newly installed sluice to allow the sea water to enter the marsh creek behind their construction, and they added a temporary reversed clapper valve to retain that sea water in the creek upstream from the aboiteau. Under these conditions, when the flood tide returned, it rose up the front of the partially built aboiteau and over its top, but instead of cascading down and eroding the inside wall, it simply trickled into a saltwater pond behind the dam. Once the aboiteau had reached full height and the running dyke walls were complete, then the sluices were adjusted to exclude sea water.

Crane described how construction in progress could be secured against tidal and storm erosion, or at night, or during high-water spring-tide periods, or during festive holidays. The surface was covered in brush, poles were laid across the brush, and these poles were held in place by cross-staking. The tips of the stakes were sharpened on one side only, and this asymmetry drew them down tightly against the poles. This same sharpening technique is evident, some 200 years later, on several of the stakes lying on top of the dyke wall in the photo of repairs at Davidson Aboiteau on Ransom Creek (Figs 4.15 and 5.10).

The foregoing details indicate how sophisticated and efficient were the Acadians' efforts and how broad and deep was their knowledge; perhaps also that dyking was not the onerous task we have been led to believe.

Easy Dyking: The Evidence and Arguments

Previously, I found it difficult to imagine a few Acadian families, equipped only with spade, fork, and oxen, ever conceiving of dyking that immense expanse. Now I believe they simply dyked what they needed, about ten acres per family, working out from the high ground on the south side of Grand Pré.

Why would these farmers enclose surplus acreage unless they were actually in the business of exporting surplus produce. We know that later on they did export hay and much produce and livestock, and that may explain why the acreage in 1701 was only 730 acres, but had reached 2,400 by 1755. Was all this increase still based on the ten acres per family formula, or were they now motivated by profit? They seemed to have dyked as far west as practical at Grand Pré and then shifted efforts to the east end of Grand Pré, where they dyked the four major creeks draining into the Gaspereau River channel.

I had wondered why the Acadians decided to enclose this relatively small east area at the cost of constructing four deep-set aboiteaux. Did they do it because it would mean more export profits, or because for them all dyking was a relatively easy and routine procedure and not a limiting consideration?

To appreciate the reasoning behind my upcoming arguments, consider the following:

First, the Acadians must have had many fields of expertise in which they were extremely knowledgeable and indeed master craftsmen. Over the previous hundreds, even thousands, of years, practically every creative and constructive human activity had evolved into an efficient, specialized craft, be it making castles or carts or clothes – think stonemasons, cartwrights, wheelwrights, shipwrights, ferriers, fletchers, goldsmiths, gunsmiths, and innumerable other masons, wrights, and smiths. The Acadians, however, were not building anything as demanding as a Roman road or a Hadrian's Wall, they were simply piling up sods to a mere height of 5 or 6 ft (1.5 or 1.8 m), and the pile was tapered from a base 12 to 15 ft (3.6 to 4.6 m) wide, to a crest 1 or 2 ft (0.3 or 0.6 m) wide. Their building materials, the marsh sods, were immediately available at the construction site in limitless supply. As the wall was raised, fewer sods were required. Viewed from a medieval perspective, we should declare the Acadians to be "sod masons" and designate their dyking spade to be their icon. From this revised perspective, I imagine the Acadians drinking lots of cider while dyking, and singing ribald songs to combat the boredom of it all.

Surely dyking would have been another honed craft, conducted with efficiency and confidence, and not the unimaginably messy, chaotic chore we have envisaged. They undoubtedly were equipped, organized, and skilled. If you closely examine certain earlier maps of Grand Pré, you will discover an unusual straight stretch of dykeland road near Horton Township, 1,500 ft in length, labelled "Acadian racecourse," which implies that they even had time to construct a recreational roadbed. Does racecourse entertainment imply gambling, and that in turn imply a prosperous market economy?

Second, Acadians thoroughly understood tidal marshes and tidal rivers, and adjusted their efforts accordingly: lower, smaller dykes along edges of the less exposed upper reaches of tidal rivers; small aboiteau logs for small volume flows; and many other minutiae of both civil and hydraulic engineering principles (Crane, 1819).

Third, Acadians probably began their dyking at the present National Historic Site, an island-like area that is slightly elevated above the adjacent marsh level. This would have been a relatively serene part of the Grand Pré tidal meadows, far from the east and west exposure of the marsh's sea edge, and much protected from the open Minas Basin by the chain of Long, Little, and Boot Islands. For these reasons, they may have been able to build those early dyke walls to the smaller riverbank standards, something nearer an 8 ft (2.4 m) base and a 4 ft (1.2 m) height, just enough to allow a narrow safety margin above annual maximum spring tides.

Fourth, the Minas Basin tidal amplitudes and dyking conditions were unique. With tides as much as 48 ft (14.6 m) over a six-hour period, the rise and fall was 8 ft per hour. Thus, if a spring tide did flood the marsh and creep up the walls to a height exceeding 3 or 4 ft (0.9 or 1.2 m), that breaching and flooding might only last about one half-hour, and in the next half-hour the upper marsh would be water-free. These rapid flood and ebb tides would be a boon in terms of hours available both for construction and for any repairs.

Fifth, if we assume the Acadians did build minimal dykes at first, that would explain why their dykes were reported as overtopped by tides during the Seros Cycle peaks of 1687 and 1705. After that they may have recognized that cyclic hazard and upwardly adjusted their dykes, for there are no reports (yet) of breaches in 1723 or 1741. However, during a storm in November 1759, the dykes were breached extensively, no doubt due to four years of abandonment and the resulting lack of maintenance, in conjunction with a Seros Cycle maximum.

Autumn and winter storms chew away at the dykes but, contrary to what one might expect, the presence of ice blocks in winter in the Minas Basin helps protect the dyke walls from erosion. The ice becomes stranded on the upper marshes during extreme high tides, and its very presence there during subsequent storms deflects and attenuates the wave action. During the winter of 1998–99, the Minas Basin was almost ice-free and the consequence was an exceptional amount of dyke-wall erosion. In 1931 the winter was mild, dyke walls did not freeze to their usual solid state, and there were no ice blocks on the marshes. A severe March storm destroyed much of the unfrozen and exposed Wickwire Dyke, and it would not be rebuilt until 1960.

Finally, consider the expediency with which the first Wickwire Dyke was constructed in 1805–06. This was done by neophyte English dykers who must have mastered all those traditional methods over the previous thirty-five to forty years. It was nearly 3 miles long (15,800 feet; 4.8 km), 16 ft at base (4.9 m), 7 ft high (2.1 m), 3 ft wide at the crest (0.9 m), and it required an aboiteau at six large creeks, one being a double sluice.

The dyking of the tidal West Marsh (the future Wolfville Wickwire Dyke) was discussed at farmers' meetings in October 1804 and February 1805. By April 1805 they were planning on a completion date of October 1. However, at a December 1805 meeting they were instead discussing what had yet to be finished. Included was the precise location of the Great Discharge Aboiteau, over which there had been much argument, resulting in resignation threats and consequent delays. (This information is taken from a J.F. Herbin school scribbler of 1911, in which he copied excerpts from a circa 1804 Proprietor's Dykeland Minute Book, which has since been lost. Appendix 5 contains a complete copy of what he recorded, with my annotations.) The entire three-mile project was probably completed in 1806, in just two seasons. A detailed survey map (size 41″ x 25″; 1.05 m x 0.64 m) of the marsh, its dyke walls, and the six aboiteaux, with each field owner listed with his acreage, was

TABLE 5.1   RELATIONSHIP OF NUMBER OF MEN, AND LENGTH OF NEW DYKE
WALL THEY COULD COMPLETE IN 20 DAYS

Work units of 6 men	Total number of men	Linear feet per day	Linear feet per 20 days*/month
1	6	16 ft (1 rod)	320
3	18	48	960
4	24	64	1,280
5	30	80	1,600
10	60	160	3,200
20	120	320	6,400
25	150	400	8,000
40	240	640	12,800

* 20 days per month was chosen as a conservative estimate of when the upper marsh would be inundated for but a short period or not at all, thus allowing construction to proceed throughout the workday.

submitted to the proprietors by Deputy Provincial Surveyor Oliver Lyman in November 1808. (The original map, recently discovered in Wolfville, is now at the Provincial Archives of Nova Scotia, Halifax.)

I no longer consider this three-mile long dyke the incredible engineering feat that I had originally believed it to be. From the above account, neither did the local farmers. The 1805 construction was done by tender to lowest bidders, in fifty-four sections of walls eight or twelve rods long. (A rod is sixteen feet. Eight rods is eight days work for one team of six dykers.) If they had employed twenty-five or thirty crews working simultaneously, the Wickwire Dyke walls could have been built in a few months, well within the proprietors' original October deadline. The entire seemingly mega-project could easily have been finished over the two seasons of 1805 and 1806. It would take 150 men only a month to build 8,000 ft of the 15,800 required.

In this context, examine Figure 4.15, showing the repair crews working at Davidson Aboiteau on Ransom Creek. In this photo, I can count eleven carts (some are horse, others oxen) and forty-one men all working at the one site. Three such "swarms" of forty men would constitute twenty crews of six dykers, which brings us to our hypothetical Wickwire estimates in the previous paragraph. These hypothetical figures are expressed in tabular form in Table 5.1.

Another deductive approach is to remember that sixteen feet is one day's effort by a six-man crew. Thus, 15,800 feet is about 1,000 crew days, or twenty crews for fifty days. At twenty work days per month, the three-mile

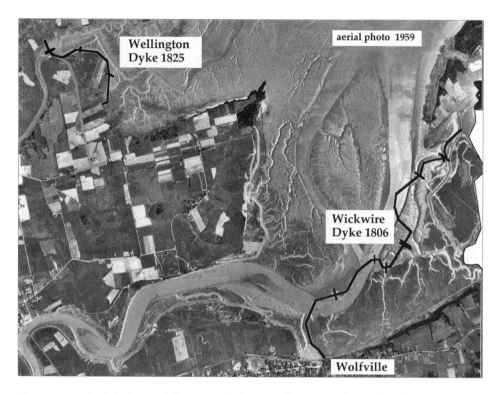

Figure 5.5   Aerial photo of the one-mile-long Wellington Dyke and the first three-mile-long Wickwire Dyke of 1806. Cross bars are aboiteau sites. River channel erosion since then has destroyed all of that original wall and the marsh beneath it, except for the section along the channel into Wolfville Harbour. (National Air Photo Library, A 16535-32)

endeavour requires only about two and a half months for construction of the running dyke walls, aboiteaux construction not included.

This 1805–06 accomplishment at Wolfville may have been the catalyst that set the stage for the one-mile-long Wellington Dyke construction of 1817–1825 (Fig. 5.5). The planning committee estimated that if each farmer provided one man and one team for each ten acres of ownership, the project could be completed in four months. This was later revised to three men and one team per eight acres. The project lasted eight years, in spite of occasional musterings of "over 100 men and nearly 50 teams." Some say it was the generous rum rations. For the full story read *The Wellington Dyke* by Marjory Whitelaw, 1997.

Figs 5.6 and 5.7 are diagrammatic representations of cross-sections of two sizes of hand-built dyke walls. The smaller one would be suitable for the upper reaches of a tidal river and the larger would be typical of estuaries

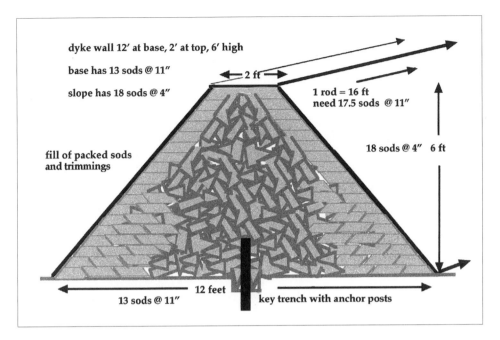

dyke wall 12' at base, 2' at top, 6' high

base has 13 sods @ 11"

slope has 18 sods @ 4"

← 2 ft →

1 rod = 16 ft
need 17.5 sods @ 11"

fill of packed sods
and trimmings

18 sods @ 4"   6 ft

12 feet

13 sods @ 11"

key trench with anchor posts

Figure 5.6   Approximately 1,900 sods would have to be cut for the construction of 16 ft of dyke wall this size. However, as few as 600 precisely cut sods would be required to face the dyke; the other 1,300 could be roughly cut as fill for the body of the wall.

opening into the Minas Basin. The diagrams are to scale, with the sods of the outer face measuring 4" x 11" (10.2 cm x 27.9 cm) exposed with a 10" to 11" (25.4–27.9 cm) length into the wall. The inner fill of odds and sods has a bit of artistic licence, for there would have been no gaps of any kind in the packed core of the dyke. At the base of the dyke are stacked outer rows and inner tiers of brick-like construction. This is sometimes evident in exposed old walls, and these multiple-layered sea faces on dyke walls presumably served to reinforce the base against severe wave action (Fig 5.8). The inner rows are slapped into place upside down, such that their bevelled surface overlapped the base of the outer exposed row of sods, thus helping to anchor the latter.

Figs 5.6 and 5.7 were used to roughly calculate how many sods would be required to build 16 ft (4.9 m) of dyke wall, this being the one-day produc-tion of a dyking team of six to eight men, according to statements in the liter-ature (Milligan, 1987; Cormier 1990).

The large dyke (Figure 5.6) would require about 1900 sods of which 600 would have to be the live, green, uniformly bevelled facing sods.

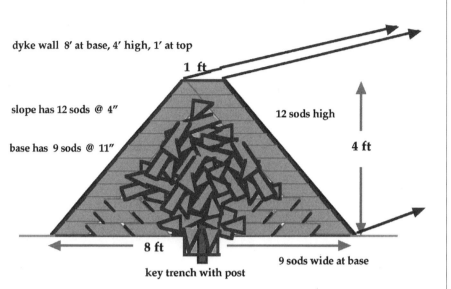

dyke wall 8′ at base, 4′ high, 1′ at top

1 ft

slope has 12 sods @ 4″

12 sods high

base has 9 sods @ 11″

4 ft

8 ft

9 sods wide at base

key trench with post

1. x-section area is 4′ x4′ = 16 sq. ft
2. 16 sf at 0.327 sq. ft/sod = 48.9 (49) sods to fill area.
3. total number sods to fill a rod (16 ft) of dyke wall is 49 x 17.5 = 857.5 sods
4. number of grassy sods required to face both sides is
      16′ x 4′ = 64 sq. ft x 2 sides = 128 sq. ft at 0.327 sq. ft/sod = 391 sods.

Sod cutting rates of a unit crew of 6 men, having 1 sod cutter
     at 1 sod per 10 seconds over 8 hr day = 2,880 sods
      at 1 sod per 15 sec .... = 1,920 sods

Two rods (32 ft) of dyke wall would require about 860 sods x 2 = 1,715 sods, which is fewer than an average day's cutting, but twice as many facing sods would be required: 391 x 2 = 782 sods.

Note: On 21 April, 1931, Robert Palmeter had a muster of 81 men and 30 horses repairing and upgrading the west Grand Pré dyke wall. Such a group could have built about 220 ft of totally new dyke wall in that one day. At these rates, they could have built a mile of small dyke in about 24 days, possibly between the two spring tides within the month.

Figure 5.7   Estimates of the sod requirements for construction of a 16 ft length of small dyke wall, and of the number of grassy facing sods to be fitted.

Figure 5.8   Old dyke at northeast Grand Pré, now storm-eroded to its base (October 1997). Note tight rows of sods facing the sea, and to the right a jumble of sod material packed in as fill.

The smaller dyke (Fig. 5.7) would require about 858 sods per rod of wall, but only about 390 of those would have to be carefully cut facing sods.

These approximate numbers raise the question "could a cutter produce that many sods in one day?" To answer that, one needs to know just how rapidly sods could be turned out at the pits. During my interviews with dykers, I asked each person how long they thought it would take to make the one side slice and the two or three width slices, and then tip the sod forward. Their collective opinions are summarized in Table 5.2.

The calculations in Figs 5.6 and 5.7 and Tables 5.1 to 5.4 indicate that about 1,900 sods are required for sixteen feet of dyke wall. This could reasonably be accomplished in five, eight, or ten hours, depending on the skill of the cutter.

From these calculations, I have chosen a rate of fifteen seconds/sod as a reasonable, even conservative, choice to work with. (This is definitely conservative, because even I have no difficulty producing four sods per minute with a sharp dyking spade.) At this rate, a cutter could achieve that goal of 1,900 sods in eight hours. If the cutter worked a ten-hour day, he could easily turn out the 1,900 sods.

Cutting Time (secs)	Sod Width Cut	Opinions
5	2 spade widths=8″	OK for experienced cutters
5	3 spade widths=11″	for experienced fast cutters only
10	3 spade widths	reasonable for fast steady rhythm
15	3 spade widths	reasonable for slow steady rhythm of 4 sods per minute
20	any size of sod	outrageously slow!

TABLE 5.3   NUMBER OF PRECISELY CUT SODS REQUIRED FOR OUTER FACING OF 16 FEET OF DYKE WALL

Single layer of sods for face of dyke
16′ x 6′ = 96ft² x 2 sides of dyke wall = 192ft² @ 3 sods/ft² = 576

If a 2nd inner row of 3 tiers is added to the sea side of wall for strengthening
16′ x 1′ = 16ft² x 3 sods = 48 sods   48+576 = 624 facing sods

If a 2nd inner row of 6 tiers is added to the sea side of wall for strengthening
16′ x 2′ = 32ft² x 3 sods = 96 sods   96+576= 672

TABLE 5.4   NUMBER OF SODS REQUIRED TO BUILD 16 FT OF DYKE WALL, USING TURF FROM TWO GRASS SPECIES

Sods Required	Black Grass (facings)	Salt Meadow Hay (fill)
1,900	576	1,324
1,900	624 (cut precisely)	1,276 (cut roughly)
1,900	768	1,132

However, it gets even easier, for not all 1,900 sods need be cut with brick-like exactness, only those for the outer wall layers with their surface of living grass. How many would that be, when the combined surface area of three sods is approximately one square foot? Table 5.3 summarizes this aspect of construction.

If we limit the master cutter to the 576 sods required to face each sixteen feet of the wall, then the statement that a six-man team could build sixteen feet of dyke a day becomes even more acceptable. Even factoring in two or three layers and tiers of facing sods, the numbers only increase to 624 and 768 "brick sods"; which is not even half of the 1,900 total bulk required. If we assume an average of 600 facing sods, then at 240 facing sods/hour the times required would be 2.4 hours for 576 sods, 2.6 hours for 624 sods, and 3.2 hours for 768 sods.

At this stage we can factor in the required number of sods of each of the two species of grasses, one for the facing quota and the other for wall fill quota (see Table 5.4).

To express this another way, 600 sods of Black Grass, at 240 sods/hour would require about 2.5 hours labour, over perhaps a period of 3 hours, whereas 1,300 sods of Salt Meadow Hay would require about 5.5 hours of cutting, at maximum. Thus, about 8 or 9 hours in total effort for one man, and less if he had an apprentice or two.

The next question is "How large must the sod pits be to produce these 1,900 sods?" Three sod pits, each 10 ft x 20 ft, which really is a rather small area (a total area of 600 square feet for all three), could produce 1,834 sods, since at the cutting surface of the marsh, each sod of "three-spitten size" (three spade widths) measures only 4 x 11 inches (0.327 sq.ft). This calcu-lated surface area could be halved if two layers of sods were cut from the one pit; the first sod layer having live grass for facing the dyke, and sods from the second depth used as fill.

In summary, a typical construction day might have proceeded as follows, with several of these activities overlapping in time:

- Laying out the centre line of a new dyke with rope, then stripping off sods six feet to either side of centre, which could be used later as fill. *Time:* 1 hour per sixteen feet of dyke.
- Digging the key trench along the centre line and driving in posts at six to ten foot intervals. *Time:* 1 hour.
- Establishing sod pits in areas of Black Grass and Salt Meadow Hay. *Time:* half an hour.

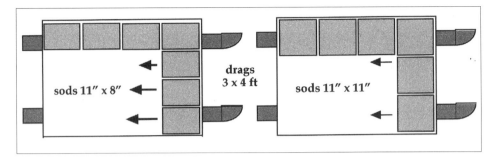

Figure 5.9   Diagrams of sod drags showing how medium and large sods would fit.

- Producing about 600 precisely fitting sods (by expert cutters). *Time*: 3 hours.
- Cutting the remainder of the 1,300 sods (these could be cut faster and/or by less experienced persons), and fill-packing them into the body of the wall. *Time*: 5 hours.

Thus, in eight to nine hours, sixteen feet of dyke wall could be completed, and the cutting of precisely shaped sods may have only occupied three hours or less of that time. If there were three skilled cutters at one pit, operating with three to six horse drags, then the wall builders and the rough-fill sod cutters could be kept extremely busy trying to keep pace with the pit production.

On the Grand Pré dykelands, the Acadians eventually enclosed 2,400 acres of the tidal marshes. In the process of accomplishing this in stages – if one accepts my hypothesis of a minimum of twelve enclosures (Fig. 6.2 and Table 6.2) – they must have built at least 95,000 ft (18 miles; 29 km) of dyke walls. For comparison, in the year 2000 there were 8,869.8 acres of dyked land in all of Kings County, contained by 161,719 feet or about 30.6 miles (49 km) of dyke walls (Lindsay Carter, Aboiteau Superintendent, Nova Scotia Department of Agriculture and Marketing). The total length of all Acadian dyke walls in Kings County in 1755 (if calculated, and this should be feasible) would certainly far exceed our current wall figures. The Acadians had none of our short major cross dykes, which function today to cut off entire estuaries such as those at Canning, Canard, and Falmouth – estuaries on which the Acadians had erected many miles of meandering walls.

Although the upper levels of most of those original Acadian walls have been levelled by bulldozers, their bases should still be there, buried beneath centuries of new turf. Perhaps dozens of the successively abandoned aboiteau

TABLE 5.5   ESTIMATES OF LOAD WEIGHT OF SODS ON THE DRAGS

Sod Width	Rows on Drag	Total Sods	@lb./ sod	1 layer	2 layers	3 layers
large 11″	3 x 4	12	28 lb.	336 lb.	24=672 lb.	36=1,008 lb.
medium 8″	4 x 4	16	19 lb.	304 lb.	608 lb.	912 lb.
small 4″	8 x 4	32	9 lb.	288 lb.	576 lb.	864 lb.
medium 8″	with 4 extra	20	19 lb.		380 lb.	
medium 8″	with 8 extra	24	19 lb.		456 lb.	

sluices still lie embedded within the silt-filled creek channels, awaiting discovery by archaeologists equipped with non-invasive electronic sensors.

One additional aspect of dyking involves the ox and horse drags. These simple drag sledges, used to transport sods from the cutting pits on the marsh to walls under construction, were described to me by the elderly dykers. From their memory only, as there seem to be no extant drags, they cited sizes of 2.5 x 3 ft, 3 x 4 ft, and 3 x 5 ft. The most often mentioned size was a 3 x 4 ft deck (Fig. 5.9) with two skids fashioned from small logs or planks. Some decks had cleats across the back and at the sides to keep sods from sliding off, which could happen when a horse started up quickly or was crossing rough terrain. These specialized dykeland drags remained at the dyke walls ready for transport of sods whenever a wall was breached by waves or tunnelled by muskrats.

Several interacting variables were involved when using the drags. Stronger horses could haul larger drags, but only where the marsh was firm. On soft marshes, smaller drags and smaller loads of sods were required. At each site, the marsh conditions, the strength and temperament of the horse, the size of the drag, and the potential sod load all had to be assessed and the dyking procedures adjusted accordingly. If not, the drags dug in or got stuck, and the horses became exhausted, panicked, or lunged to get free and spilled the remaining sods.

I expected the oral accounts of how many sods were piled on a drag to vary, but they varied beyond reason. Everyone seemed unsure of the actual numbers and how high they were piled. The sod numbers were nine, twelve, sixteen, "never over twenty-four," and one statement of "hundreds, well maybe fifty." Likewise, recollections of how many layers of sods were placed

Figure 5.10   Repairs to Davidson Aboiteau, Ransom Creek, Grand Pré, circa 1913. Many sod-cutting spades are evident, as well as two lightweight sod pallets termed hand barrows (arrows 1 and 2).

on the drags varied from "oh, never more that one layer," "always two or three layers," to "piled up pyramid-like." The truth must lie somewhere in between. The basic drags in Fig. 5.9 nicely accommodate the two common sizes of sods and, knowing average sod weights, it was possible to calculate how much various loads would weigh (Table 5.5). The weight of the sods quickly adds up, with a mere thirty-six large sods weighing an impractical 1,000 lb. (450 kg). No wonder the drags were small and that it was forbidden to add more weight by riding on them – a regulation that my interviewees loathed as teenage drag drivers.

It may be possible to extrapolate these sod weights to the paintings by Lewis Parker and Azor Vienneau of Acadians engaged in dyking activities and to obtain estimates of the loads on the hand-barrow pallets and on the oxen drags. The pallets, which are already large and heavily constructed, seem to be carrying an unreasonable number of sods. In the circa 1913 photograph of the Davidson Aboiteau repairs (Fig. 4.15), the hand-barrow pallets appear reasonably small and lightweight (Fig. 5.10).

CHAPTER SIX

Sequence of Dykeland Enclosures at Grand Pré

Building the Aboiteau

Now is the tide returned with angry face ...
Lo! in its road an earthy gate is turned.
It gathers force and lifts its vengeful height,
Leans full against the portal with vain might.
Vain pressure on the salty forces now,
The dyke o'ertops it with its lofty brow.
So for the hours like giants in embrace,
Breast beats on breast and face is unto face ...
While far within the sheltering of its wall
The cattle graze and endless harvests fall.

J.F. Herbin, 1909, 65

Up to now we have covered the basics of the mechanics of dyke construction, the nature of the botanical building blocks, the uniqueness of the tidal regimes, and the relative ease with which dyking was executed. Having established the *how* of dyking, in this chapter we address the *where* and *why* and *when* of the enclosure of all the Grand Pré marshlands.

My present consummate interest in this subject had a modest beginning. In July 1994, while beachcombing and bird watching along the shores of northeast Grand Pré, my wife and I discovered a small diameter aboiteau log (eight-inch outer diameter, five-inch inner diameter) and nearby a matching trench and cavity in the eroded face of the old marsh. We notified the Grand Pré National Historic Site staff, and the then director, Jocelyne Marchand, had it moved to the basement of the church museum. Its small size and location prodded my curiosity.

In 1999 I met a professional antique dealer and fellow beachcomber, Basil Rogers of Hantsport, who had spotted this same aboiteau protruding from the bank a few years prior to my discovery. He had tried to remove it but could not. When he next returned to Grand Pré it was missing and he assumed it had washed out to sea, not knowing it had washed into my hands. He was present in 1991 when a large Acadian aboiteau, which had been dug up while deepening drainage ditches, was being cut into shorter more manageable sections and dragged away and dumped over the dyke wall into the sea. He salvaged enough to make some kitchen cabinets and some panelling and to carve out smaller items such as spoons. He has slabs of this wood as yet unused, all of which I have seen. These examples and another early 1990s dis-entombment of a large aboiteau on Grand Pré lend credence to my contention that many original early eighteenth-century Acadian aboiteaux may still be in situ, but buried beneath the current level of the Grand Pré farmland drainage creeks.

Grand Pré Drainage Patterns

The base map I am using is derived from the National Air Photo Library 1963 photos series A 18060 59–61. Those 1963 transects were flown especially to record the intertidal topography at an extreme low tide of 0.0′ Datum, on 25 May, between 8 and 9 A.M. On this outline base map I have plotted the creek drainage patterns based on examination of many aerial photos from as many years as possible. Originally, I tried to use information from Harcourt Cameron's 1956 publication *Nova Scotia Historic Sites*, which includes a large format map folded in a map pocket. It was originally drafted from 1945 government aerial photos (A 8645) and partially updated from forest inventory aerial photos of 1955. Cameron also had enlargements of these, and many stereo pairs. I was given two of his enlarged 1945 aerial photos, and those marked-upon working copies match the details drafted on his base map, even though the legend on his published map refers only to 1955 aerial photos. A more serious omission is that of a scale bar, as his map simply states that 1 inch = 660 ft. However, that was only correct for the original draft and not for the published map, which was reduced photographically to accommodate the journal map pocket. The scale on the latter is nearer 1 inch = 965 ft. Finally, the persons who compiled his map were not thorough, for segments of creeks were omitted and others were connected incorrectly.

I redrafted the creek drainages from old maps and from old and recent aerial photos, and I believe I have resolved most of the mistakes (Fig. 6.1, p. xx). The drainage features on my map are colour-coded to emphasize that most of the nearly 3,000 acres of original tidal marsh meadows were drained by only two creeks, the Great Discharge Creek (green) and the larger Ransom Creek (blue). Thousands of years ago a watershed elevation must have run north and south near the east side of Grand Pré, as evidenced by the four short creeks in red, draining east. I have added features and dates of the recent changes in location of the mouth of the Great Discharge where it empties into the Cornwallis River. Erosional changes can explain the shift on the map from the 1760 discharge channel to that of 1928, but the sudden appearance on 1945 aerial photos of the present discharge location, that long south-to-north channel opening adjacent to Ransom Creek, is as yet unexplained. In the southeast corner of Grand Pré, the original outlet of "Deportation Creek" was shifted to the north in 1947–48.

The value of Cameron's map lies in his plotting of elevations. His stereo examination, his specialty at the time, revealed ridges crisscrossing Grand Pré. He concluded that all these were old dyke walls (Fig. 6.2, p. xxi). I doubt this because it would mean that the Acadians were inconsistent in their dyking practices, erecting several sets of walls in a few areas, but enclosing large areas everywhere else. The latter situation is what was reported by eye witness Otis Little in 1748. I have therefore assumed that some of Cameron's "dykes" are access roads, which may have been built up with brush to support the weight of their loaded carts (Crane, 1819). The tidal marsh is a soft substrate, and Crane's comment about creating a firm roadbed that could support loaded ox carts is understandable. The Acadians would have required arterial roadways to major construction sites such as at the aboit-eaux and at submerged road crossings to Long Island. Those same roadbeds could then serve as collector roads for their cart and wagon traffic to and from adjacent arable fields. Roadways are not crop land so they were, and still are, kept to a minimum, which meant that these few major tracts bore much of the wagon traffic and would have been constructed accordingly. Once established, it would be sensible to retain and maintain them on and on for centuries.

Three historic Acadian roadways run south to north across Grand Pré, and when they are plotted over the creek drainage map (Fig. 6.1, p. xx), it becomes evident that they track along the watershed areas between creeks (Fig. 6.3, p. xxii). This would be the least wet ground on a tidal marsh, the highest and driest once the land was dyked, particularly if it had a brush and pole base. The east road and the west road cross the barrier of creeks by the two most direct watershed tracts available. They terminate at Long Island, where their original submerged bridges would later become aboiteaux causeway bridges. The central road terminated at the east-west dyke wall that skirted south of the many gullies at Ransom Creek. There are two possible routes for its historical connection to the mainland, neither of which was detectable on the photos. In contrast to the location of roadbeds, most of the dyke walls track along the edges of the creeks, at their tidal overflow crests, the only exception being along those few wide creeks that have gently sloping sides with many gullies, such as Ransom Creek (RC in Fig. 6.4).

If the Acadians did construct what are locally referred to as "corduroy roads," then a series of archaeological test trenches at Grand Pré might expose those distinct differences between the construction of the base of an Acadian roadbed and the base of a dyke wall, the latter usually having a central trench with posts and brush in single layers. In a few cases, the Acadians may have transferred old dykes to new locations by mining the old dykes for sod fill and then converting an old dyke base to a roadbed. The Toye Dyke in east Grand Pré is now an elevated roadbed. Trimming down an old dry dyke wall to obtain a firm roadbed seems reasonable, but I doubt they would have used the old sods as fill in new walls, because dried sods would not meld together into that necessary solid mass, as do fresh moist sods. (The names Toye and Ransom were taken from local surnames at that time.)

In Fig. 6.2, in light of the above observations and comments, I have colour-coded in brown those sections of Cameron's "dyke walls" that I consider to be not dyke walls but roadbeds, either primary or secondary. Where dyke walls cross creeks, an aboiteau sluice system must be installed, whereas when roadbeds cross creeks, all that was needed was a brush base, a culvert, and cap of stones and fill. In 1977 just such a structure was found by archaeologists at the Grand Pré National Historic Site, immediately south of the statue of Evangeline. That test trench exposed a brush and pole base (and a leather shoe), a log-framed culvert, and a cobblestone roadbed to the adjacent hillside.

I am not certain about the southwest corner of Grand Pré, because it would have been more typical of the Acadians to run a low dyke east and west (along my brown line, below 9, Fig. 6.2) at the top of that north slope of Great Discharge Creek, and thereby avoid the construction and maintenance of a major aboiteau. The same aboiteau avoidance philosophy is evident at 8B at the top centre in Fig. 6.2 of Grand Pré, where numerous creeks dissect the south slope of Ransom Creek. However, judging from the Planter maps of 1760–61, those two major aboiteaux had been installed sometime before 1755 (Fig. 6.4).

I have accepted Cameron's logical determination of where the first dyked enclosure was built, adjacent to an island of high ground that is now the National Historic Site, and have taken my reasoning for subsequent dykes from that starting point. The Historic Site probably sits on a bulge of Wolfville Sandstone. In 1975 D.E. Eagles (35) recounted that around 1922,

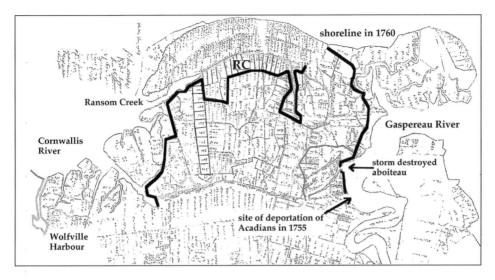

Figure 6.4   The 1760 Planter allotments map showing east, west, and north dyke walls, the aboiteau gap at "Deportation Creek," and the Ransom Creek area bypassed by the original Acadian dyke (RC). The deeply dissected marsh area to the west of Grand Pré, bordering the Cornwallis River, was dyked by the Planters in 1806. (Nova Scotia Department of Natural Resources, Kings Co., Plan no. 5-13-A 1760)

when excavating for the foundations of the present church museum base-ment, workers struck what one of the men, Leslie Harvey, described as "concrete footings" that delayed the new construction work, expanding the project from six weeks to fifteen weeks. Would not the construction of concrete footings at Grand Pré in the 1700s be an unreasonable assumption, especially if stones and sandstone bedrock were present? In 1922 could Leslie Harvey have mistaken the sandstone for "concrete"? Surface excava-tions in 2001 by archaeologist Jonathan Fowler revealed Acadian stone foundations situated on upland gravels, without any trace of concrete or tidal marsh layers. A few fifteen-foot-deep bore holes would soon reveal the true geological foundations beneath this historic island mound. This higher ground directly adjacent to the tidal meadows and a major drainage creek would have been the ideal location to begin dyking.

A third prime source of information, after the 1963 aerial photos and Cameron's map, was the 1760 map prepared by New England Planter John Bishop (Fig. 6.4). The depiction of Grand Pré marshland and creeks is of such accuracy that much can be directly superimposed over the 1963 aerial photos. This particular map has made it possible to decipher topographic changes of the shorelines at Grand Pré over the past 300 years.

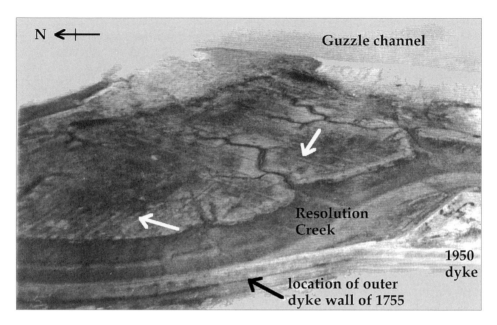

Figure 6.6 Low-level aerial photo (1959) of the Guzzle channel looking towards Boot Island, showing parallel dale and dale ditch patterns. These plowed areas are outside all historical records of dyke walls, yet they must have been enclosed at that time. Shoreline erosion has removed all evidence of such a dyke. (Nova Scotia Department of Agriculture and Marketing, MMRA photo 3-459-73)

I have proposed twelve bouts of Acadian dyke construction (Fig. 6.5, p. xxiii, and Table 6.2) as the minimum plausible number to accomplish the dyking limits discovered and surveyed by the first New England Planters. This proposed sequence of dyking, from about 1680 to 1755, was formulated after many hours of contemplating and correlating the patterns on my drainage map, the detailed Planter map, and Cameron's map of marshland ridges. My analysis should be viewed as a hypothesis to be refined and expanded through archaeological digs, drill-core sampling, newly discovered documents and maps, and more detailed examination of topographic features in aerial photos and on the ground. There is 1959 and 1973 photographic evidence of earlier dykes at the west end of Long Island, to the south of Little Island (Fig. 6.6).

During this investigation, four dykeland fundamentals were revealed and they should be kept in mind when conducting research involving Bay of Fundy tidal marshes and when examining aerial photos.

First, because of the unusual rise in sea level over recent centuries in the Bay of Fundy, structures built on tidal marshes often have *not* been eroded

Enclosure	Aboiteau	Blockages	Canal Links	Comments
1	1 major 2 small	5	1	Cameron believed this was first enclosure
2	1 large 1 small	0	0	Included more of same creek
3	1 large 1 small	1 or 2 minor	2 ?	Included much of inland Ransom Creek
4	2 small	1 or 2	0	Included east branches of Ransom Creek
5	2 large 4 small – or – 3 blockages		2 ?	Skirts wide gullied parts of Ransom Creek
6	2 large	2	0	Skirting more of east Ransom Creek
7	1 major 1 small	0	1	Enclosure of all of eastern Ransom Creek
8A	2 large 3 small	0	0	Into difficult deep west creeks
9	1 major 1 large 2 small – or – 2 blockages		2	May have been part of #8; major project
10	2-3 large 2 small – or – 2 blockages		0	Enclosure of part of the east drainage
11	1 major	0	0	Finished enclosure of all of east side
8B	1 major	0	0	Enclosure of gullied portion of Ransom Creek
12	Boot Island has not yet been studied			

Total aboiteaux installed: 30–33

away but have been entombed by subsequent marsh deposits. On the Enclosures Map, Fig. 6.5, I have indicated by black and red banded bars where aboiteau sluices were probably installed. Their Enclosure location number and their relative sizes are listed in Table 6.1, along with other information. Many of these original sluice logs should still be there, deep in the creek channels. In support of this assumption, in 1990 and 1991, when drainage ditches were being deepened with drag lines, large log sluices, about 45 ft long, were dug up at two separate sites on Grand Pré, far inland from the present-day dyke walls.

Second, because the tortuous course of each marsh creek is unique and evidently is immutable over hundreds of years, collectively they reveal precisely the progress of coastal erosion as well as the relative placement of old dyke walls. The entangled root matrix of marsh grasses resists the easy water course meanderings typical of streams with their unconsolidated substrates of silts, sand, or gravel. Even creeks on the broad intertidal "mud" flats, such as those off Starr's Point, show little change since the 1931 aerial photos. This suggests that those flats are in fact submerged marshes. Recent changes in the position of the adjacent Cornwallis River channel does not appreciably alter them, it simply slices through these time-frozen creek patterns (Fig. 6.7). These intertidal creeks are so persistent that they have had permanent names assigned to them by duck hunters, names passed down from father to son. I have traced back some of the creek names from the 1990s to 1841 (Fig. 6.7, caption).

Third, the shape of each dykeland farm field is constrained by the often tortuous path of the original marsh creek drainage configuration, established centuries prior to dyking. After the initial years of plowing and crowning efforts by the Acadians, the drainage pattern of each large field unit was firmly established and, as it probably could not be improved upon by subsequent farming families, has not varied for hundreds of years. Fig. 6.8 (p. xxiv) offers a comparison of the field-block boundaries from the 1760 map and the 1963 aerial photo, with a few selected fields colour-coded.

Fourth, a special plowing procedure (appendix 7) was used for improving drainage on flat fields. It creates long narrow strips within each field block and these are evident on aerial photos as parallel lines. They consist of long ridges about 30 ft apart, termed dales, and they are flanked by narrow dale ditches. These were first established by the Acadians and are still recognizable in the 1945 and 1963 aerial photos. The enlarged 1945 photo of the National Park Historic Site area (Fig. 6.9) illustrates an entire spectrum of photographic signatures of dales and ditches, from the hardly detectable to brilliant white. For scale, several small insets of a 200 ft-long warehouse are included. At the far right of the photo, many of the original 30 ft-wide dales are still detectable in the new 150 ft-wide (white) dales. Just below these wide strips, across the diagonal creek and above the inset, the dark dales and pale ditches are also the original 30 ft-wide field units, from the days of plows drawn by horses. Note also the landscape trace of an original Acadian dyke wall, in all probability the east wall of their first enclosure.

This special plowing procedure gradually moves soil towards the centre of the field strip and creates a drainage ditch to each side. Rain washes away sea

Figure 6.7   Aerial photos of intertidal creeks at Starr's Point that have remained essentially unchanged, except where a subsidiary channel of the Cornwallis River has shifted west, cutting into the old marsh patterns. These creek channels are so persistent that generations ago farmers and duck hunters assigned them names: 1 – North Cove; 2 – South Cove; 3 – Starr Creek; 4 – First Cut Off Creek; 5 – False Channel; 6 – Blind Channel; 7 – Shad Creek; 8 – Alison Creek (Ellison in 1841); 9 – Ford Creek; 10 – Deep Creek. (National Air Photo Library A 8645-57; 92302 21H/1)

Figure 6.9   Examples of dale and dale-ditch patterns evident in fields near Grand Pré National Historic Site in 1945. They vary from barely detectable (1, 2) to sharply defined (3), from original 30 ft widths of horse and plow to bulldozer-crowned and tractor-cultivated units 100 to 200 ft wide (4). For scale, small inset photos show a 200 ft long warehouse at 2, bottom centre. (National Air Photo Library A 8645-54)

salt from the surface soil via the ditches. Through consultation with Hank Kolstee (Nova Scotia Department of Agriculture and Marketing), I learned that over the years the same surface runoff adds organic matter to those ditches and, even when buried by bulldozer crowning centuries later, their moisture-holding properties and organic content are often evident in an otherwise uniform crop by the widely separated rows of healthier plants, those whose roots are near or in the old dale ditches. Whereas the crowned surface of a crop field may readily lose water, the moisture reservoir in the buried dale ditches keeps wicking upwards and is detectable by satellites. These strips of moisture-retaining soil produce the distinctive parallel linear patterns seen on satellite and aerial photo images.

Canada's observation satellite, Radarsat, using a sensor known as Synthetic Aperture Radar (SAR) that records topographic and moisture differences, registers the same irregular patterns in its imagery as those field boundaries on the 1760 survey map. Thus these ghosts from the Acadian farming presence of 300 years ago still haunt the Grand Pré dykelands.

Tidal Creek Drainage Patterns

In the early 1680s, when the first Acadians came from Annapolis Royal to assess the tidal marshes at Grand Pré, they must have been thrilled on the one hand at the prospect of 3,000 acres of flat, fertile, rock-free, stump-free land, and apprehensive on the other hand at the magnitude of the twice daily tidal exchange. Dyking such a unique terrain might seem daunting to us today, but the local topography greatly favoured the Acadian's task. From the advantage of the hillside on which they soon established their town site (south of the present National Historic Site and eastward towards Horton Landing), they had a near aerial view of the entire Grand Pré tidal marsh. A telescope would have revealed all of the creek patterns. By studying the ebb and flow of tidal water along the creek channels during spring and neap tidal phases (twice a month) they could, with such thorough topographic fore-knowledge, easily devise a sequential dyking plan for the entire marsh.

The Acadians would have quickly recognized that most of that vast tidal marsh drained from east to west via two major creek systems: one along the north boundary; the other along the south boundary of the marsh. The east end of the marsh drained by a series of short deep creeks (Fig. 6.1). Ideally, if they ran a dyke wall across each end of the marsh to Long Island, the entire marsh would be secured for farming. That could have been done, but would have required a large workforce, which they certainly did not have at the outset; or it would have taken many years with a small workforce, and they undoubtedly wished to put plow to land as soon as possible.

By happy coincidence, one of the two major creeks lay at the base of their hillside village, and ran parallel to it. Any site chosen for construction of an aboiteau along this creek was immediately accessible from the adjacent high ground. Timber and sods were at hand. A minimal height for dyke walls could be established by locating tidal-height marker posts along the lines of an intended dyke. As water seeks its own level, the daily tidal influx would have delineated all relative elevations on a minute by minute basis. Thus, topographic surveying was unnecessary, only the recording of direct observations was needed. It was truly a dyker's dreamland.

Relatively few interruptions would occur during wall construction, as the upper levels of Minas Basin tidal marshes are often flooded only a few days a month, and some months not at all. This is not surprising when one learns that during the year the height differences between a spring high tide and a neap high tide can be as much as 10 to 12 ft (3–3.6 m) in the Bay of Fundy. As well, with mean tides of 39 ft (max 52 ft) (11.8–15.8 m) in Minas Basin, the times of submergence at high water are much shorter than on most coastlines, where the tide drops only 4 to 6 ft (1.2–1.8 m) over the same six-hour ebb period. Near Digby and Annapolis, from whence the Acadians moved to Grand Pré, the mean tide is 22 ft (6.7 m) and the maximum 30 ft (9.1 m). At Grand Pré, the tide drops at a rate of 8 ft (2.4 m) per hour on a 48 ft (14.6 m) tide.

Placement and Sequence of Acadian Dykes at Grand Pré

Where did the Acadians place their dykes and why at those particular sites? Fig. 6.5 depicts a series of twelve large enclosures that could have been completed by the 1730s. The black and red bars indicate where aboiteaux would likely have been installed. As mentioned previously, many are probably still in position, but now buried.

I reason that the dykers progressed north then east, then north again, but stopped short of the wide and deep east-west drainage gully of Ransom Creek that follows along the south side of Long Island. Then they began an approach towards the many wide, deep drainages at the west end of Grand Pré, and there they skirted along the tops of the creeks, avoiding the need to construct the huge aboiteaux that the Planters found necessary to enclose those same marshes farther westward as far as Wolfville Harbour (see Figs 9.5.1 and 9.5.5). Finally, the Acadians enclosed the four deep creeks of that narrow strip of watershed that forms the eastern boundary of Grand Pré, each of which at that time drained into the Gaspereau River. To gain access to Long Island, they may have postponed construction of any major aboiteau causeway by simply building a rocky submerged roadbed across Ransom Creek (near the present Palmeter Farm). Such a road crossing could be used whenever the tide had receded enough to expose it, which in the context of Minas Basin tides would be most of the time. The construction of roadbeds across tidal creeks, roadways that periodically became submerged, was common in Europe and North America. An early Acadian road to Windsor is reported to have crossed the Gaspereau River near Wallbrook by such means (R.W. Starr, 1891; A.W.H. Eaton, 1910; J.F. Herbin, 1911). However, being both a river crossing and a tidal crossing and thus buffeted by strong currents from two directions, it presumably was a natural river fording of exposed bedrock, and not constructed of stones. If so, it should be possible to relocate the site.

Except for the creek gullies, most of a tidal marsh is sea-level flat with watershed boundaries that are hardly noticeable. Therefore, it is an easy matter to cut canals and link up with adjacent creeks to divert drainages in other directions. This procedure reduces the number of aboiteaux needed, saving time and money. Such links are evident on topographic maps for 1928 and 1967 in the Wickwire Dyke and Horton Landing areas. Even in Crane's 1819 article, he recommends a cost-cutting procedure of blocking off an aboiteau sluice that needed replacement and diverting the water to another aboiteau further along the dyke wall. In Fig. 6.5 I have plotted four such canals, and there must have been other smaller ones.

Table 6.1 lists the number of creek blockages created by each Acadian enclosure and the potential created for useful canal linkages. The Acadians also seem to have deliberately taken advantage of the fact that the rims of creeks are usually higher than the adjacent marsh, for it is here that tidal sediment loads are first dropped and ice blocks with their silt loads often go aground. When they melt in spring, they contribute quantities of sods, silts, and stones. Building walls on these crests (as evident in Fig. 6.5) may have reduced the number of sods required by one or two layers.

Based on a synthesis of my 1997 drainage pattern map and various other maps depicting dyke walls, it seems plausible to me that the following reasoning may have guided the Acadians in their deliberations prior to and during their dyking of the Grand Pré tidal marshes. Each of the twelve proposed enclosures is discussed in turn.

Enclosure 1

Block the most accessible and shallower major creeks first because of limited manpower

What is now known as the Great Discharge Creek at the foot of the hill at the Grand Pré National Historic Site was an ideal starting point (see the drainage creek watershed colour-coded in green in Fig. 6.1).

Because they worked at first in the south central area of the Grand Pré tidal meadows, the potential for destructive wave action against any partially or fully completed walls would be nil, for the following reasons:

- the dykes were too far from the outer exposed shoreline to the east and west for any direct effect, and that great distance in itself also served to attenuate wave action;
- the dyke walls were constructed on the upper-level marsh surface, which is flooded only at higher tidal phases;
- the tides turn and ebb so quickly in Minas Basin that any destructive phase would be short-lived and easily repaired.

- in addition, the marsh was storm-protected from the open Minas Basin to the north by the presence of the interconnected Long, Little, and Boot Islands.

For these reasons, these first dyke walls would need to be only 4 or 5 ft high. As I have said, this was a dyker's dream terrain.

Enclosure 2

Extend enclosures to the north to include more of that first watershed

The question is, were the expansion steps small or large or a mix of both? Milligan, 1987, states that the Acadians cooperated to enclose large areas, then divided them up into smaller field lots. This seems to be the historical consensus and it fits well with Cameron's stereo photograph analysis of old ridges on Grand Pré.

Many of the earliest dyke walls cut across and thereby blocked the upper reaches of drainage creeks (Figs 6.2 and 6.5). How may the Acadians have coped with this trapped rain and sea water?

Did they simply let it sit there to form fish ponds or to evaporate to form salt crusts? Much of it would be rain runoff, except when certain monthly spring tides flooded over the entire marsh and in behind their new walls. The rainwater itself quickly becomes saline because it washes salt crystals off the blades of marsh grasses (Bleakney and Meyer, 1979).

Such no-outlet creeks could have served as fish traps because during marsh flooding many fish species (minnows, smelt, gaspereaux, herring, eels, sea bass, even dogfish sharks) swim through the grasses, feeding. When the tide begins to recede, these fish retreat to the creeks to escape, or into the nearest marsh pool, where they await the next tide (Brown, 1983). In many cultures, harvesting such supplemental food sources was the prerogative of children.

Did they construct a small entrance aboiteau and let the sporadic rain or tidal waters enter the dyked enclosure, where it would simply flow through via the original creek system and drain out through the discharge aboiteau at the other side?

A basket screen placed over such an "entrance" aboiteau could serve as a stationary sieve trap for fish.

However, aboiteau drainage boxes were not always set, as one might expect, at the lowest level in a creek. They were often set high enough in the wall to create freshwater reservoirs for pastured livestock. In winter, blocks of ice could be cut from these ponds. Besides, as Crane explained, the higher in the wall an aboiteau sluice was located, the shorter and smaller could be the log from which it was adzed.

Any of those reclaimed creek sections totally enclosed by dyke walls would likely develop into freshwater cattail-bordered ponds that would attract ducks and other waterfowl, as well as muskrats and mink. The Acadians undoubtedly were hunters and trappers as well as farmers.

Did they dig canals to connect a blocked creek to an adjacent creek drainage system? Such an excavation could serve double duty, the second being to provide a source of more sods. Some of the older enclosures, including the first one, make little sense unless cross-connections were contemplated and constructed. There is obvious potential for one to the north of the northeast corner of Enclosure 1, at the pink bar, where an extensive terminal area of Great Discharge "green" creeks (Figs 6.2 and 6.5) could easily have been canal-connected to the "blue" Ransom Creek drainage to its north.

Enclosure 3

Extend walls to the east and south

This may have been done in two stages, if one presumes that the west-east dividing road in Enclosure 3 was once a dyke. An archaeological test pit could verify whether the foundation structure of a dyke lies beneath this road.

At the northeast corner of Enclosure 3, the present road jogs north then east. It also crosses several creeks, which would involve the chore of aboiteaux construction if building a dyke, but would require only a few open culverts if building a roadbed. It seems to me that a straight dyke eastward would have avoided the creeks and fit in better with the dyke wall on the east side of Enclosure 3. On my original map, I had added a dotted line to indicate just that option and opinion, and even added a circle where an aboiteau would have been placed. Seven months later, I was pleasantly surprised to learn that a large aboiteau log had been dug up at that exact site during ditch deepening in 1990. However, Cameron did not record any stereo evidence of a dyke or road at this location.

Enclosure 4

Add the rest of the Ransom Creek watershed to the east of Enclosure 3

This would leave a large creek for shipping and receiving goods by sea, a creek that has received the misnomer of "Deportation Creek" (see appendix 8). I had been told of planks being plowed up near the head of this creek, and when I examined the area I found a flat, deck-like topographic feature on the south side of the creek, where one would expect a sloping bank if the site were unaltered. All this is near the Iron Cross Deportation Memorial. A test trench would soon settle any ambiguities about a wharf, and old pilings might provide tree rings that could date the structure.

Enclosure 5

Block the deeper northern creeks last

These were conveniently on the far north side and at either end of the marsh. At first, the Acadians logically ran a dyke east-west along the top of the south bank of the deepest creek, Ransom Creek. They established an access road northward to Ransom Creek (central road in Fig. 6.3), and from this they dyked east and south along the edge of Ransom Creek, as well as to the west and south, joining up with Enclosures 3 and 2, respectively. Their access roads ran along the central watershed lines between larger creeks, because there the beginnings of the drainage creeks were shallow and broad and easily crossed by simple bridges.

Initially, they assiduously avoided that wide, deeply gullied section of Ransom Creek by dyking along its southern crest (Fig. 6.5). However, on the 1760 Planter map (Fig. 6.4), there seems to be an aboiteau blockage on Ransom Creek that separates the field dales from the adjacent sea bay. This new acreage is blanketed with twenty-three long narrow lots. These lots and the nearby north-south row of eleven square lots do not have any topographical constraints relative to their creek gullies, which is most unusual. These may have been bureaucratically imposed by the Planter surveyors on the last Acadian enclosure (Enclosure 8B), within which the Acadians had not yet established field boundaries and dale ditches. Because of these ambiguities, I have not included the 8B aboiteau in Fig. 6.11, p. xxv; it depicts a situation more representative of that relevant long period of Acadian occupation when tides enticed marine fish and mammals far into the Ransom Creek drainage, as far as the walls of Enclosure 4.

Netting and hunting could have provided a secondary reason for avoiding the construction of any aboiteau across these larger creeks. These deep tidal inlets, especially Ransom Creek, would have been attractive to Beluga Whales, Harbour Porpoises, and even Harbour Seals, for each species will pursue schools of fish up creeks and rivers undeterred by brackish or freshwater environments. The Acadians could have more easily hunted these mammals in such confined quarters. Herbin (1911) reported that Acadians extracted oil from local 17 ft-long white whales (Beluga Whales) to burn in their lamps, and for lucrative trade purposes. How were these large mammals captured? Did the Acadians harpoon or net or shoot porpoises, whales, and seals? Are there any accounts in the literature that would verify these hunting activities?

Enclosure 6

Extend the dyke walls along the east side of the large north-south Ransom Creek gully (opposite Enclosure 5), build a submerged stone bridge and access road to the east end of Long Island, and then curve the dyke wall back to Enclosure 4

In 1990 or 1991 an Acadian aboiteau sluice log was dug up at this site, which is at the junction of Enclosures 6, 7, and 10. The log was about 40 ft long and intact. Because of a lack of interest at that time, this Acadian artifact was dumped into the sea at the Guzzle, where it sat perched on the upper marsh for several years until it was finally carried away by the tides. Fortunately, its large clapper gate was saved and is on display at the Kings County Heritage Museum, Kentville. Thus, this incidental discovery is on record and substantiated by a period artifact.

Immediately downstream from that aboiteau sluice, the same ditching machine scooped up buckets of compacted white snail shells. This was probably an accumulation of thousands of shells of the marine Mud Dog Whelk, *Ilyanassa obsoleta*, killed by the installation of the aboiteau, which changed their creek habitat from saline to fresh water. The dead snails would have been flushed downstream and compacted into the aboiteau spillway pool. I have a similar report from another Ransom Creek ditching operation near Robert Palmeter's farm on Long Island, during which aboiteau planks and masses of white shells were extracted.

Enclosure 7

Enclose outward from the northeast corner of Long Island along the shore and then south back to Enclosure 6

This eastern line was labelled Toye Dyke on Cameron's map. The area is now a prominently elevated roadbed. To reclaim this section of marsh, the Acadians would have had to exclude the sea with a large causeway and aboiteau sluice located near the present Palmeter farm. This would have served as the first dry road bridge to Long Island. If a previous submerged road to Long Island nearby existed, its rocks are probably still there and possibly detectable using appropriate sensing instruments.

The aboiteau location indicated by the red bar at the upper corner of Enclosure 10 in Fig. 6.2 is probably the small one I found in 1994. It was unusual in that it drained to the north, from a relatively high elevation. It probably functioned to quickly discharge rainwater from the high marsh between Long Island and Little Island, as otherwise that water, rain or tidal, had to drain tortuously southward all the way to the Gaspereau River, or alternatively westward via Ransom Creek across the full width of Grand Pré to the Cornwallis River.

Enclosure 8

Undertake a major project at the west end of the marsh, possibly in two stages

However, with the increase in population and its available manpower, a two-stage operation may not have been necessary. From its northeast corner, an aboiteau with a causeway road to Long Island would have divided this area into the original western 8A section and a new Ransom Creek 8B northern portion, located along the south side of Long Island. However, as Ransom Creek is wide and deeply gullied in this region, the Acadians probably opted to forgo, for as long as possible, a major aboiteau causeway in order to retain that creek as a productive hunting and fishing asset. In Fig. 6.10 (p. xxv) note the potential extent of tidal flooding up Ransom Creek in the absence of an aboiteau, as indicated by the marine colour-coding. In any case, they could easily have constructed a submerged bridge to Long Island, and the presence of a well-developed, watershed-positioned, north-south road here hints at such a historical connection.

Enclosure 9

Undertake a further major project at the western side of Grand Pré

This established the limits of Acadian dyking efforts between there and Wolfville. The 1760s maps indicate an aboiteau causeway across Great Discharge Creek, but that too may have been a late Acadian construction effort. The previous dyke configuration in this area may have been a wall running parallel to that creek along its crest on its north side, later converted to a major roadway, as evident on several maps.

Enclosure 10

Proceed with another major dyking project to include the north-south strip of land at the eastern boundary of the marsh

All of this land emptied southward into the Gaspereau River in the 1700s. There were four deep but rather narrow creeks to dam, but as they had small watersheds, the aboiteau sluices would not have had to be large.

It has always been assumed that the Acadians were ever expanding their dykelands up to the moment of deportation. Thus, the positions of their dykes as plotted on the excellent survey map of 1760 were considered their outermost limit of construction. However, in September 1998 I discovered that the marsh areas to the east and south of Little Island had many parallel lines, indicating previous crown plowing within the protection of dyke walls (Fig. 6.6). The lines are evident on this photo because it was taken in April well before the marsh grasses began growing and obscuring such subtle contour details.

The dashed line to the north and east of Little Island on my Enclosures map (Fig. 6.5) indicates where I believe that wall might have been. Unfortunately, shore erosion has removed any easily detectable trace of this dyke, except at its extreme southerly end, where it is revealed on aerial photos of July 1946 (Nat. Air Photo Library A 10178-6). It seems unlikely that the inexperienced Planters would abandon the Acadian line of the 1755 dyke wall, even if it were broken in places, and opt to build a new line of dykes on an eroding shore, well outside of what the Acadians had considered a construction safety zone. It is, then, reasonable to assume that the Acadians had moved their dykes back from this area prior to the arrival of the Planters.

Enclosure 11

Work on a final phase to enclose the eastern marsh to its shore line
This is an area of much historical confusion because of the misinterpretations in the general literature, the misleading labels on Cameron's 1956 map, and the placement of the Iron Cross Memorial. New information and revised interpretations by myself and historian/archaeologist Jonathan Fowler indicate that in 1755 a dyke wall and an aboiteau blocked sea access to this so-called "Deportation Creek" (appendix 8).

This final block of enclosed marshland had probably been under cultivation since 1735, or within five years of that date, and for that reason the Acadians could not have been rowed down a nonexistent tidal creek to ships at anchor. When the aboiteau was destroyed in the November 1759 storm, tidal waters became reestablished in the mythical "Deportation Creek." Because the creek still had its redundant wharf from an earlier time, and since it was not dyked again for at least another generation or two, (either in 1814 or as late as the 1850s), that deep tidal creek became identified as the site of the deportation, thereby misleading future historians, cartographers, and memorialists. Recent evidence indicates that the Acadians were deported from a rocky shale outcrop on the bank of the Gaspereau River, previously known as Black Landing, but currently referred to as Horton Landing. In 1755 the river channel would have turned sharply east towards Oak Island, traversing a large marsh, and would have had more the appearance of a narrow tidal creek than of the broad stretch of river it presents today. All this is depicted in Fig. 9.1.1. Hence those crucial historical references of Acadians "marching to a creek bank" need not have referred to the much smaller "Deportation Creek." (This topic is discussed in chapter 9 and at length in appendix 8.)

Marsh Enclosure 11 has long been known as Dead Dyke, and Cameron tagged its dyke walls "Dead Dyke" on his map. Many persons mistakenly assume the word "dyke" refers exclusively to the actual walls. It certainly can, but for the generations of farmers who owned these lands, the terms Wellington Dyke or Wickwire Dyke or Grand Pré Dyke encompassed the entire area, including walls and aboiteau and fields and creeks. Thus, in a historical cultural context, "Dead Dyke" should refer to the entire Enclosure 11, so why the name? I believe it was assigned by the New England Planters and the connotation was that a dyked section of land, previously farmed by the Acadians, was now "dead" because of the twice daily saltwater incursions. It is significant that the term was used on a 1760 map and text document describing the land holdings of Theofilus Sutherland (Fig 9.1.3).

Enclosure 12

This undocumented block encompasses all that was dyked on Boot Island. It must have been considerable, for that same 1760 document shows that roads and fields and dyke wall boundaries were well established on the island. Encouragingly, many old dyke features stand out sharply on 1946 and 1963 aerial photos. I have not yet examined that island terrain on foot or attempted calculations for Table 6.2, but I have included space in that table and an estimate of the total area dyked.

From Table 6.2, the average length of wall built annually was 7,850 ft. The table indicates that sixty men could accomplish this in just forty-nine days. This may be impressive, but in real terms it is meaningless because the averages ignore the sliding scale of construction that would have taken place as the population base expanded. That aspect is summarized in Table 6.3.

When Tables 6.2 and 6.3 are examined in conjunction with my estimates of construction efforts, they add some social detail to those historical events.

TABLE 6.2   GRAND PRÉ DYKELANDS IN 1755
SUGGESTED SEQUENCE OF ENCLOSURES

Enclosure No.	Metres	Feet	Millions m²	Hectares	Acres
1	2,348	7,701	0.428	42.8	106
2	2,044	6,704	0.437	43.7	108
3	2,971	9,745	1.32	132	326
4	2,217	7,140	0.912	91.2	225
5	3,979	13,051	1.38	138	341
6	3,723	12,211	0.923	92.3	228
7	1,478	4,848	0.437	43.7	108
8A	3,085	10,119	0.856	85.6	211
8B	145	475	1.03	103	254
9	1,992	6,534	0.838	83.8	207
10	3,093	10,145	1.19	119	293
11	1,176	3,857	1.18	118	291
12	?	?	?	?	225
Total	28,251	92,530 av. 7,710*	10.931	1093.1	2,923 av. 244

* Sixty men would take only forty-nine days, spread over two months of tidal cycles, to achieve the annual average of 7,710 feet of new wall construction.

TABLE 6.3   COMPARISON OF CENSUS FIGURES AND HYPOTHETICAL ACREAGES

Historic Records				Enclosure No.	My Acreages	Years
arrived 1680						
1686 census	125 acres	10 families		1	106 acres	6 yrs
1693 census	540 acres	55 families		1, 2, 3	540 acres	13 yrs
1701 census	728 acres	79 families		1, 2, 3, 4a	730 acres	21 yrs
1755	In final 54 years Acadians enclosed an additional 2,193 acres making the total 2,923 acres in 75 yrs					
	At 244 acres/enclosure/year, they could have finished in 9 years, by 1710					

1686 census

In six years about 7,800 feet of dyke enclosed 125 acres. But there were only ten families then, and undoubtedly fewer in previous years. How many construction crews could they muster, even assuming large families? For the sake of argument, if we use a minimal average number of one man and one strong boy (boys drove the teams) per young family over those six initial years, then ten families could muster a crew of twenty.

A crew of eighteen is the equivalent of three dyking teams, and thus could construct 960 ft in twenty days (Table 5.1).

A crew of twenty, building a dyke 8 ft by 4 ft (not 12 by 6) could perhaps equal the linear efforts of a crew of twenty-four, which is 1,280 ft in twenty days.

So, after a mere six months (each month with a conservative estimate of twenty dyking days), the dyke could be 7,680 ft long. In some months they could work twenty-five days without tidal submergence, and occasionally thirty days, but they must have had other things to do, so perhaps twenty days is more reasonable. If anything, this is a conservative estimate.

Thus, Enclosure 1, of 7,701 ft, could have been finished in two years by fewer than ten families, if they devoted sixty days a year to dyke construction.

1693 census

This is only seven years later and already 434 more acres have been added via 16,450 ft of wall. By then there were fifty-five families. What if we now raise the family team contributions to one father and three sturdy sons.

Using similar reasoning, then fifty families could easily do 8,000 ft in a season, in their "spare time."

1701 census

By this time, the eighty families could reasonably muster hundreds of "men and boys" whenever their assistance was required for that minor mundane chore of enclosing another 250 acres or more.

If we use the average of 244 acres per enclosure (Table 6.2), then it would only take the annual construction of one of these enclosures, over a period of nine years, to complete all the proposed 2,900 acres of Acadian dyking on the Grand Pré tidal marshes. In theory, but unrealistically, they could have finished by 1710, but available information suggests that the Acadians sensibly enclosed more land only as they needed it. For example, a map of the Bay of Fundy, printed by Thomas Bowles, London, based on observations made in 1711 and 1712, depicts Long Island (labelled Charles I) as an island separated from Minas Town by a band of sea marsh. If this map is correct, then by 1711 Grand Pré was not yet dyked all the way across to Long Island (Fig. 8.2).

J.F. Herbin, in *The History of Grand Pré*, quotes a 1720 eye witness reporting that part of Grand Pré was dyked, and the rest could be. The date is not finite because the actual observations could have occurred several years prior to publication. More interesting is Herbin's statement that nearly *all* available marshland at Minas had been dyked by the beginning of Lieutenant-Governor Mascarene's administration, which began about 1740. The phrase "nearly all available marshlands" could have referred to the undyked 700 acres of the future Wickwire Dykeland portion of the western tidal meadows, which the Acadians avoided dyking, but probably used as a major source of salt hay.

The above suggests that the Acadians did not add a new enclosure each year but rather developed a new enclosure and brought it into production before adding another one. It is possible that much of the Grand Pré tidal meadows were dyked by 1725 and the remainder by 1735–40. If each family required about ten acres, then there would be an incentive to construct new dykes only when additional families moved into the area, or when their own children and grandchildren added to the population pressure.

Another pressure that could have stimulated a rapid bout of dyke construction after 1720 would have been the Acadians' developing and burgeoning export business (Wynn, 1979). Whatever the stimuli and constraints, by 1755 the Acadians had proven to all who visited the Minas Basin that their below-sea-level pastures, grain fields, and garden produce were the finest in quality, and in quantity per acre, of any farms along the Eastern Seaboard.

In theory, the Acadians had fifty-four years (1701–55) to complete the nine years of dyke-wall construction required to enclose most of Grand Pré and Boot Island. As the population grew, the total annual construction could have been accelerated or the time required for completion of a new enclosure greatly reduced. Therefore, if we accept that they were under no time constraints, and only periodically needed to enclose new blocks of marsh, then hypothetically they would have had time to dyke the marshes all around Little Island as well as on Boot Island, and even time to retreat from some previously dyked areas. All this prior to 1755.

By 1755 the final configuration of dyke walls at Grand Pré could have reached the stages represented in Fig. 6.11. In this figure, I have depicted only the final two hypothetical phases of construction because, when isolated from the previous seventy years, they dramatize the Acadians' elegant dykeland engineering achievement. Having built a total of 17.5 miles (27.4 km) of dyke walls and installed possibly as many as thirty aboiteau sluices during their step by step enclosure of Grand Pré marshlands, the Acadians finally achieved their goal with a mere 4 miles (6.4 km) of wall. They closed off intertidal Grand Pré on the east side with 2.2 miles (3.5 km) and on the west side with 1.8 miles (2.9 km) of wall (the black lines in Fig. 6.11, p. xxv). They reduced the number of aboiteaux to only three large ones in each of the two walls. The gray lines in Figure 6.11 represent the tidal excluding walls prior to the installation of the two major aboiteau barriers at Ransom Creek and Great Discharge Creek. The Ransom Creek aboiteau would have sacrificed that large fish trap inlet for the convenience of not having to patrol and maintain those three miles of dyke walls with their ten aboiteaux (numbered 1 to 10 on the map).

The advantage of the final Great Discharge aboiteau is less obvious to me. It would add a few acres and would mean less wall to maintain, but it meant the construction and maintenance of a very large aboiteau. However, if that aboiteau was part of the original construction phase of Enclosure 9, it would mean that there had never been any dyke walls along the north side of this creek, walls that would later be converted into roadways.

Chapter 7 discusses why the Acadians evidently began retreating from earlier dyke wall positions and why the New England Planters and the United Empire Loyalists were destined to suffer similar setbacks.

CHAPTER SEVEN

300 Years of Rising Sea Levels

The Broken Dyke

In vain the strength and virtue of its years!
O'er fence and furrow, through the broken walls,
Across the verdant fields, the tide has thrown
Its torrent arms; and the awed listener hears
Through the deep night the herds' mad cries and calls,
As the fierce river leaps to claim its own.

J.F. Herbin, 1911, 60

The 50 ft (15 m) rise of high water level in Minas Basin over the past 5,000 years, which caused the burial of mature forests, is discussed in chapter 3. The gradual nature of that process is easily imagined, and at an average of one ft/century (30 cm) it would hardly be noticed. My imagination, therefore, was not prepared for what I discovered on the steep bank of the Cornwallis River at Wolfville.

A low ridge traverses the marsh from Wolfville Harbour to the riverbank, long considered to be an old roadbed to a wharf built at the beginning of the twentieth century. At the eroding riverbank, this ridge is exposed in cross-section, and I was looking not at a roadbed but at a buried dyke wall. I later located a cross-section of the original wharf road farther to the east, where it is buried beneath 30 inches (0.76 m) of marsh soil that has accumulated since the dyke broke and was abandoned in 1931.

Exposed at the base of the cross-section of the dyke wall were three alternating layers of brush and hand-cut sods, and above that 5 to 6 ft (1.5–1.8 m) of dyke-wall sods. There had even been a later addition of a protective

Figure 7.1   This dyke at entrance to Wolfville Harbour was built by Planters in 1805–66 and abandoned in 1931; now it is almost entirely entombed by a 6 ft (2 m) accumulation of marsh turf, a consequence of rising sea levels. Note the base construction of three layers of brush and sods, and the later addition of a storm facing of slabwood (S) and boards (B).

facing of slabwood (Fig. 7.1). What was unimaginable were the implications. This slightly protruding dyke, which now resembled a roadbed, was constructed in 1805–06, and at that time its base sat *on top of* the marsh surface. Now its base is 5 to 6 ft (1.5–1.8 m) *beneath* the present marsh surface. This was undeniable proof that sea level and the marsh surface had risen at the unprecedented rate of nearly 3 ft/century (0.9 m), not at the accepted 1.2 to 2.3 inches (3–6 cm)/century worldwide, or at the accepted 20 cm/century in the Bay of Fundy as calculated by Dalrymple, Amos, and Yeo (1992).

As yet, there is no satisfactory explanation, the facts seem so improbable. Compaction may be a contributing factor, but there are no studies, and any hypothesis that suggests compaction as a contributing elevation factor has to contend with the fact that those small hand-built dykes of old were constructed on metres of firm root matrix, the latter packed with fine silts, and often sitting on bedrock or glacial till deposits.

Dr John Shaw (Bedford Institute of Oceanography, Dartmouth, Nova Scotia) suggested to me that perhaps the Minas Basin is a special case, because of its miles of dyke walls that now deny the twice daily tidal surges any access to their former extensive flood plain meadows. The waters are thus restricted to moving up and down the dyke walls, not back and forth across vast marsh meadows. This restriction may somehow translate into increased local tidal amplitudes, increased silt loads in the water column, and increased deposition across the remaining undyked marsh areas.

Another approach is to argue that because the present 50 ft (15 m) amplitude increase over the past fifty centuries (5,000 years) averages only one foot (0.3 m) per century, then my calculation of 2.5–3 ft (0.75–0.9 m) per century is unacceptable. However, there must be a strong positive correlation between tidal amplitude and sediment transport capabilities. Thus, it is possible that during the lesser tidal amplitude periods of 5–3,000 years ago (Fig. 3.1) the quantity of suspended sediment transport in the water column and the subsequent silt deposition across the marshes was minimal. Subsequently, during the last thousand years or so, it has gradually approached one metre per century, due to the cumulative effects of rising sea levels in general, land submergence, marsh compaction, effects of dyke wall enclosures, and an accelerated increase in tidal amplitudes in the semi-enclosed Minas Basin in particular.

The implications of this discovery for investigations of local biology, geology, oceanography, history, and archaeology were exciting. In the archaeological context, the presumed paucity of dyke-wall remnants was not necessarily the result of their rapid erosion, but more often of their rapid burial beneath tidal sediments. By extrapolation, Acadian dykes of the early 1700s would now be covered by 8 to 9 ft of marshland deposits and thus completely out of sight, but nevertheless present and intact. There is one such dyke at Wolfville (Fig. 7.2).

A follow-up to this discovery was a 1999 co-operative survey, with archaeologist David Christianson and assistant Steven Powell, of the Nova Scotia Museum of Natural History, to determine the elevations of these features. Analysis of that data evolved into interesting graphics depicting events at four separate local sites. Every case confirmed the initial 3 ft/century observations. Recent studies in the Cumberland Basin at the head of the Bay of Fundy, by Jeff Ollerhead and his students (Proosdij, Ollerhead, Davidson-Arnott, 2000), revealed that over a four-year period vertical growth of the marsh surface varied from 0.6 to 1.6 cm/year. If averaged, these figures provide another example of the possibility of a marsh rise of about 3 ft (0.9 m)/century.

Before discussing each locality, some observations that apply generally should be mentioned. Throughout the area, the strand line (high-tide drift

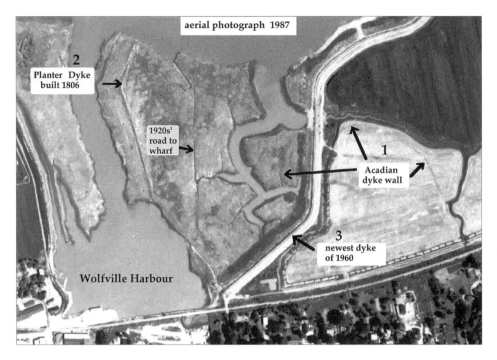

Figure 7.2 Aerial photo of Wolfville Harbour showing a series of three historic dyke walls. The straight-line marsh creek developed from a roadbed leading to a government lighthouse and wharf. (National Air Photo Library A 87323)

line along the shore where all the interesting beachcomber stuff can be found) is at the same elevation of 25 ft above the geodetic base level, a standard permanent reference elevation used by all land surveyors. (They do not use mean sea level, as that varies over time and location.) Unexpectedly, the elevations of the different marsh surfaces were *not* the same. The much higher levels of suspended sediment loads in the river channels could account for the differences. Daborn and Pennachetti, 1979, found that suspended silts ranged from <10 mg/litre in the Minas Basin to >100 mg/litre at the mouth of the Cornwallis River to a maximum of 4,900 mg/litre only one kilometre up river. I am assuming it is these tidal sediment loads that have added an additional 1 to 1.5 ft (0.3–0.45 m) of elevation to the Wolfville tidal marsh, above the marsh levels observed at east Grand Pré.

The value of these graphs lies not in their precision but in their generalities. Even if extrapolated elevations and actual survey levels differ by as much as 6 inches (15.2 cm), that would not invalidate the dramatic evidence of rapid increment of marsh levels in the Minas Basin over such relatively short periods. The graphs suggest that archaeological test trenches or simple coring

Figure 7.3 Eroded face of the present marsh at the bank of the Cornwallis River at Wolfville. In 1931 the original 1806 dyke was breached and abandoned. Note the discontinuity at the ledge of compacted pasture soil and above it the seventy-year accumulation of non-compacted tidal silts in a matrix of marsh-grass roots.

efforts, at these and similar sites on other dykelands in Atlantic Canada, could reveal profiles that further the documentation of historical events. Carbon dating and tree-ring correlations would add even more information.

The 1806 Wolfville dyke at the eroding Cornwallis River bank would make an ideal site for developing and testing marsh profile survey methods and interpretations. It has a 40 ft (12.2 m) exposed section of marsh and river deposits, and we already know that:

- half-way down the bank is a layer of clam shells 750 years old (Bleakney, 1986);
- about 6 ft (1.8 m) down is the base of a dyke wall 195 years old (Fig. 7.1);
- 2.5 ft (0.75 m) beneath the present marsh is a pasture profile (Fig. 7.3) as well as the gravel surface of the old wharf road, from seventy years ago (Fig. 7.2).

There are also laminated silts that are often contrastingly coloured and textured, reflecting the presence of grass, roots, logs and branches, snail and

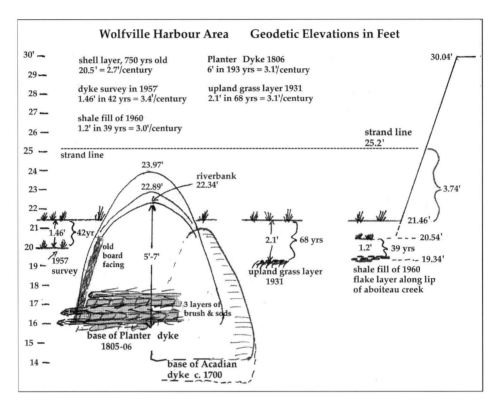

Figure 7.4   Original composite sketch of five sites where rapid deposition of tidal silts provided evidence of a rapid rise in relative sea level in Minas Basin.

clam shells, and marine foraminiferan shells. Chemical tests would further expand the tales that each layer could tell.

There are two Wolfville marsh graphics: an earlier hand sketch version that includes five observations that substantiate my belief in a marsh elevation rise of nearly 3 ft/century over the past 300 years (Fig. 7.4); and a computer-generated diagram with a more historical interpretation (Fig. 7.5, p. xxvi).

The initial hand-drafted graphic depicts two old dykes: one built by Acadians and one by Planters. The computer-generated graphic adds a third wall, the present Wolfville dyke, and plots their elevations, derived from our survey data: an Acadian dyke circa 1700; a Planter dyke of 1806, and the machine-built 1960 dyke wall (Fig. 7.2). The general working assumptions in the boxes to the left of the elevations column were extrapolated from the same survey data.

In aerial photos of 1931 and 1952 this old Acadian dyke still protrudes conspicuously above ground, even casting a shadow in the 1931 photo. It would have been added to by the Planters until the 1806 dyke was completed. After the machine-crowning of these fields in the 1970s and 1980s, the Acadian dyke was no longer visible at ground level. However, it is easily traced on 1987 and 1992 aerial photos through its landscaping signature, related to differences in moisture and vegetation, which imparts a different colour-reflectance value in the soil above it, both in the plowed fields and on the marsh.

In Fig. 7.5, each dyke construction date is indicated on its baseline. The relative elevation of the tidal marsh surface can be determined from the vertical geodetic scale. The green tufts of grass are marsh elevations at those dates, and the dashed orange lines lead up to a horizontal strand-line level. The hypothetical vertical advance of the strand line, the marsh surface, and the base and top of each dyke, over that 300-year period, are founded on survey facts and my extrapolations.

The solid black lines in the dyke wall diagrams represent the original wall, and the solid orange lines are the hypothetical additions that I deemed necessary to keep the top of the dykes about 2.5 ft above strand line (high-water level). On the 1700 and 1806 dyke diagrams, the uppermost short black horizontal lines, marked 1755 and 1931 respectively, are estimates for wall elevations in those years. Finally, the adjacent green bars are the present elevations at the top of those dykes.

With more detailed surveys of these and other dykes, the emerging patterns on these graphics could be refined into a useful general hypothesis. However, other variables must be considered. For example, one can assume that the long sections of old dykes that are most exposed above marsh level today were those that escaped storm destruction. When a dyke is breached, a gap quickly develops, but the adjacent wall sections may remain intact for the next 100 or more years – recall the basic integrity of those root-reinforced marsh sods.

If those damaged dyke walls were soon abandoned because a new wall was being constructed behind them, then as sea and marsh levels gradually rose the top of the old dyke eventually became submerged at high tides. The question then is, did these abandoned dykes enter a phase of gradual erosion of their crests, or did the undisturbed plant cover trap detritus and actually add to the height of the dyke? I believe that both probably occurred, based on personal observations at Wolfville and Grand Pré; it is a matter of relative exposure to storm action.

If one assumes that the top of a functional dyke would have been maintained at 6 or 7 ft above marsh-grass level, then in 1931 the dyke at Wolfville would have been at an elevation of 25.5 or 26 ft geodetic (7.7–7.9 m). Today the top of that old wall is at 23 to 24 ft (7.0–7.3 m), so at some period it was reduced in height by 1.5 to 2 ft (0.45–0.6 m). In support of this, its crest is now rather wide and rounded, whereas originally it would have been steep and narrow, with a 1.5 to 2 ft-wide footpath (Fig. 5.3). The old wall may even increase in width from new turf and a general detritus accretion along each side. An archaeological dissection would probably answer that question.

Once rising sea levels begin to regularly overtop an old dyke, the uppermost sods may be lifted by storm action, as they have no further sods above to hold them down, but their roots would help anchor them to some degree. This peeling off of topmost sod layers can be seen today at northeast Grand Pré, but this is a special case, an area of exposure to severe wave action (Fig. 7.6, p. xxvii). On the other hand, abandoned dyke walls are no longer grazed by cattle, or mowed, or used as footpaths, and their crests may be invaded by Salt Marsh Elder (*Iva frutescens*) and Wild Rose (*Rosa virginiana*). These are woody growth forms with roots and rhizomes that bind the sods together. They often form a continuous hedgerow, as at Wolfville Harbour and at the Guzzle, thereby advertising themselves as sites of old dykes.

In both summer and winter, their clusters of tough stems sieve out plant detritus from tidal flood waters, trapping quantities of dead *Spartina* as well as algal mats from marsh pools, and they also accumulate their own dead leaves, stems, and roots. What is the relationship atop an abandoned dyke wall between the rate of erosion, the rate of new plant growth, and the rate of detritus accretion? To answer that would require a long-term study. Therefore, while an examination of that cross-section of the 1806 Wolfville dyke may provide some exciting general measurements, the following are still unknown:

- the height of the original wall;
- the amount added to the dyke by the Planters to compensate for sea-level rise;
- the amount removed (if any) by the 1931 storm;
- the post-abandonment erosion since 1931 (if any);
- the amount added by shrubbery sieving out detritus over decades and centuries.

With rising sea levels, the old walls eventually become tidally submerged so regularly that Marsh Elder and Rose are killed. Their position is then occupied by a floral crest of the more salt tolerant Sea Lavender (*Limonium Nashii*). In the Grand Pré area, I have observed that hedgerows of intertidal

Figure 7.7   The present east Grand Pré rock-faced dyke wall, looking south to the Gaspereau River estuary, showing relative elevations of a Planter dyke topped with Marsh Elder and an Acadian dyke with Sea Lavender on its crest.

Marsh Elder are always sitting atop a Planter dyke, whereas the older and lower remnants of Acadian dykes sport a crest of clusters of Sea Lavender (Fig. 7.7).

Some of these questions could be answered by a botanical test trench dug into the 1806 Wolfville dyke. If Marsh Elder root remnants could be identified down to a sharp discontinuity, then we could conclude that Marsh Elder contributes to its own specialized habitat by trapping detritus and adding height to the dyke wall. If it forms but a single thin layer, then Marsh Elder establishment is a one-time event that adds little to the crest of an abandoned dyke before it dies out and the Sea Lavender takes over.

Some basic archaeological endeavours could advance our ability to analyse and interpret the history of dykelands. Two crucial bits of data are the year a dyke was constructed and its geodetic elevation. The first may be dug up in libraries, but the second involves digging or coring in the marshes and surveying. If cores were taken, or test trenches dug, just to each side of an old abandoned dyke wall, then on the landward side of the wall, beneath the present layer of tidal marsh turf, one should find a pasture grass profile, and beneath that the identifiable hollow aerenchymous roots of the original marsh grasses. In chapter 4, I have shown that aerenchymous roots of *Spartina* and *Juncus* can be identified in 200-year-old dyke wall sods. After determining a hay-field/marsh-grass boundary, one could then determine how much pasture turf, as well as how much tidal marsh sod, had accumulated during the intervening years. This could be done on a grand scale at Grand Pré with the old Acadian dyke enclosures, starting at the National Historic Site and progressing north to Long Island. This could provide a sequential marsh-level and pasture-level profile from about 1680 to 1730, with perhaps one anomaly, the Saxby Tide marine deposits of 1869.

In 1993 the Nova Scotia Power Corporation replaced their line of power poles that cross the enclosed Grand Pré marshlands from the National Historic Site to Long Island. They dug pits 12 ft (3.6 m) deep, and I was informed that "snail and clam shells were noticed from a depth of about 4 ft (1.2 m) to the bottom of the pits." However, these figures are after-the-fact recollections by the supervisors. I examined forty-one of the piles of excavated marsh deposits and identified nine species of marine molluscs. Thus, cores extracted from fields on Grand Pré will have shells as well as roots of marsh grasses. The Rough Periwinkle snail (*Littorina saxatilis*) lives amongst the grasses of the flat tidal marsh and, in the cores, could serve as an indicator of marsh level at the time of dyking. The depth of accumulated soil since then would, I am certain, reveal something of the natural fertility of enclosed marshlands. In spite of centuries of plowing, soil compaction, erosion, and harvesting of crops, the power pole pits indicated that nearly 4 ft (1.2 m) or more of new upland turf has been added to the original marsh elevation. How does this relate structurally and chemically to the original marsh beneath? The roots of the non-marine grasses are tapping into the nutrient-rich layers beneath, but what are the differences after hundreds of years? A comparison with the rate of accumulation and fertility of adjacent upland soils, disturbed and undisturbed, would be illuminating.

The second computer-generated graphic (Fig. 7.8, p. xxviii) is of an area at east Grand Pré, where the Guzzle joins the Gaspereau River. It differs from the Wolfville area in that its marsh surface is 4.5 ft lower than the high-tide line, and that is about 1.5 ft (0.45 m) lower than on the Wolfville marsh. The reason for this difference is that, on an equivalent tide, a greater amount of silt is transported and deposited at Wolfville than at east Grand Pré. At this Guzzle site, the actual elevation of the basal layers of the Acadian and Planter dykes is as yet unknown, but their crests are exposed and I have extrapolated back from known profiles at other sites.

The lower Acadian dyke is unexpectedly located *between* the Planter dyke and the 1940 dyke (the latter enlarged in 1960) (Fig. 9.2.3). It has a long section missing, which I presume was removed by the November 1759 storm. I suggest that when the Planters finally began to rebuild the outer dykes, they built a new one that looped slightly outside of the old Acadian line to include more of that relatively sheltered marsh. Today, the latter wall remnant has a crest of Sea Lavender whereas the Planter dyke has one of Marsh Elder. The location of both of these old dykes is dramatically revealed during higher high tides, when for a brief time their respective floral crests protrude above the gradually submerging marsh (Fig. 7.7).

Two other areas, one near Horton Landing and another termed Palmeter's Dyke on the short north shore section of Grand Pré, are only in sketch format and are not presented here, but are worth a brief discussion.

The Horton Landing area is in a different category from the others for it has the only extant Acadian dyke *inside* today's protective enclosures (Figs 9.1.5 and 9.1.6). According to local legend, it has never been disturbed with the exception of being pasture land for over a century. However, cattle traversing its length have created a trough on its crest, which complicates reconstructing the history of its elevations. This east-west wall would have been the south boundary of Enclosure 10 and would have been built by Acadians about 1730. It became redundant with the construction of the new north-south Acadian wall and aboiteau at the mouth of "Deportation Creek," possibly about 1735. Its dyke and aboiteau broke in November 1759, returning sea water to the fields of Enclosure 11 and up to the previous Enclosure Walls 4, 6, and 10 – walls that once again became the outermost dyke walls of southeast Grand Pré (Fig. 6.5). Our survey of elevations indicates that the accretion of pasture turf behind this wall, over the subsequent 270-year period, has been about 1.7 to 2 ft/century, reflecting the remarkable fertility of dykeland soils.

The present sea-wall dyke at Horton Landing is in its original Acadian location and, because new walls have been added over older ones, a test trench excavated from behind or within a small coffer dam should reveal the following sequence: an Acadian brush, post, and sod dyke; a Planter sod addition, and a later plank facing; a thick turf layering from the heavy-equipment period of the 1950s to 1990s, which created wide road-width crests in place of the narrow footpaths of old; and finally, the heavy rip-rap rock facing of today.

The north shore of northeast Grand Pré is the most complex to depict in vertical section. It is fully exposed to the Minas Basin and has experienced much erosion. Its marsh is advancing vertically and horizontally inland, but at the same time the oldest sections are being severely undercut on its seafront (Figs 4.7 and 10.2). Newly exposed, just off the beaches, are two levels of old forests that I judge to be about 430 and 560 years old. Beach sands and gravels are being storm-driven inland and now cover the remains of older dykes.

Figure 7.9   Dyke between Long Island and Little Island in 1942. The dyke was
breached and abandoned in 1944. This was the only section of Grand Pré dyke wall
fully exposed to the open Minas Basin; sixty years later the sod wall has been levelled
and the plank face reduced to stubs (see Fig. 7.10).

   To the north of the present dyke wall, remnants of a major Planter dyke,
breached and abandoned in 1944, protrude from several areas in the tidal
marsh. In 1942 I took photographs of the dilapidated condition of the high
plank facing on that wall (Fig. 7.9), not knowing that in two years it would
be abandoned, and not imagining how I would value that photo fifty-seven
years later. The wall is now reduced to the level of the marsh surface (Fig.
7.10). With each passing winter, new portions of this old dyke are exposed,
providing a rare ongoing opportunity to view the progressive dissection of a
dyke wall. There are layers of sods and brush and poles, as well as a facing
of planks and posts, and even the iron rods that anchored the plank facings
to "deadman" logs buried in the core of the dyke. In May 2001, even old sod
pits were newly exposed (inset, Fig. 4.2).
   Jim Eldridge considers installing these deadman anchor logs as the worst of
any dyking procedure. A pit had to be dug straight down into the dyke wall,
not much larger than the log or timber to be inserted, but large enough for a
man to squeeze in and guide the threaded rods being driven through the sod
wall into holes drilled in the logs. By reaching and feeling, the washers and
nuts were threaded onto the rod ends and then the fill had to be packed back
into the pit. It was a messy, strenuous, and frustrating operation. The present
large dyke walls along the north and northeast shore of Grand Pré were built
over major sections of this type of plank facing. Thus, the engineering details
of this type of construction have not been lost, only entombed.

Boot Island

Little Island

Figure 7.10   The dyke wall in Fig. 7.9 photographed in November 1999. It was first built by the Planters (but when?) to replace a threatened section of original Acadian dyke, and it traversed the marsh to link up with an Acadian wall at the end of the black arrow. Not only was a plank face added some time later for protection but also a breakwater consisting of a row of large posts was installed well out in front.

The outer shore of this marsh is a series of erosional steps cut into a 10 to 12 ft (3.0–3.6 m) thick deposit of marsh grasses. Within that accumulation are several bands of black plant remains, the black onion-like corms of Salt Marsh Bulrush (*Scirpus maritimus*) (Fig. 7.11, p. xxix), indicating periods of sandy beaches hundreds of years ago. Tidal currents and storms still transport fine sand to this particular area, as is evident in aerial photographs (Fig. 9.3.4). At the very base of this ancient marsh turf, a non-marine gray clay containing many roots and rhizomes of Wild Rose (*Rosa virginiana*) is exposed. Accepting a sea-level rise of 2.5 to 3 ft (0.75–0.9 m)/century, these rose roots could be nearly 400 years old. To add some finer detail to the charting of sea-level changes, it would be helpful to have these roots carbon dated, as well as the tree trunks and stumps on the adjacent tidal flats.

A variety of old sod pits lie at the top of this outer marsh, as well as a revealing section of dyke wall built from hand-cut sods. Several rows of carefully laid sods faced the sea side of this dyke wall, whereas the core section has a fill of loosely jumbled sods (the effect of recent storms) as well as a few posts, planks, and stakes driven in at intervals along the wall (Fig. 7.6). This dyke may be worn down nearly to its original base, because it now has an

18 ft (5.5 m)-wide exposure. On the other hand, these many rows of sods may be a reflection of a century of adding height and width to an original dyke to compensate for sea-level rise and an exposed coastline.

The same local erosional forces have also exposed an interesting layer of wood chips, the type created by sharpening posts with an axe. This extensive layer is slightly lower, but is to the sea side of the base of the old dyke wall. This implies that, at the time, this stake sharpening yard was on dry ground and therefore inside a previous dyke wall. This site has not been carefully surveyed for relative elevations and the tree species of the wooden posts have not been identified. The chips may be related to an old shad fishery that would have required numerous tall poles and tie-down stakes to support long lines of gill nets set across the adjacent intertidal flats (Figs 1.1 and 3.4).

In summary, the effect of rising sea levels has been to bury and preserve the old dykes at many locations, but at other sites shore erosion has reduced them or even removed them entirely. The challenge is to be able to recognize the various remnants when exploring the dykeland terrain.

The next chapter deals with examples of how poorly cartographers have depicted this sea-level history. Fortunately, aerial photographs have precisely recorded its effects.

CHAPTER EIGHT

Coping With Cartographic Errors

An Expedient Survey Method of 1760

We have also the peculiarity in the laying out of the North
Mountain lands from the base line ... the side-lines were
run by that torment of surveyors the conch-shell line ... The
line was blazed through the forest by following the sound
of a conch-shell used as a horn.

A.W.H. Eaton, 1910, 81–2

Don't believe everything you see on a map, any more than you believe everything you read. The spectrum of accuracy of cartographic renditions of dykelands is astounding, from near aerial-photo quality through figments of
imagination to total omission. Compounding this confusion is the revision of
older maps without a revision of their dykeland areas, leading to the omission of changes caused by shore erosion and relocation of dyke walls.

Even when a new topographic map is published, the lag time between the
surveys and publication can be significant relative to dykelands. For example, much of the surveying for the 1911 topographic map (13 A, Province
Nova Scotia, Hants and Kings Counties, Kingsport Sheet no. 84) was done
by Hugh Fletcher in the 1890s and published in Geological Survey Reports
of 1901, 1904, and 1905. Nevertheless, authors will refer to geographic
conditions of 1911 at Grand Pré as "according to Govern. Topo. Map 13 A,
Kingsport Sheet 84, 1911." This is an accepted conventional convenience,
but can become misleading cartographic information, particularly when

dykelands are the topic. A fifteen to twenty-year lag time could exclude significant bouts of dyke-wall construction.

A pertinent example in the context of this book is the 1967 topographic Wolfville Sheet based on a 1959 aerial survey according to map legends. But with shore erosion at potentially 3 ft (1 m)/year (Table 9.4.1), twenty or more feet of erosion could occur over that eight-year time lag, with consequent construction of new dykes and relocation of aboiteaux. This is precisely what happened at Grand Pré. The final 1967 map depicted the new 1960 dyke wall at west Grand Pré, the most recent version of the Wickwire Dyke (see chapter 9). However, at east Grand Pré the wall depicted was an obsolete pre-1960 dyke. That particular map information was derived from the 1959 aerial survey photos, thereby omitting the relocated walls and new aboiteau that had been installed in 1960.

I eventually sorted out all of this confusing cartography using an "obscure" series of 1963 aerial photos. The word obscure is in quotes because the 1967 map legends do not mention any aerial photos other than those of 1959. However, I realized that the new depiction of the extensive intertidal flats on that map could only have come from early morning photography during an extremely low tidal phase. It took considerable persistence to convince the National Air Photo Library that, in spite of there being no mention of other flights on the map, such a set of photos must have been used to generate the new intertidal rendering. The file was finally located and, as predicted, the flight was flown during the hour of a 0.0′ Datum tide, between 8 and 9 A.M., on 25 May 1963. This set of photos (A18060) has proven to be invaluable, because the early morning low-angle light has enhanced every contour and the resolution is suitable for excellent enlargements.

Prior to the 1940s standard government aerial photos are a rarity, but because dyke walls endure for so long they show up well on the 1940s and 1950s photos and their positions can verify the location of cartographic depictions on older maps. However, I have devised a quick method for assessing old maps of the Grand Pré area by involving marsh creeks. As each drainage creek in the tidal marshes has a unique configuration and as these channels have not changed appreciably over the past 300 years, the accuracy of historical maps regarding dyke walls, field boundaries, and shore erosion can easily be determined through comparison with the specific creek patterns of these four particular maps:

• Horton Township map of 1760, surveyed by John Bishop, including all of Grand Pré;

- West Marsh Dyke of 1808, surveyed by Oliver Lyman, from west Grand Pré to Wolfville;
- Wolfville Sheet 21 H/1, 1928 topographic;
- Wolfville Sheet 21 H/1 W, 1967 topographic.

Selected prints from the National Air Photo Library photos of 1945–46, 1953–59, 1962–67 also apply in some cases (appendix 9).

For an almost instant assessment of the quality of any local Kings County map, first examine the depiction of Boot Island and the Guzzle channel. Originally, in 1760, two major parallel creeks dissected the Boot Island marsh from east to west. If they are not accurately represented, ask for your money back. A narrow Guzzle channel first formed around 1860. By the 1960s the northern creek had been eliminated through shore erosion. If you find a 1960s map with the two creeks, ask for double your money back. (See historical sequence in Fig. 9.2.1, p. xxxi).

A second feature that reflects the spectrum of interest and disinterest that surveyors had for marshes is the depiction of dyke walls. Dyke walls have bordered these marshes since the time of the Acadians, yet on some maps dykes are partially or entirely omitted. They are not omitted from the aerial photos, so where have these walls been hiding in the interim?

The following are eleven pertinent local examples of the pitfalls of believing what you read. These revelations are not accompanied by the relevant maps, as those maps are too large and their reduction to page size would obscure the details being discussed. My comments are such that the omissions and mistakes on the maps can be appreciated without having the maps at hand.

- A few old maps correctly depict Long and Little and Boot Islands as one island, isolated from the uplands to the south by an extensive tidal Grand Pré marsh. One such map of 1649 (printed by Thomas Jefferys in 1755) correctly has French settlers plotted at Annapolis, but not at Grand Pré (Fig. 8.1). A map of 1711–1712 (printed by Thomas Bowles, London) has the French at Grand Pré with a church and mill, and the three connected islands are still isolated from houses and fields by a band of tidal marsh, as they should be at this early occupation date (Fig. 8.2).
- The 1834 Great Map of Nova Scotia, a standard and important resource, has a Grand Pré shoreline suspiciously similar to that of the 1760 John Bishop map, but it does not really matter, because all tidal creeks and dyke walls were omitted on this set of maps.

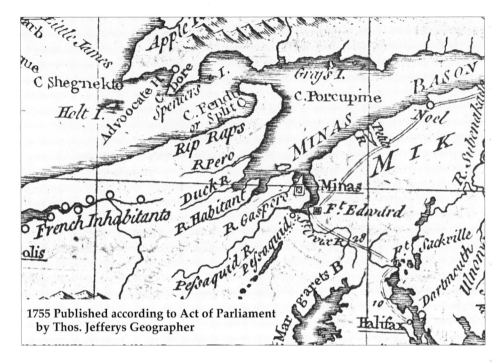

1755 Published according to Act of Parliament
by Thos. Jefferys Geographer

Figure 8.1   Map published in 1755, but based on observations of Bressani in 1649, Brattle in 1700, and Chabert in 1751. The depiction of one large island off Grand Pré reflects the period of 1649 or 1700 and not 1751, by which time the marshes would have been dyked and the island geographically connected to the mainland.

- The 1863 hydrographic map, Sheet 2 Bay of Fundy, was surveyed in 1860 and updated and reissued as recently as 1942 (Sheet 353). Although the bathymetric figures and contours for the seabed were revised over those eighty years, the topographic portions of the map hark back to the 1860s, and closely resemble the Church map of 1864, even to its major misrepresentations (who copied from whom?). The 1942 edition definitely is *not* a map of dykelands of the 1940s.
- The 1864 series of Nova Scotia maps by A.F. Church, famous for having so many property owners' names on the maps, are geographically atrocious for the Grand Pré area. Boot Island does have the two creek-like indentations, but they are on the north side of the island instead of on the west. His road to Boot Island takes an imaginary course straight across two major creeks, creeks that are conveniently omitted from his map. The drainage courses of Great Discharge Creek and Ransom Creek are unbelievably distorted. The only dyke wall depicted is from Horton Landing to

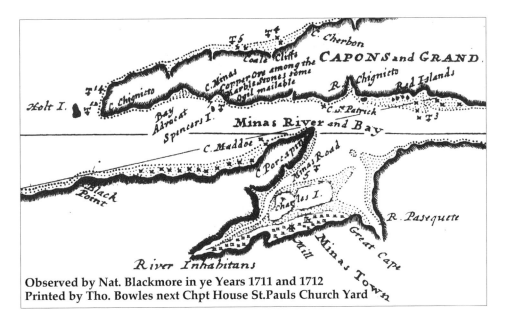

Observed by Nat. Blackmore in ye Years 1711 and 1712
Printed by Tho. Bowles next Chpt House St.Pauls Church Yard

Figure 8.2   Map of 1711 and 1712 published by Thomas Bowles, London, "By Her Majesties Special Comand," thus limiting it to the reign of Queen Anne, 1702–1714. Grand Pré has houses, a church, a mill, and one large Charles Island (consisting of the then contiguous three islands of Long, Little, and Boot) separated by marsh.

Little Island, leaving the entire Grand Pré and Wickwire marshlands fully exposed to daily tidal flooding.

- An 1867 Grand Pré area map, prepared by Dominion Atlantic Railway engineers, depicts their rail line and almost everything else that could be of historical interest. There are Acadian roads, an Acadian racetrack, 1860s roads, wharves, the Cornwallis River ferry crossing, various ford crossings at rivers, and so on but, astoundingly, absolutely no dyke walls are drawn on that otherwise informative map.

- The 1953 government topographic map has retained the details of the Guzzle, Boot Island, Oak Island, and Horton Landing from the old 1928 topographic map, in spite of considerable changes evident in 1945–46 aerial photos. The map does not even include a large new 1944 dyke extending from Long Island to Little Island. However, the west side of Grand Pré actually was revised to depict the remnants of the derelict Wickwire Dyke of 1931, but the map does not include that vital section of the wall extending from the bank of the Cornwallis River into Wolfville Harbour, where it did then, and still does, connect to the railway roadbed.

- The interesting 1891 MacKinlay coloured map of Nova Scotia & Island of Cape Breton lacks a Guzzle channel, which had been present since the 1860s. He also neglected to include any dyke walls at the west side of Grand Pré, in spite of their presence since the 1720s.
- The 1911 topographic map (Kingsport Sheet 84, Map 13 A) is a peculiar mix of omissions and errors, although superficially it appears acceptable. It lacks all creeks on Boot Island, has only a partial dyke wall at east Grand Pré, and once again the west Grand Pré and Wickwire dyke walls are missing. There is even an access road to an aboiteau that is mistakenly labelled as "Dyke."
- Not until the 1928 topographic map (Wolfville, Sheet 21 H/1) is there any evidence of an attempt to survey dykelands with some accuracy, and even then the results did not equal those of the 1760 surveyors. Nevertheless, the quality and quantity of detail in this 1928 map are why it was used as a base map for many decades. The 1966 Soil Survey Maps for Kings County (Report No.15, Canadian Department of Agriculture, 1965, Truro, NS) is colour-coded for the marsh soils under cultivation behind dyke walls and for soils exposed to tidal immersion outside the walls (Fig. 8.3, p. xxx). Surprisingly, as their base map, the makers used the 1928 topographic map with its unmistakable double-creeked Boot Island.

The 1928 base map was adjusted in one area. Someone on the survey team or cartography team was aware that the Wickwire Dyke wall had been destroyed about 1930 and that a new one had recently replaced it. They apparently did not conduct a ground check of the area, but simply moved the 1928 dyke wall arbitrarily further inland on the soil map, but not far enough to be accurate. They created, with the stroke of their pen, several hundred acres of additional farmland, which in fact were under tidal waters. They also neglected to "install" aboiteau dams across the major creeks of the new 1960 Wickwire Dyke, leaving gaps on the map that in reality would allow flooding of the entire 3,000 acres of Grand Pré farmlands.

In spite of these misrepresentations, the map is significant because the enclosed marshland soils are colour-coded a dark green, and this essentially demarcates all the lands in Kings County dyked by the Acadians. It is the most visually striking map plot of the Acadians' dyking accomplishments that I have found.
- The 1968 book by Andrew H. Clark, *Acadia: The Geography of Early Nova Scotia to 1760*, is a major reference for Acadian history. It contains a map (Fig. 6.2) of the Acadian population of 1714 plotted on a map

prepared by the University of Wisconsin Cartographic Laboratory. The source of this Grand Pré base map, which is used throughout the book, is not identified. Geographically the map is not of the 1714 period, but is adapted from the Canadian 1967 topographic, as evidenced by the wide Guzzle gap between Boot Island and Grand Pré marshlands. Clark's map has but one shoreline indentation, implying one creek on Boot Island; that indicates that the 1928 and 1953 topographics were not consulted, as they depict both historical Boot Island creeks.

• When government bodies assumed responsibility for dyke walls and aboiteaux in 1950, they began surveying and soon produced maps whose detail focused specifically on dykelands. Their base maps are updated after each construction project and thereby generate a historical record of dykeland changes, be they natural or man-made. These maps are not in general circulation as they are intended for use by owners of dykeland and government surveyors.

These large maps have information features unobtainable from other maps. One Grand Pré series consists of four maps, each 3 ft x 4.5 ft (0.9–1.4 m). They usually have the location of geodetic benchmarks, elevations of land surface both inside and outside dyke walls, direction of drainage flow in the creeks, dates of installation of new aboiteaux and their elevations, lists of property owners, and other data. The older editions from Maritime Marshlands Reclamation Administration files even plot the derelict remnants of pre-1950 dykes. The relative positions of dyke walls can be compared with previous maps and with recent aerial photographs for a precise determination of erosional changes.

One could be seriously misled by innocently documenting the historic sequence of dyke construction and destruction in a specific area by relying solely on a series of historical maps. Unfortunately, most maps need to be cross-checked with other maps, with minute books of annual meetings of dykeland associations, and with old newspaper articles, journals, and other sources. Even J.F. Herbin's map notes are at times unreliable. While reading items he had copied into his notebooks, I began to find conflicting dates and unreasonable calculations.

For a man of so many accomplishments, and a quintessential historian, author, and archivist, he had two unfortunate afflictions. First, he was an obsessive collector of the printed word and he scissored away at journals, books, and newspapers. His scrapbooks abound with original historical gems, but those items are orphaned because they are without page, age, or name. His clipping technique was so meticulous that he removed all margins, and what ended up on the cutting floor included all titles, publication dates, and page numbers.

His second affliction was a form of astigmatism that had him misreading the numbers 3, 5, 6, and 8. This played historical havoc when he copied numerical information from documents. In a 1911 school scribbler, he copied out pertinent information from the 1804 and 1805 minute books of meetings that planned that first three-mile-long Wickwire Dyke wall. He mentions no source, but from those minute books he transcribed fascinating construction costs and geographic details, and a list of original owners of the salt hay dykeland lots. However, in spite of having in his collection the original Oliver Lyman survey map, dated 1808, he recorded it as 1803. He even went so far as to surmise it must have been a dykeland "proposal" map, because according to the minute book the dyke was built later in 1805–06. He copied out the length of the dyke as 3,168 yards, whereas it was 5,168. Lyman's map records the acreage of each lot and Lyman's total is 687.2.13 acres, yet in Herbin's notebook it reads 637 acres. In contrast, T.C. Haliburton (1829), who apparently had access to Lyman's map as well, correctly reported the new acreage as 687 acres.

With the above guidance and precautionary words, it is hoped that others may be encouraged to take up this cartographic challenge of deciphering dykeland history in their particular area. By way of encouragement, chapter 9 offers six examples of the kind of information that can be extracted from maps and aerial photos.

CHAPTER NINE

History of Dykelands at Six Locations

District of Horton

The attention of the traveller is arrested by the extent and beauty of a view, which bursts upon him very unexpectedly, as he descends the Horton Mountains ... The variety and extent of this prospect, the beautiful verdant vale of the Gaspereaux, the extended township of Horton interspersed with groves of wood and cultivated fields, and the cloud capt summit of the lofty cape that terminates the chain of the north mountain, forms an assemblage of objects, rarely united with so striking an effect.

T.C. Haliburton, 1829

The dykeland histories described in this chapter are a distillate of information gleaned from diaries, documents, marshland ledgers and minute books, maps, newspaper articles, postcards, old photographs, on-site field investigations, interviews, and aerial photographs spanning 1931 to 1999. The approach is both biological and cultural, interspersed with comments and questions. It may seem surprising that dykeland history differs within the limited area of Wolfville to Boot Island, but the erosional regimes along this portion of the Minas Basin shoreline differ substantially, and these account for the diversity in degrees of preservation of dykeland construction artifacts.

This chapter has an abundance of illustrations, with labels and legends to make them as informative as possible on their own. The illustrations are the focus of the text and they contain a wealth of information. The six localities present a wide variety of dykeland aspects that provide excellent material for exercises in photo interpretation and map deciphering.

The six geographic localities are outlined in Fig. 9.0.1. Their special discussion features are as follows:

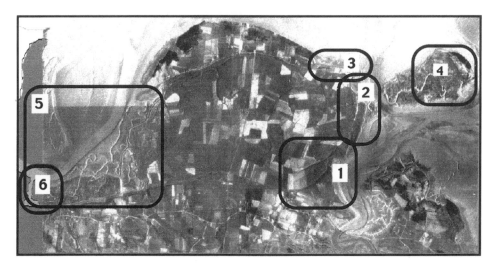

Figure 9.0.1   Composite of 1963 aerial photos with outlines of the six localities
discussed in detail in chapter 9: 1. Horton Landing area; 2. Gaspereau River Estuary
and the Guzzle Channel; 3. Northeast Grand Pré shoreline; 4. Boot Island; 5. Wolfville
and West Grand Pré tidal marshes; 6. Wolfville Harbour area.

Locality 1   Horton Landing area: recent deportation site discoveries and
the potential for locating other undocumented sites.

Locality 2   Gaspereau River Estuary and the Guzzle Channel area: location
of old extant Acadian and New England Planter dykes; and the urgent need
for their documentation and archaeological excavation.

Locality 3   Northeast Grand Pré shoreline: a complex patchwork of dykes,
ditches, sod pits, plank facings, a small aboiteau, and drowned forests.

Locality 4   Boot Island: eroded to half its 1760 dimensions, but with undisturbed remnants of dykes, and possibly of aboiteaux.

Locality 5   Wolfville and West Grand Pré tidal marshes: a challenging area
to dyke, avoided by the Acadians, but later dyked by the New England
Planters.

Locality 6   Wolfville Harbour area: aerial photos have recorded an unusual
assemblage of historical remnants.

While reading of these historical changes, keep in mind that since 1700 relative sea level and marsh level have risen by 8 to 10 ft (2.4–3 m) in Minas Basin.

9.1   Locality 1: Horton Landing Area

In the 1884–1950 ledger of the Minutes of Annual March Meetings of the Proprietors of the Grand Pré Dykeland, the secretary's report always began with a description of the boundaries of that reclaimed tidal marshland with the words "Namely, from *Horton River* near *Black Landing*, thence westerly."

Those italicized words have proven to be the clues to deciphering key historic events at Horton Landing. At this site, the history of the Acadians at Grand Pré commenced, flourished, and terminated. The focal point is a long intertidal exposure of layers of black shale rock, 360 million years old (Horton Group, Horton Bluff Formation, Middle Member ECHh/m, of late Devonian-early-carboniferous).

At the time of the Acadians, the Horton River (now the Gaspereau River) executed a sharp bend at Horton Landing (Fig. 9.1.1) that swept away sediments from this outcropping of blue-black shale, creating a gently sloping bedrock riverbank. This site provided an unprecedented firm access to the upper shore, at any tidal level, in an otherwise inherently slippery riverbank environment.

The two maps in Fig. 9.1.1 illustrate how the river channel has changed from a long curving creek adjacent to Oak Island in 1760 to a broad channel leading directly into the Gaspereau River. This change has created new current and eddy patterns that have contributed to silts obscuring the shale, and has enabled the marsh grasses to extend out over the rocky outcrop, building to depths of 6 ft (1.8 m) and more. I first explored this typical "muddy" riverbank in June 2000, and discovered a shale bedrock exposure just beneath a camouflage blanket of silts. Black Landing is no longer conspicuously black except at an extreme low tide, and then only if explored on foot. Local historians were unaware of this geological explanation for the name "Black Landing," as opposed to "Black's Landing."

This strategically located landing site determined the location of future Acadian homes (some foundations still exist and artifacts surface during plowing operations), as well as the location of the adjacent Fort Montague and of a connecting road running inland and over the hill into Gaspereau Valley. This road is still in use, running from the riverbank past the Fred Curry farm and across the railway track. By a similar geological fate, the

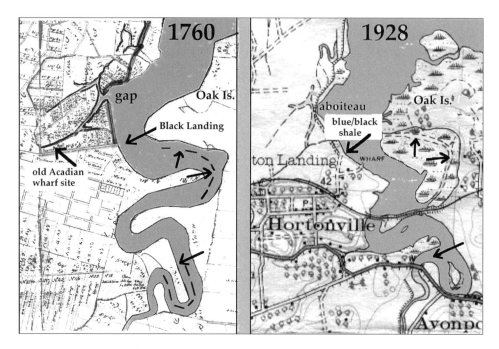

Figure 9.1.1   Maps showing changes in the channel of the Gaspereau River relative to
the site of a black shale outcrop referred to as Black Landing, and then as Horton
Landing. A major deportation of Acadians took place from this landing. On the 1760
map, note the gap in the dyke wall where an aboiteau was destroyed by storms
in 1759.

bank of the Cornwallis River at Starr's Point has an outcrop of sandstone
bedrock known as Boudreau Landing, which is why that site was chosen for
docking ships, why a town was established, and why a major road ran diagonally inland from that particular landing area.

The Acadians who settled Grand Pré found not only this firm shore ramp,
which at that time extended from high to low water line, but also an adjacent deep creek extending inland towards two hills on which homes could be
built. This direct access, at high tides, into the village area, must have been a
boon when transporting goods to and from ships. There is anecdotal evidence of a wharf on this creek (the "Deportation Creek" of most literature),
and I have an account of planks being plowed up. Even today, a broad flat
area at one side of the creek looks suspiciously like a wharf deck. It would
be worth a test trench effort to establish its existence.

Between 1735 and 1740 the Acadians had closed off that creek with a
major aboiteau. The 1760 maps of Charles Morris and John Bishop plot the
presence of dyke walls here and an aboiteau dam, but there is a gap in the

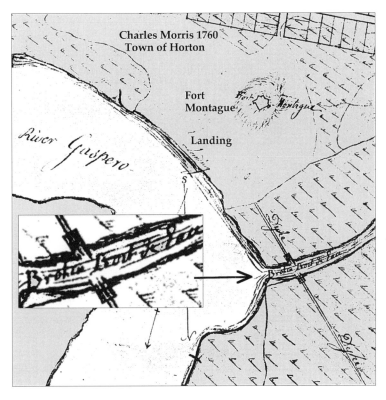

Figure 9.1.2   Charles Morris map of 1760 with dyke walls drawn in to
either side of "Deportation Creek." In the creek are the words "Broken
Boit de Eau," referring to a water box or sluice. This is irrefutable proof
that the Acadians could not have been deported from this particular
creek in 1755. (Nova Scotia Department of Natural Resources)

aboiteau with the words "Broken Boit de Eau" (Fig. 9.1.2). The French
rendering could be Morris's phonetic spelling of "boîte d'eau," a water box
or sluice, or his phonetic rendering of the spoken word "aboiteau."

Other circumstantial evidence is the larger 1760 map by surveyor John
Bishop depicting all the Grand Pré field boundaries. Only in the area of
"Deportation Creek" are very small fields plotted on that map (Fig. 9.1.3).
The straight line between the two creeks bounded by those rows of narrow
fields is a road, not an incomplete dyke wall. This identification came from
a 1760 property map depicting the various lots of Theofilus Sutherland of
Horton (Sutherland, 1760). Many lines on that Sutherland map are invalu-
ably labelled as to creek, road, old dyke wall, or salt marsh, and thus can be
cross-referenced to other maps with the same lot boundaries, but otherwise
undesignated as to function.

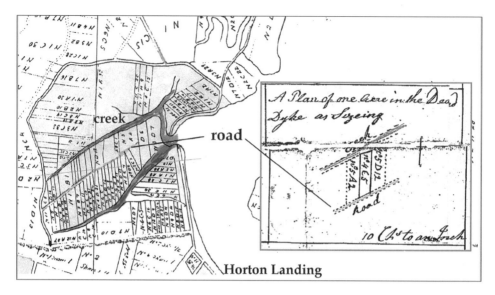

creek

road

A Plan of one Acre in the Dead Dyke as Sizeing

road

10 Chs to an Inch

Horton Landing

Figure 9.1.3   Portion of the 1760 Planter map (Fig. 6.4) with an inset of part of a small survey sheet of the various land lots owned by Theofilus Sutherland in 1760. Note the match of road and creek labels, and the reference to "one Acre in the Dead Dyke as Sizeing." This is interpreted to mean that a previously enclosed area of dyked land was now "dead," flooded by sea water after the loss of the aboiteau. (Nova Scotia Department of Natural Resources)

The field patterns in the Dead Dyke area on these 1760 maps match those on 1963 aerial photos, so this section of Grand Pré must have been desalinated prior to 1755 and under the plow for some time. There had to be an established aboiteau because once land has been dyked, crowned, and drained, creating dales and dale ditches, future generations follow those hard-won contours. If the telltale parallel lines of dale ditches are recognizable, either from the ground or from aerial photos, then the area must have been behind a protective dyke wall at some time in the past.

The reason for the fine subdivisions in this area may relate to "sizeing" of land allotments. To make up an even "share" of land allotment, a final small lot or two were often added to "fill in" the total deed size or land quantity, thus the term "sizeing." The Theofilus Sutherland map includes a plot of what appear to be three dales and the plan says "A Plan of One Acre in the Dead Dyke, as Sizeing" (Fig. 9.1.3, small inset). I wonder whether these Dead Dyke lots were to become garden plots eventually, after reconstruction of the aboiteau, as they were conveniently near the town site.

J.F. Herbin believed that, as the Acadian population increased, the fields became subdivided in keeping with inheritance traditions and that some

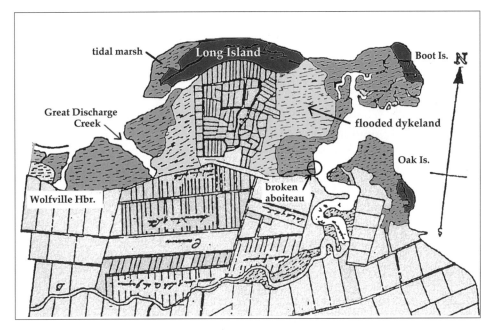

Figure 9.1.4   Horton District in 1760-61. The central block of demarcated fields is presumed to be the acreage not flooded by the 1759 storm-breaching of dyke walls, the only agricultural marshland available to the Planters when they arrived in June 1760. The accuracy of this map is confirmed by its close match to field patterns in 1963 aerial photos (Fig. 6.8). (Nova Scotia Department of Natural Resources)

families found it necessary to move to other localities. Karl W. Butzer (in correspondence) believes that agricultural land was becoming scarce and terribly subdivided. This hypothesis has three possible problems: first, there seemed to be more than enough land to support the population, for they were in the agricultural export business; second, why was this supposed family subdivision of Acadian lots restricted primarily to portions of Dead Dyke (Enclosure 11) and not generally all across the dyked land; and third, after 1759 the Dead Dyke fields were under salt water and thus an agricultural "waste land" of farm fields that no one would care about, but the land grant officials could conveniently top up allotment totals with these "valuable" salt-hay lots with their established access roadbed (Fig. 9.1.3).

In November 1759 a severe storm breached many Acadian dykes. I have concluded that the aboiteau at Horton Landing creek was also destroyed at this time; it is recorded as such on the 1760 John Bishop map, as mentioned above. Sea water would have flooded the fields up to some previous barrier system of dyke walls. Probably all redundant dyke walls were retained by the Acadians as back-up insurance to diminish damage from unexpected storms. One extant map (Fig. 9.1.4) depicts a huge block of fields only in the centre of Grand Pré, implying that areas outside were subject to tidal flooding. The precision is almost as if the cartographer had taken a flight over the marshes at high tide, in contrast to other maps of this period that seem to have been surveyed at low tide when all the old field boundaries were exposed. Whatever the situation, the inner Dead Dyke walls would have been well maintained until the completion of Enclosure 11 and thus would have been easily repaired. However, the reconstruction of an aboiteau dam and its sluices across the entrance to that deep navigable creek was probably beyond the capabilities of the newly arrived Planters.

A dispiriting sight must have greeted the New England Planters in June 1760. The Dead Dyke fields had been flooded daily by sea water all winter. By springtime, their upland grasses and any perennial crops would have been salt killed and in that brief period the marine marsh grasses would not have had time to become established. Thus that previously dyked area was truly dead, which I believe accounts for its historical name of Dead Dyke. The aboiteau was finally rebuilt about 1855, according to the Fred Curry family history and their grandfather's recounting of events. It may have been earlier, for the famously informative but undated *Johnson Scrapbook* (Provincial Archives of Nova Scotia) contains a cryptic comment that "The 'Dead Dyke' was opened June 14, 1814, after 3 years work." If this is true, then as a boy the Currys' grandfather had witnessed a replacement, or repair operation, in the mid-1850s, some forty years after an initial reconstruction in 1814. By 1806 the Planters had built the impressive three-mile/six aboiteaux New Dyke wall from Wolfville to Long Island (formerly termed the West Marsh and latterly the Wickwire Dyke), so there is reason to wonder why they would have waited until 1855 to replace the Horton Landing ("Deportation Creek") aboiteau.

In whatever year it was replaced, the farmers who were responsible formed their own marshland management group, the Proprietors of Dead Dyke Marsh. They did not merge with the Proprietors of the Grand Pré Marsh until 1898, at which time the Grand Pré marshlands secretary crossed out his annual "Items Pertaining to Proprietors of the Dead Dyke Marsh," and never referred to that marsh body again in his minute book.

In 1947 that Planter aboiteau at Horton had to be replaced. This was done by relocating the site north of its original position and cutting a deep channel from another creek through to the river. In 1987 that aboiteau was weakening and was replaced by constructing a new one slightly behind it and then tearing out the old dyke wall and sluice box.

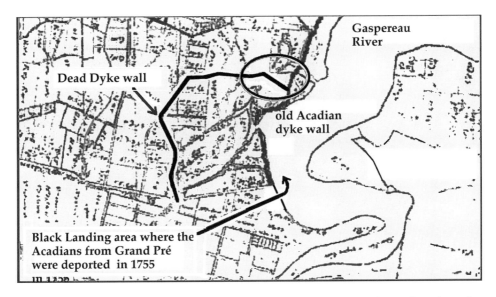

Figure 9.1.5   1760 survey map. The diagonal wall section within the circle is the only extant Acadian dyke on the Grand Pré, all others have been levelled. The original structure would be within this mound, beneath a cap of subsequent Planter sods.

The northeast boundary of Dead Dyke is today unique, because it is the only standing Acadian dyke protected by the present dyke walls (Fig. 9.1.5). All other old dyke walls have been flattened for agricultural purposes or reduced to roadbeds. This Horton wall section is extant because for three generations the Curry family has purposely preserved this ridge in their pasture, as instructed by their grandfather, to be their personal memorial to the Acadians who first wrestled with these tides and proved to others the benefits of farming below sea level.

The 1963 aerial photo of this area (Fig. 9.1.6) has other instructive features, such as the plowing patterns and the field boundary outlines that they create, which remain so distinctive for centuries. These field boundaries are constrained in several ways, such as by a deep and steep-sided creek at A; or a previous dyke wall at B; or an arbitrary lot line at C. The broad, shallow gullies at D were simply plowed across.

This photo also shows an example of a connector drainage diversion canal, above E. Originally, a large collector creek at F in the extreme upper right drained into the Gaspereau River estuary. To reduce the labours of aboiteau maintenance, the Planters closed it off and its waters were channelled southward into an adjacent drainage system that is still functioning.

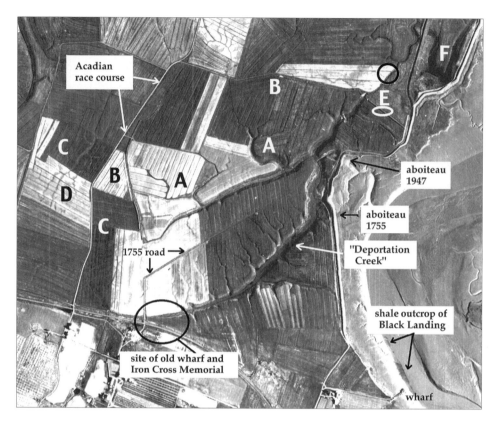

Figure 9.1.6   Aerial photo of Horton Landing area in 1963, showing the black shale outcrop, the racecourse, two aboiteau locations, "Deportation Creek," and a 1755 road. The dale patterns in the fields are determined by such factors as deep creeks (A), previous dyke walls or roads (B), and land ownership boundaries (C). D illustrates how much detail of drainage creek patterns is evident under certain conditions. The white circle above E is a canal connecting two watersheds, and the oval below E is the only surviving Acadian wall at Grand Pré. F is a large pond created by blocking that aboiteau and draining its surplus water via a canal into the adjacent watershed and out of the 1947 aboiteau sluice. (National Air Photo Library A 18060-59)

The freshwater pond that formed at the closed-off aboiteau became a productive cattail marsh, attracting ducks, muskrats, and mink.

The abandoned Horton Landing log wharf may be very old and possibly had an Acadian origin. The oldest section is the main body of the wharf, with a later addition to its north; the latter has taken the brunt of subsequent erosion. The original was so well constructed that it seems not out of square in any direction; its placement on the solid shale bedrock accounts for some

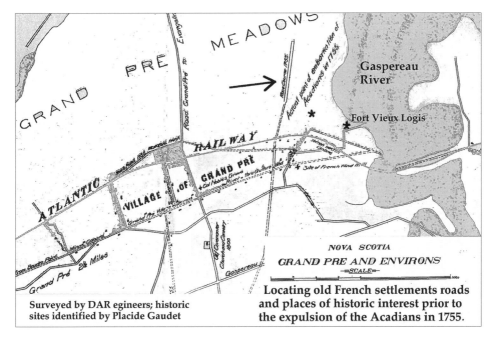

Figure 9.1.7 Dominion Atlantic Railway map of about 1867, to which they added many Acadian features including the "racecourse 1755" at arrow. Disappointingly, they did not include dyke walls or creeks. (Provincial Archives of Nova Scotia, D.A. Railway Map)

of that stability. Growth rings from the larger logs of this wharf, and from its deck additions, could have dendrochronological potential, as could the adjacent old elm tree.

The Acadians were known to have exported the excess of their produce, but from what kind of a shoreline site? Because they had blocked their inland creek with an aboiteau, they would not have been using small tenders from that inland wharf site. They had to be loading and unloading ships either from the black shale slope or from a wharf. Are there any wharf references hidden away in early first-hand accounts of periods either before or after the deportation?

One other interesting historical map feature is that unusually straight road on the dykelands in Fig. 9.1.6 labelled "Acadian racecourse." On a few old maps, including the Dominion Atlantic Railway survey (Fig. 9.1.7), it is labelled "racecourse 1755," and is about 1,750 ft in length. Did the Acadians actually have time for such frivolous pursuits? Were they so affluent? Did they place bets?

Figure 9.2.2   The west side of the Guzzle channel in 1951, when stumps of a forest cover of hemlock and white pine from about 3,500 years ago were being exposed by rapid widening of the channel and removal of old marsh deposits. (Nova Scotia Department of Agriculture and Marketing, MMRA photo)

9.2   Locality 2: Gaspereau River Estuary and Guzzle Channel

This is an unusual area because, until the 1930s, it was sheltered from erosional forces from the north. Although the Guzzle channel broke through from the north in the 1860s, it remained a narrow and shallow channel for the next fifty years (Fig. 9.2.1, p. xxxi). Erosion of the thick deposits of marsh turf was a slow process, but once it was through these and into glacial till, the Guzzle began to widen and deepen rapidly. In the process it removed sections of abandoned Acadian dyke walls and their aboiteaux at the eastern side of Grand Pré. Those walls are tantalizingly evident in the 1945–46 aerial photos, but become much reduced by the 1963 aerial survey. As the Guzzle widened, it exposed a forest of large stumps on its western slope. They were a prominent feature in 1951 (Fig. 9.2.2), but none remain fifty years later. Today the erosion is threatening the present rock-faced dykes to such a degree that during 1999 and 2000 an unprecedented rock breakwater was erected on the tidal marsh, well out from the actual dyke. This structure has

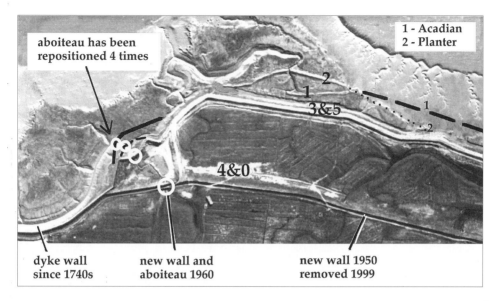

Figure 9.2.3   Aerial photo of the east side of the Guzzle, indicating the many historic features still evident after hundreds of years of sea-level changes, shore erosion, and farming practices. Dyke 3 was built in 1940, breached in 1958, and upgraded in 1960. The four white rings are the positions of four successive aboiteaux installed on this creek. (National Air Photo Library A 18060-59)

buried portions of an Acadian dyke that was included in our dykeland elevations survey of 1999.

Nevertheless, interesting remnants of Acadian and Planter walls, and probably aboiteaux as well, remain and should be surveyed, documented, and excavated, as they too may be gone within a decade or less. Their traces are best seen on the 1945 and 1963 aerial photos. Fig. 9.2.3, from 1963, has been labelled with numbers and letters to facilitate discussion.

The sequence of dyke wall construction in this area has been complex, and in Fig. 9.2.3 the steps have been numbered 1, 2, 3+5, and 4+0. The first dyke (1) was built by the Acadians possibly around 1740, and today a long section is missing. This gap may be from the storm of 1759, for it resembles the pattern of wall destruction in the aerial photos of 1931 at Wolfville (Fig. 9.5.3). I had wondered whether the Planters had mined that section of wall for its sods and used them as fill when repairing the nearby large aboiteau. However, the clay in these old dykes becomes compacted and rather firm. The 1806 dyke wall at Wolfville resists probing by a metal rod, whereas the adjacent marsh turf does not. Even today, tractors plowing on reclaimed marshland come to a shuddering near-halt when they hit an old dyke wall just beneath the surface.

Some eyewitness accounts, such as Haliburton's of 1829, support the contention that the Acadians left their redundant dykes in place. He likened the pattern of the many old dykes on Grand Pré to that of a giant honeycomb. Any back-up dyke would be an asset whenever outer dykes were broken. This precautionary attitude carried over even into the 1960s, when the new "indestructible" machine-built Wickwire Dyke wall was completed; the farmers still insisted that the west Grand Pré dyke wall, an original Acadian wall, not be flattened. They had not forgotten the previous Wickwire Dyke that gave way in 1931, and how disaster was averted only by the presence of that old Acadian west Grand Pré wall.

The second dyke (2) is Planter in origin and could have been part of the dyke refurbishment done in the years 1763 to 1770. The northern and southern ends of this wall are exposed to erosion and key trench posts now protrude at regular intervals. These posts are the type driven into a central "key trench" over which the walls are constructed. The trench and posts serve to anchor the wall against lateral tidal pressures. A small marsh drainage creek cuts through both of these walls (immediately above 1 and 2 in Fig. 9.2.3) and the original brush is visible. With a little digging and probing a sluice log or sluice box might even be located. The line of black dashes is the probable line of the Acadian wall, and the adjacent black dotted line is the Planter wall that Robert Palmeter tied into when he built wall 3.

In 1939 Robert Palmeter, the Grand Pré Marsh Commissioner responsible for dyke maintenance, feared that dyke 2 would not hold much longer. In spite of dire predictions that any heavy equipment on dykeland would simply sink out of sight, he had wall 3 built with a drag line. He was the first person to attempt such an operation. His successful example has been followed ever since.

Farther out in the marsh lie remnants of even older dyke sods and brush, and a few in-line key-trench posts. This should be the earliest wall, which means that the Planters set their replacement dyke *inside* the Acadian dyke in this area, probably because the latter was too close to the riverbank. Just to the north, where the marsh was widest, the Planters located their new dyke *outside* the Acadian dyke. If we could find the Marshland Minute Book for the period prior to 1884, speculation might graduate to affirmation.

At the northern ends of these two dykes, the Acadian and Planter dykes converged and then crossed a large creek where many brush and post remnants are still evident. Then the dyke turned northeast where it is lost to erosion. It could go nowhere from there but northward parallel to that major creek, Soldier's Creek, draining both Boot Island and east Grand Pré, and then it would have to cross Resolution Creek via an aboiteau and either join onto the lee side of Little Island or circle north around that island to join a dyke from Long Island. The strongest evidence for such a scenario is the series of parallel dale ditch patterns in a low level 1959 aerial photo (Fig. 6.6). Perhaps some old documents somewhere will eventually substantiate and expand on this lonely evidence.

Who plowed this section of marshland, and when? This is a conundrum for a number of reasons. If the dales and ditches are Acadian, then the Acadians must have abandoned that outer dyke wall and retreated back to the 1760 map position, which is the same dyke line as today. That in turn means that the dale ditches are older than 1755 and must have persisted for more than 200 years. This at first seems unreasonable, based on present meagre knowledge of the persistence of dale ditches in this Minas Basin area, with its history of rising sea and marsh levels. For example, at Wolfville the dale ditches that became tidal again in 1931 are barely evident in 1992 aerial photos, after only seventy years. They are, however, detectable at ground level, where they drain into creeks that run at right angles to their direction. Presumably the runoff in the ditches keeps eroding and perpetuating the notching effect at the edge of fields, even as the marsh becomes higher with rising sea levels. Because the marsh surface today is 30 inches (0.76 m) higher than it was in 1931, this truly is a phenomenon of perpetuation of ditches.

Could it be that old dyke walls become buried by the rising sea levels and rising marsh turf, whereas the contours of dales and dale ditches actually rise in company with the marsh elevations, via replication, decade after decade? Such a confirmation should be of interest to archaeologists, for it would mean that plowing patterns on aerial photos from the Bay of Fundy region are not at their original marsh levels.

The aboiteau dam at Resolution Creek has been set back at least four times (Fig. 9.2.3). In 1755 it was located at the outer position, and I think I have found traces of it. At some later time, as yet unknown, the Planters set that Acadian one back to just in front of the zigzag configuration, possibly in that 1763–70 period of repairs. The zigzag wall, the third location, indicates that it is the second aboiteau constructed at this site, possibly as late as the Saxby Tide of 1869. This configuration was necessary to connect the new aboiteau and sluice box to an original and still functional running dyke. In 1960 there was a major relocation of dykes in this area to their present positions and the aboiteau was again moved, but much farther back this time. Its sluice box was last replaced in 1994. Repair and replacement of sluice boxes is part of basic maintenance and has its own history of evolving methods and

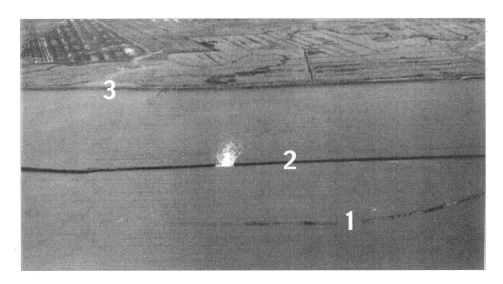

Figure 9.2.4   Aerial view from above the Guzzle channel looking west on 6 April 1958. Dyke 1 is a Planter dyke from 1760–70; the breached Dyke 2, where water is foaming through the gap, was built by Robert Palmeter in 1939–40; and Dyke 3 was the new, larger one constructed in 1950. The entire Grand Pré farmland was threatened by the Seros Cycle extreme tide in 1958. (Nova Scotia Department of Agriculture and Marketing, MMRA photo no. 16-028)

materials, which continues to this day. It would provide an interesting study in itself.

Dyke 3 of 1940 was massive in comparison with the hand-built dykes, but Palmeter's machine-built dyke did not hold up as well as did hand-built dykes with their carefully laid sods with a living grass turf surface. In response to that specific problem, Robert Palmeter later developed a formula of grass-seed mix that was applied to the surface of machine-built dykes with great success. In 1950 a larger dyke was raised at 4, and as predicted, dyke 3 finally breached on 6 April 1958 (Fig. 9.2.4). It was the new dyke 4 (no. 3 in Fig. 9.2.4) that prevented a massive flooding of the entire Grand Pré marshland acreage.

After strong arguments that the acreage between dykes 3 and 4 was too valuable to abandon, in 1960 old dyke 3 was upgraded by having dyke 5 superimposed upon it. Subsequently it had to be rock-faced, and now, forty years later, its northeast corner has required the construction of a separate rock breakwater, set out on the marsh, to dampen the brunt of winter storms. This Guzzle location no longer has the insurance luxury of that 1950 wall, because it was flattened in 1999–2000. (Hence dyke wall 4 logically becomes dyke 0.)

A final important feature of this area is that many dyke walls of the post-1760 period were built atop the original Acadian and/or Planter dykes, which in consequence are entombed in perpetuity. Theoretically they are available for excavation and examination. All one would need was permission, a research grant, and a substantial coffer dam.

9.3   Locality 3: Palmeter Dyke and Little Island Area

The historically crucial feature of this area is the sandstone elevation known as Little Island. It forms the extreme northeast corner of Grand Pré marshlands, and for over 200 years it supported farms and was surrounded by fields. Rising sea levels and shore erosion have greatly reduced its acreage, but it is still the anchor point for the north and east Grand Pré dyke walls. As sea levels rose, Little Island itself became a seawall, and in the 1884 Marshlands Minute Book dykes are described as running to it from the west and then away from it on its south side. There is no mention of dykes surrounding it. Thus the detailed 1760 survey map is curious in that the New England Planter surveyors plotted a dyke wall circling the west side of Little Island. We know that there was no urgent need for such a wall, for one was not built until the 1960s. Perhaps their depiction was a cartographic rendition to establish the legal boundaries of the marshland, as Little Island had to be excluded because it was a farmstead site. Even by 1884 it had only a cattle-excluding fence on its west side. In 1963 the west slope of the island was bulldozed to form a ridge higher than the rest of the island. In doing so, the workmen cut into the old farm site (Fig. 9.3.1) and inadvertently incorporated old pearl ware, cream ware, clay pipes, and glass into the new wall. After rainstorms, these items surface in the old roadbed that traverses diagonally up the back of the wall.

One can assume that, as the fringes of the island gradually changed status from high ground to tidal marsh, dykes were erected to secure the farm sites and fields. This scenario would help to explain the complex of dykes evident in the 1946 aerial photo (Fig. 9.3.2). This quantity of short dykes at various angles and the different directions of dale ditches bespeak a lot of modifications to walls, as well as outright retreats.

Fig. 9.3.3 is my interpretation of the history of these walls. The New England Planters may have, during their repairs to dykes damaged by the 1759 storm, extended their acreage by running dyke 1 due east off the old Acadian dyke to join the high ground on the west side of Little Island, not realizing the per century magnitude of sea-level rise. They would soon have had to erect dykes around their island fields at 2, and later actually retreat to

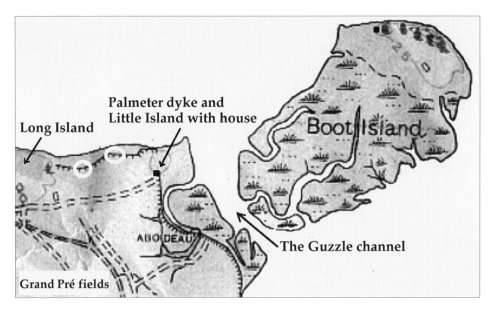

Figure 9.3.1　Enlargement of a 1928 Wolfville topographic map (no. 21-H/1) of northeast Grand Pré. At that time the Guzzle was increasing its rate of widening and deepening. Note the geodetic contour rings on both Little and Boot Islands, and how the dyke wall was connected to the north side of Little Island. That dyke was destroyed in 1944, and remnants are now exposed at the two white rings.

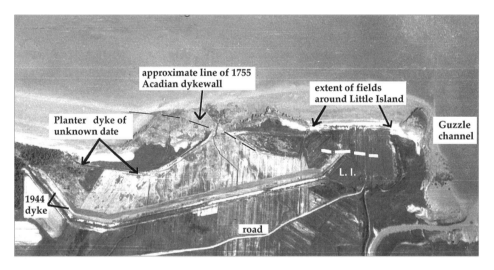

Figure 9.3.2　This 1946 aerial photo of the Little Island area of Grand Pré shows the complex of dyke walls and fields around Little Island (white L.I.), a shoreline exposed to storm erosion. By 2002, only fifty-six years after this photo was taken, the north shore of Little Island had eroded to the line of white dashes. (National Air Photo Library A 10178-7)

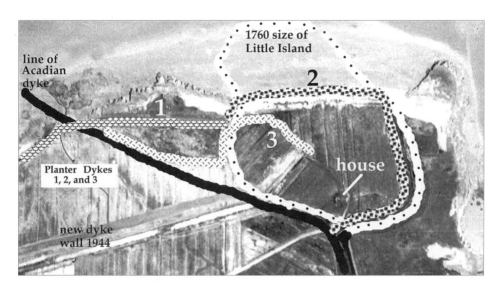

Figure 9.3.3 This 1946 aerial photo of Little Island demonstrates my hypothetical explanation of the many dyke walls there. The size of the island in 1760 is the dotted white line, and the black line is the Acadian dyke in place at that time. Planter dykes 1, 2, and 3 have different patterns: the first was repairs in 1760–80; the second was to protect the fields from rising sea levels; and the third was a retreat from sea levels and storm effects. Major upgrade construction occurred in 1944, 1960, and 2003. (National Air Photo Library A 10178-7)

new locations at 3. I have tentatively concluded that 3 was the last dyke built by hand, the one that gave way in 1944, a few months after the present dyke was established. Evidence for this is the area between 3 and 1, which is not plowed, and also the physical prominence of wall 3 in comparison with 1. It is wider and higher; it is casting shadows; and it has adjacent borrow-pit pools, indicated by the three white indicator arrows in Fig. 9.3.4 (p. xxxii). The black arrow points to an old sod pit. Without archaeological test trenches and an elevation survey, the question of which is the older wall remains hypothetical. The west section of wall 3 may have been built on the old 1750s Acadian wall.

Even a cursory examination of aerial photos from 1946 through 1992 reveals the degree to which Little Island was fast diminishing. By 2000 its former crop fields already had areas thick with salt spray-tolerant Bayberry shrubs and roses. The rest of the island is low and grassy and now so soaked by spray and tides that Black Grass and Salt Marsh Bulrush are the dominant ground cover over some sections. In May 2003 high tides actually swept across the island and passed close to an old well now hidden by Bayberry

Figure 9.3.5   Northeast Grand Pré, November 1999. A breakwater barrier of large posts set in a deep trench in the marsh. The dyke it was meant to protect is out of the photo, to the left. It was breached in 1944 and abandoned.

shrubs and roses. The rim of the rock-lined well is about 8 inches (0.2 m) beneath the present turf surface and has a 5 ft wide (1.5 m) inside diameter. It may prove useful as another baseline indicator of rising sea levels.

To the west, that outer wall 1 may be sitting on an original Acadian dyke, and the answer may soon be forthcoming because a deep erosional slot is cutting into the bank and under this wall. From the air, these slot trenches have the appearance of a row of shark's teeth (Fig. 9.3.3). This is the same dyke-wall site (shown in Fig. 7.6) with many hand-cut sods so carefully laid in rows. The recent undercut has already exposed a layer of large wood chips, the type produced when sharpening posts with an axe. So many chips lie over such a wide area that it may have been a site where shad net poles and stakes were prepared in the 1880s and 1890s. However, just to complicate the picture, the chip layer is on the sea side of the adjacent old dyke, so either the chips were trampled into a tidal marsh and thus prevented from floating away, or a previous dyke wall lay out beyond this one, and the men were trimming their poles in a dry hayfield. Examination for the presence of either upland hay grasses or diagnostic marine grasses and foraminiferans beneath the chip layer could help to determine the type of surface on which the men were standing.

At first glance, the western half of this dyke towards Long Island seems far less confusing, for there is but a single long curved section of wall (Figs 9.3.2 and 9.3.4). This curved dyke replaced the Acadian dyke of the 1760 map, but in what year was it built? Was it prior to the 1869 Saxby Gale or immediately afterwards? It was finally breached in 1944 at the gap in the outer-

Figure 9.3.6   The west end of the Palmeter dyke that was abandoned in 1944. Erosion has exposed sod and brush layers, posts, plank facing, and threaded iron rods used to anchor the planks to a "deadman log" buried within the dyke wall.

most centre section, just a few months after a new dyke was completed much farther behind it.

A prominent, compact row of large pilings lies just north of the old breached 1944 dyke (Fig. 9.3.5). At present it consists of 131 pilings, some broken at ground level, some short, and nineteen others 6 to 8 ft (1.8–2.4 m) tall. They are mostly 4 to 6 inches (10.2–15.2 cm) in diameter and separated by gaps of 1 to 4 inches (2.5–10.2 cm). This structure is no part of any dyke, but because most persons view it at a distance, the collective assumption has been that it is a remnant of the old 1944 wall. None of the older local residents had any other suggestions as to the origin or purpose of this structure. It is, in fact, a type of storm-breakwater barrier that is set up in exposed marsh areas of the Bay of Fundy. Cormier (1990) refers to them at Grand Pré and in Albert County, New Brunswick. The fact that men in their seventies and eighties have no oral historical record of this endeavour suggests a structure of considerable antiquity.

At the extreme western end of this marsh (Fig. 9.3.4), a sandy beach cuts across an old dyke wall, the one breached in 1944. This cut has exposed a wonderful sampling of construction techniques, including heavy and fine brush layers, sod layers, and plank facing with iron rods anchored to deadman timbers embedded within the walls (Fig. 9.3.6). Once again, it must be emphasized that the storms of each winter season remove forever much of what was observed the previous year.

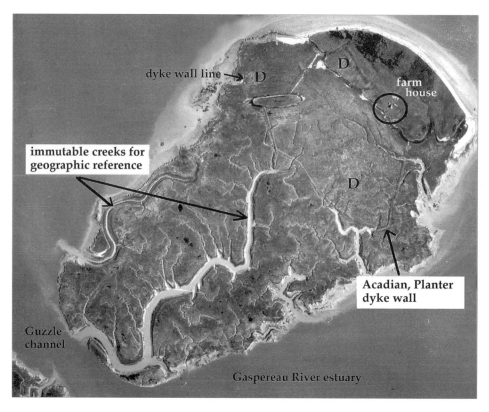

Figure 9.4.1   A 1946 photo of Boot Island showing old dyke walls, farm buildings, and extensive areas with parallel patterns of dales and dale ditches at D. (National Air Photo Library A 10178-5)

9.4   Locality 4: Boot Island

A severe storm on 30 October 1913 provided the impetus for the families residing on Boot Island to move to the mainland in 1914. Their broken dykes were abandoned and have never been repaired or altered. Aerial photographs from 1946 to 1992 record the cultural changes as the deserted farmhouses and outbuildings became derelict and then crumbled, and as the plow patterns in the fields became invaded by forest and progressively obscured. The island is now a wildlife preserve and posted with No Trespassing signs.

The aerial photos also show well-defined dyke walls and traces of older ones that ran northwards from the island to land no longer there (Fig. 9.4.1). I have not explored the island on foot, but I suspect that old aboiteau sluices may lie deep in the creeks that now slice through those abandoned dykes.

TABLE 9.4.1   SHORE EROSION AT BOOT ISLAND NATIONAL WILDLIFE AREA
FOR 1998–2000 AND 1990–2000

Stake No.	Stake Name	Direction to Cliff*	Measurement to Cliff		Decrease	
			1998	2000	1998–2000	Annual
1	Field	68	69' 4"	63' 6"	5' 10"	2' 11"
2	Field Edge	60	83' 6"	81' 0"	3' 6"	1' 9"
3	Outhouse	58	76' 6"	63' 0"	13' 6"	6' 9"
4	Gap	42	103' 6"	97' 2"	6' 4"	3' 2"
5	Forest	40	67' 0"	55' 9"	11' 3"	5' 8"
6	Old Chair (Blow-down)	32	57' 3"	49' 2"	8' 1"	4' 1"
7	Open Glade	24	44' 0"	39' 0"	5' 0"	2' 6"
8	End of Island	18	50' 0"	48' 6"	1' 6"	3' 5"
Average					6' 11"	3' 5"

* Degrees Magnetic

Stake No.	Stake Name	Average Annual Decrease Between Surveys				Overall
		90–92	92–96	96–98	98–00	90,92–00
1	Field	4' 1"	3' 8"	2' 1"	2' 11"	3' 2"
2	Field Edge	–	3' 3"	2' 9"	1' 9"	2' 9"
3	Outhouse	–	4' 7"	2' 0"	6' 9"	3' 11"
4	Gap	4' 8"	3' 11"	3' 0"	3' 2"	3' 9"
5	Forest	–	3' 0"	3' 3"	5' 8"	4' 0"
6	Old Chair (Blow-down)	6' 2"	5' 2"	4' 8"	4' 1"	5' 0"
7	Open Glade	–	5' 10"	4' 10"	2' 6"	4' 5"
8	End of Island	4' 3"	6' 5"	3' 9"	0' 9"	3' 10"
Average		4' 9"	4' 6"	3' 3"	3' 5"	3' 10"

Source: Report by A. Macfarlane, Canadian Wildlife Service, Sackville, NB, 2 June 2000.

The old dykes themselves may be well buried and well preserved. Then there is the question of Acadian home sites. If some remain, they may be less disturbed than sites on the mainland. When did the Planters first occupy this island, and how many families were there? Did they ever report cellars and artifacts in their diaries? It is also probable that Acadian cellars may occasionally become exposed in section along Boot Island's eroding cliff faces.

The Canadian Wildlife Service has kept records of shore erosion at Boot Island from 1990 to 2000, and the ten-year average has been a startling 3 ft 10 inches (Table 9.4.1). These measurements are from eight stations on the north side of the island. In the two-year period from 1998 to 2000, cliff loss to erosion varied amongst stations from a low of 0.9 inches to 6 ft 9 inches.

Boot Island is now half the size it was in 1760. Unfortunately, we will never know the extent of the original Acadian dyke walls because, in that area of the 1760 map, no cartographic distinction is made between dyke walls and lot boundary lines. However, the Theofilus Sutherland property map does provide one interesting bit of information, and other extant deed maps may also have similar helpful labels. The Sutherland map depicts the property lots at the east side of Boot Island as bordered by a roadway running along the edge of the eastern shore, which is rather surprising, as this is an exposed cliff that rapidly erodes. Probably that original Acadian road, when first cut through the forest, was set well back from the crumbling sea edge.

That bit of roadway may be part of an intriguing cartographic mystery in connection with Boot Island. Where was the road that connected Boot Island to Long Island, a road mentioned in the literature, but never carefully or even reasonably plotted on old maps? At ground level, some evidence of a road leading from the Boot Island farm site west, or north across the marshes, should remain. I have searched in vain on aerial photos for a satisfactory clue.

9.5   Locality 5: West Grand Pré and Wickwire Dyke

The history of this western block of 800 acres of tidal marsh is the tale of two cultures. It is where the Acadians left off dyking and where the Planters began, in earnest and with a new-found confidence.

The Acadians stopped dyke construction at the west end of Grand Pré when they reached those large discharge creeks that collected nearly all of the water from the Grand Pré marshes. By 1804 the Planters had established many lot boundaries on this tidal marsh for salt-hay harvesting, with a total deeded area of about 460 acres owned by thirty-eight farmers (J.F. Herbin's notebooks, 1911). In that year, they decided to convert this marsh section to sweet upland hay and to expand the area to nearly 800 acres by constructing a running dyke from Wolfville to Long Island. This was a distance of three miles and required the additional construction of six large aboiteau sluices to span major creeks (Fig. 9.5.1). According to Herbin's extracts from the original accounts, it was built over the two-year period of 1805 and 1806, and may well have been the impetus for the smaller one-mile-long Wellington Dyke project of 1817 to 1825 (Fig. 5.5). By this time, the Planters had about thirty-five years of dyking experience and should have been aware of the rate of riverbank erosion, but if so they dismissed the potential consequences. They did build one of the longest dykes in Atlantic Canada, but it was to be

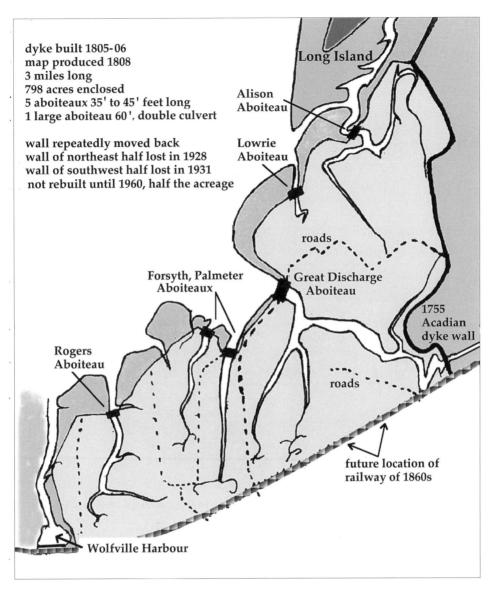

dyke built 1805-06
map produced 1808
3 miles long
798 acres enclosed
5 aboiteaux 35' to 45' feet long
1 large aboiteau 60', double culvert

wall repeatedly moved back
wall of northeast half lost in 1928
wall of southwest half lost in 1931
 not rebuilt until 1960, half the acreage

Long Island

Alison
Aboiteau

Lowrie
Aboiteau

roads

Forsyth, Palmeter
Aboiteaux

Great Discharge
Aboiteau

1755
Acadian
dyke wall

Rogers
Aboiteau

roads

future location of
railway of 1860s

Wolfville Harbour

Figure 9.5.1   Bank of Cornwallis River at Wolfville shoreline, from 1760 Planter map. Dyke from Oliver Lyman's 1808 map. The area between Wolfville and Grand Pré enclosed by Planters in 1805–06. It was three miles in length and had six large aboiteaux. Its history became one of retreat from riverbank erosion.

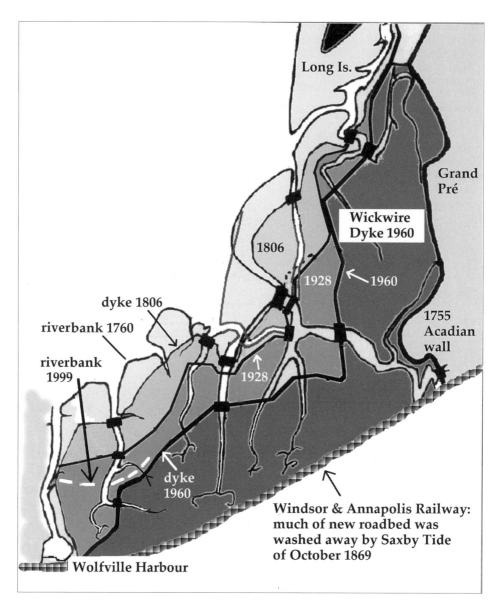

Figure 9.5.2   Bank of Cornwallis River at Wolfville shoreline – changes 1760–1999. Dyke walls of 1806, 1928, and 1960, three of the many locations of the Wickwire Dyke wall during its history of retreat from the Cornwallis riverbank. Based on maps of 1808, 1928, and 1967. Erosion forced sections of dyke wall to be moved back again and again: 1869, 1882, 1902, 1907, 1913, 1920, 1917, 1928. By 1931 there was full retreat to the Acadian wall of 1755. Note the position of the riverbank in 1760, in 1999, and at the white arrow, where it threatens the present 1960 dyke wall.

one of the shortest lived. Its history became one of repeated retreats from the river and repeated reconstruction. The caption of Fig. 9.5.2 gives a sample list of the piecemeal patching of this doomed dyke, extracted from newspaper accounts for the limited period 1869 to 1931, when all was lost.

Fig. 9.5.2 depicts several major changes over the period 1760 to 1999: the 1760 riverbank shoreline; the 1806 dyke wall (based on an 1808 map); the dyke position in 1928 just prior to its abandonment and the retreat to the 1755 Acadian position; and the latest Wickwire Dyke wall, finished in 1960. The magnitude of loss of farm acreage to river erosion is strikingly evident through comparison, in the lower left of Fig. 9.5.2, of the change in location of the riverbank in 1760 and 1999.

In the minute book of the meetings of dykeland proprietors at Wolfville in 1804 and 1805, what was previously referred to as the "West Marsh" was renamed the "New Dike," and later became the "Wickwire Dyke" named after Zebediah Wickwire (1730–97). But why this particular Wickwire person, and in what year it become official, has yet to be determined.

With the construction of the "New Dike" in 1806, the original Acadian north-south guardian wall at west Grand Pré became redundant, but fortunately it was not flattened to create more arable land, as is the practice now. Over the ensuing years the proprietors of the Wickwire Dyke spent a fortune maintaining a dyke that took the brunt of all storms from the west. As their efforts were providing a valuable dyking service to the proprietors of the Grand Pré farmlands, they often requested financial remuneration for that service, and often received an unenthusiastic response. In March 1927 they requested an increase in the current $73.97 annual stipend they received for protecting the extensive Grand Pré farm fields. It was, however, too little and too late, for in late December 1928 a storm broke through the Wickwire at its northeast corner. The southern half, nearer Wolfville, was salvaged for two more years by erecting a division dyke, presumably along the south side of the Great Discharge Creek channel.

An attempt was made to repair the lost aboiteau in that northern section (also referred to as the eastern section in some documents) of the Wickwire wall. On 1 April 1929 a contractor from Falmouth, W.J. Alyward, convinced the Dykeland Commissioners that with a workforce of one hundred men and thirty teams, he could repair the broken dyke at Alison Aboiteau in one week for $2,500. Other submitted estimates for repairing the aboiteau and the walls ran from $12,000 to $15,000. In spite of Alyward's eventual "cost overrun" of $9,600, his newly completed aboiteau collapsed on 31 August 1929. But his walls held up, and so did his invoice of $11,494.80 dated 31 December 1929. The infuriating outcome for each owner of the now salt-

Figure 9.5.3 Extreme enlargement of corner of an aerial photo taken by R.T. McCully, June 1931, showing the effect of a 4 March 1931 storm on Wolfville Wickwire Dyke. So many large sections of wall were washed away that the dyke was abandoned. The white wall sections are plank facing reflecting sunlight late in the day. (C. Byers Collection, Parrsboro, NS)

soaked and abandoned northeast half of the Wickwire Dyke was a bill for $20.60 per acre owned, "for recent repairs" to their farmland (Acadia University Archives: Dykes and Common Fields Collection, Accession 1900.018.5).

On 4 March 1931 after a mild winter and no frost in the dyke walls, a storm tore through many soft sections of what was left of the western portion of the Wickwire, and the entire marsh had to be abandoned (Figs 9.5.3 and 9.5.4). Concerted efforts to find financial resources were to no avail. The final demise of that ambitious three-mile-long Wickwire Dyke is pathetically documented in the last pages of the 1882–1936 ledger of Minutes of Meetings of Proprietors of the Wickwire Dykelands. In 1932 the secretary devoted his energies to collecting the proprietors "payments in arrears"; in 1933 and 1934 there were meetings, but no new business; in 1935 not even

Wolfville Harbour

lighthouse

sewer
shaft

flooded pastures

footpath on
1806 dyke

Road to the Wolfville Light March 1931.

Figure 9.5.4   Postcard photo showing the massive destruction of Wickwire Dyke in
March 1931. Note wall sections missing to right of the lighthouse. This flooded
pasture area has been tidal marsh since that time. It is contiguous with Wolfville
Harbour waters to the left of the old wall.

an entry. On 4 April 1936 the last entry in the book records a special meeting
at which Robie W. Tufts, local Federal Migratory Birds Officer, presented an
impassioned plea to turn over their flooded marsh to the federal government
as a bird sanctuary. A motion from the floor to do so was defeated and so
were the Proprietors of the Wickwire Dykelands. They were destined to wait
until the early 1960s before government funding once again made it possible
to plant crops on that marshland.

After 1928 the Grand Pré farmers had to pay for a refurbishing of their
entire west-end dyke, including a plank facing that took several years to
install. They financed this undertaking with bonds and debentures, paid off
over ten years (Minute Book, 28 November 1931, 397). During these
repairs, however, they apparently "stole sods" from the Wickwire side of
their Grand Pré dyke wall. At the 1935 Annual March Meeting of the Grand
Pré Proprietors, they discussed the appointment of an arbitrator to settle
compensation claims from Wickwire proprietors for the sod they had used to
repair and enforce their Division Dyke. In 1959–60, a new Wickwire dyke
was erected further inland than the 1928 line, but this time the dyke enclosed
only 400 acres between it and the 1755 Acadian wall. Today, this new wall
in turn is threatened by the river and requires tons of rockfill to delay its
inevitable fate. But now there is no longer an established older wall to fall
back to, because by the 1980s farmers valued the potential crop acreage
beneath that old Division Dyke wall (constructed on Acadian roots) more
than they valued its flood insurance potential, so they had it flattened.

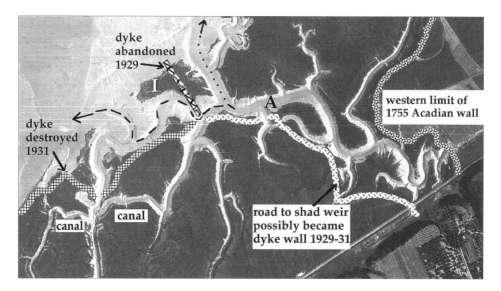

Figure 9.5.5   Wickwire Dyke, 1945. Dykeland area between Wolfville and Grand Pré showing the same drainage creek patterns as on the Planters' 1760 map. When these dyke walls were abandoned in 1929 and 1931, the original Acadian dyke saved the Grand Pré farmlands from flooding then and for the next 29 years. See text for detailed discussion. (National Air Photo Library, A8645-56)

Nevertheless, the original base of that Acadian dyke must still be there, and possibly identifiable.

Changes in tidal currents and in the deposition of silts have twice necessitated the relocation of the outlet of Great Discharge Creek. In 1760 it emptied into a square-shaped bay half way along the riverbend (Fig. 9.5.1). This area silted up, so the dyke wall and aboiteau were moved back and a channel cut through to an adjacent creek, one with a prominent loop that discharged into the Cornwallis River further to the west. The riverbank continued to erode and the farmers continued to retreat and build new dykes. At some point, they realized that the expenses of construction and maintenance of aboiteaux could be reduced by cutting canals from one collector creek to another, thus allowing one aboiteau to service as many as three creek drainages. This canal accommodation can be seen on the 1928 and 1967 topographic maps, and on the 1946 and 1959 aerial photos these canal link-ups are identified (Fig. 9.5.5).

Although much has been learned of this 1806 Planter dykeland enclosure, other major events are, as yet, undeciphered enigmas. The first involves how the southern half of the Wickwire Dyke was "saved" in 1929–31, while at the same time the northern half was "let out to sea." A substantial dyke wall must have divided the two areas, but it is difficult to find a divisional wall in post-1931 aerial photos. However, after the exceptionally destructive Saxby Tide of 1869, walls may have been built along each side of the Great Discharge Creek during a step-by-step process of refurbishing local dykelands. Frustratingly, the minute books covering dykeland activities on the Wickwire during that 1870s period are currently listed as missing.

The Great Discharge Creek formed a wide and deep natural boundary between the two marshland areas, and it would have been quicker and easier in 1929 (and after 1869) to throw up dyke walls along each side of the creek than to attempt reconstruction of a huge new aboiteau, which could be done any time later. There may have been a redundant temporary Saxby repair wall from the 1870s that could have been upgraded rather quickly in 1929. But where was it located?

In this connection, the 1945 aerial photos show an access road in this area. Cameron labelled it "Wickwire Dyke" on his map; perhaps during its long history it has been both. It runs north from the railway line along the west side of the Great Discharge Creek to where the latter turns west at A in Fig. 9.5.5, but from there it is difficult to trace. The most suggestive evidence is a broken line set back slightly from the bank of the creek. It may be a derelict dyke. If so, it could have connected to the dyke walls to the west, those depicted on the 1928 topographic map. What is missing is any topographic indication of where it may have crossed several wide creeks.

Originally, this track may have been a road to a major shad trap mentioned in the minutes of the meetings of 1804–06 (Herbin's 1911 school scribbler; appendix 6). The dykeland owners could not agree on where to place the double-sluiced aboiteau in the Great Discharge Creek, whether up stream or downstream of the "shad weir." Specifically, their choice was either "a point opposite the island, over the [illegible word] or false channel of the island" or "the site at the shad weir, higher up." In Fig. 9.5.5 the probable island is labelled 1 and the shad site could have been near A. If the fishing weir was at site A, it must have had a suitable wagon access road crossing the marsh, one that could have been refurbished in the 1870s and in 1929. In 1959–60 this same road was upgraded to provide access for heavy equipment for construction of the present Wickwire Dyke wall and for installation of the new Great Discharge aboiteau.

Addendum: Notes from Robert H. Palmeter's 1931 Time Book

In relation to the disastrous final breaching of the Wickwire Dyke on 4 March 1931, a unique little book records the emergency repairs made to the old west Grand Pré Dyke (alias Division Dyke; alias Acadian Dyke), a dyke that had not been in use since 1806. It is a Time Book for men and horses employed for dyke wall maintenance for the period January to June 1931. It belonged to Robert H. Palmeter and is now part of Jean Palmeter's extensive collection of local historical documents, many of which she has generously shared with me. This little book, 3.75 by 6.5 inches, is one of the most unusual historical items that I have examined and may be the only one surviving of the dozens that once were in Palmeter's possession. It provides rare insight into how dyke-wall maintenance was organized and conducted during those critical months of the destruction of the Wickwire Dyke. The results of my analyses are summarized in Tables 9.5.1, 9.5.2, and 9.5.3. A copy has been deposited with the Kings County Heritage Museum, Kentville, Nova Scotia.

The Time Book records who worked each day, for how long, at what rate, and whether with or without a horse. The horses were usually paid $2/day and the men $2.40/day. After compiling a list of the names in this book (Table 9.5.1), I was astounded to discover that over this six-month period, a total of 203 different local men had been employed. Most of the labour was done by a hard core of 161 recurring names, but even this is a revelation of the labour pool that Robert Palmeter had at his disposal as a Commissioner of Grand Pré Dykelands. His Time Book reveals that he could muster fifty to eighty men on short notice. The Acadians must have had a similar organization of manpower for dykeland maintenance and repair.

When I showed the name list to Jean Palmeter, she was able to provide a biographical sketch of nearly every person, knowing the families through her position as a local schoolteacher. She even knew how many of these men were still alive in that summer of 2000, and where they now resided, and she then accompanied me to personally interview the four survivors. Only the eldest, Walter Kelly, who was eighty-eight, had spent his life on Grand Pré, and he had been a master sod cutter. (One can only imagine interviewing a group of these men just ten short years ago. Their minds were a veritable library of how things were done, and why done in that particular manner.)

Through Jean Palmeter's further invaluable input, we know who were hired hands and who were landowners. Table 9.5.2 indicates that owners rarely participated in dyke-wall repairs, but sent men and horses.

Table 9.5.3 is a compilation of Palmeter's notes integrated with my details of tidal information for the critical months of March and April 1931. It tabulates his activities relative to daily tidal heights, over the period that destroyed the Wickwire Dyke in March and again in April when it overtopped the now vital West Grand Pré Dyke. An immediate upgrade of this latter old

TABLE 9.5.1 ROBERT H. PALMETER'S GRAND PRÉ DYKELAND TIME BOOK (14 JAN–26 JUNE 1931)

Allen, Fred [father, England]	Brown, R. [hh]	Coldwell, Cecil [farmer]	Dykens, Freeman [hh, Eye Road]
Allen, F. Jr	[excellent carpenter; went with	Coldwell, Clifford [farmer]	Dykens, Judson
Allen, G.W. [bros, WWI vets]	Palmeter to Amherst]	Coldwell, Delmar	Dykens, Noble
Allen, J.		Coldwell, Edwin	
	Buchanan, Arthur	Coldwell, Harry	Eagles, Elias A.
	Buchanan, Norman [bros. hh]		Eagles, Nat F.
Atwell, Austin	Buchanan, Walter	Crowell, Clyde	[why no John Eagles? no dyke?]
Atwell, Carl	Buchanan, William	Crowell, Daniel [all hh, from	
Atwell, Earl [all hh]	Buchanan, Fredrick	Crowell, George Hortonville]	Eye, Basil
Atwell, Elden		Crowell, Gordon	Eye, George [father]
Atwell, Russel	Cahoon, Frank [hh]	Crowell, James	Eye, Vernon
Berry, Caleb	Cavanagh, Harold	Corkum, Cecil [hh]	Farmer, Lawrence [black]
Berry, Roy [all hh]			
Berry, William	Clayton, Austin [hh]	Crane, Fred H.	Forsyth, Rupert
	Clayton, W.		
Best, Roy [hh]		Curry, Lee H.	Foster, George
Best, Joseph	Clowry, Hib		
		Davidson, Frank	Fullerton, R.R.
Beatty, Fred	Coffill, Albert	Davidson, Nat	
Beatty, Freeman [all brothers]	Coffill, Hebert [farmer]		# Fuller, Burpee [son of Lev.]
Beatty, Kinsman	Coffill, Horace [farmer]	Dennison, Lewis P.	Fuller, Clarence
Beatty, Perry	Coffill, John [bros, cousins]	Dennison, L. Crandall	Fuller, Frank E.
	Coffill, Vernon		Fuller, Guy P.
Biggs, William [from England]	Coffill, Walter	Dunn, Lester [hh]	Fuller, Howard D. Sr
			Fuller, Jack [son of Guy]
Blair, George			Fuller, Leverett
[father of Harry Blair]			

Gertridge, Peter G.
Gertridge, P. John
Gertridge, Randolph

Golar, Cranswick [part black]
Golar, William [all hh]

Gould, E. Vernon

Guptill, Harry
Guptill, Manning [all bros]
Guptill, Otis
Guptill, Scot

Guy, Earnest [black] Shelburne

Hardacre, John [farmer]
Hardacre, Orland [son?]

Hartling, M. [hh]

Harvey, Fred
Harvey, Graham R.

Henderson, Frank [hh]

Higgins, Lawrence

Hughes, Clarence

Hutchinson, Avard [bros]
Hutchinson, Emerson

Jennings, K. [hh]

Keddy, Alden
Keddy, Grant
Keddy, Norman

Kelly, Albert
Kelly, Brenton
Kelly, Ralph
Kelly, Robert [father]
Kelly, Walter [Ding]

Kennedy, Robert

King, Curtis
King, Harding
King, James
King, Ralph

Laird, Edward [father]
Laird, Sydney

Lockhart, David
Lockhart, Harold [bros. to Murry]
Lockhart, Murry

Lowe, Herbert

MacIntosh, Fred [father]
MacIntosh, Stewart

Maitland, James A.

Messom, Lewis
Messom, Ralph [all hh]
Messom, Robert
Messom, Tom

Miles, Aleck [all hh]
Miles, Hardy
Miles, John

Miner, John [Gaspé farmer]
Miner, Johnston [Hortonvale farmer]

Morine, Daniel
Morine, Edward

Neil, Ernest [black]
Neil, John [black]

Norman, H.

Palmeter, Charles [son of Fred]
Palmeter, Fred A.
Palmeter, Harry M.
Palmeter, Robert H.

Parsons, Joseph [black]

Patterson, Arthur H.

Pinch, Cecil [all hh]
Pinch, Edward
Pinch, Fred Jr
Pinch, Fred Sr
Pinch, George
Pinch, Gilbert
Pinch, Harding
Pinch, Henry
Pinch, Victor

Reid, Don [son]
Reid, Percy B. [father]
Reid, William [son went west]

Rhyno, H. [both hh]
Rhyno, L.

Rogers, Henry

Rogerson, Cyrus [Bedeque, PEI; had 2 daughters]

Schaller, R. [mystery name]

Schofield, Max [son?]
Schofield, Otis [farmer]

Sherman, Gordon
Sherman, P.

Smith, Donald
Smith, Edward
Smith, Edwin [all hh ?]
Smith, Ivan
Smith, James

Snyder, Luke [of Bridgewater]

Spencer, Herbert

Starratt, Oscar
Starratt, A. [not Albert]
Starratt, Albert [bro. to Percey]
Starratt, Percey

States, Ray [black]

Stewart, Annie M.
Stewart, Steven G. [brother]

Sweet, Albert
Sweet, Med [all hh]
Sweet, Robert
Sweet, William

Terfry, Bert
Terfry, Corey

Townsend, Grant
Townsend, Hardy

Trenholm, Bruce [son of Scott]
Trenholm, George
Trenholm, Gilbert [a Coldwell "adopted" by Scott Trenholm]*
Trenholm, John [bro. to Leslie]
Trenholm, Leslie E.
Trenholm, Scott H. [bro. to Stewart]
Trenholm, Stewart L.

Van Buskirk, Burton
Van Buskirk, Cecil

Veno, E. [hh, Lunenburg Co.]

Walker, John

Walsh, J.
Walsh, Kenneth [all hh]
Walsh, Paul
Walsh, Robert

Weagle, Kenneth

West, E. V.
West, Horace

Wilkens, Roy

Woodman, Roy R.

Zwicker, B.
Zwicker, J.

Total: 203

PHONETIC SPELLINGS
Betty = Beatty
Buchman = Buchanan
Burpy = Burpee
Clary = Clowry
Claton = Clayton
Coffel = Coffill
Colwell = Coldwell
Gennings = Jennings
Guptil = Guptill
Hues = Hughes
Hutcheson = Hutchinson
Mackantosh = MacIntosh
Oschar = Oscar
Parson = Parsons
Reno = Rhyno
Scofield = Schofield
Starrat = Starratt
Starret = Starratt
Syrus = Cyrus
Townshend = Townsend
Welsh = Walsh
Wiggle = Weagle

#: alive in year 2000
hh: hired hand

* Gilbert born Coldwell, raised as a Trenholm then back to Coldwell as adult.

203 different men are recorded in the book. If the 42 "land owners" are subtracted, then most of the dyke work was done by 161 men and boys, plus 15 owners at times; 176 men on call for repairs.

TABLE 9.5.2 ROBERT H. PALMETER'S GRAND PRÉ TIME BOOK (JANUARY–
JUNE 1931)

#Allen, F. A.	Fuller, G. P.	Reid, P. B.
#Allen, G. W.	Fuller, H. D. Sr.	#Reid, William
Biggs, William	Fuller, Leverett	Schofield, Otis
Buchanan, William	#Fullerton, R. R.	#Starratt, A.
#Coffill, Herbert	Gertridge, P. G.	#Starratt, Albert
Coldwell, Clifford	Gertridge, P. J.	#Starratt, Percey
Coldwell, Cecil	Gould, E. V.	Stewart, Annie M.
Coldwell, Delmar	#Hardacre, John	#Stewart, S. G.
Crane, F. H.	Laird, Edward	Trenholm, George
Curry, L. H.	#Maitland, James A.	Trenholm, John
#Davidson, Frank	#Palmeter, F. A.	Trenholm, L. E.
#Dennison, L. P.	Palmeter, H. M.	Trenholm, S. L.
Eagles, E. A.	#Palmeter, R. H.	Trenholm, Scott
Fuller, F. E.	Patterson, A. H.	Woodman, Roy R.

Persons and horses were paid at various rates: 30¢/hr; $2/day; $1.75 for 7 hrs.
Sometimes a horse was paid the same rate, but usually less: man $2.40/day; horse $2/day.

The men on this list [42] rarely worked for pay; only those 15 marked # were ever on the payroll, and not often at that. But they often sent a horse and/or a hired hand. Apparently they were the affluent landowners and horse owners.

Acadian wall suddenly became Palmeter's full responsibility, as it alone served as barrier between sea and farmland.

Robert Palmeter would have been worried about the predicted extreme tides of March 4, and this is expressed by his special two-hour night patrol of his dykes. His East Grand Pré Dyke was directly exposed to the sea, whereas his West Grand Pré Dyke was supposedly protected by the underfunded Wickwire Dyke. He paid himself $1. On the second evening he was accompanied by E.V. West and they shared a $4 disbursement for their four hours of inspection. On March 10, the two repeated their inspection, having some real concerns now that the Wickwire Dyke was seriously breached and irreparable. Their old West Grand Pré Dyke wall, which had been resting since 1806, was now the only seawall protecting all their farmland. To prepare their dyke for the next set of extreme tides on April 4 and 5, Robert Palmeter had crews working from March 25 to April 1, taking advantage of the low neap tides. The work crews must have been proceeding on schedule, for he gave them Saturday and Sunday off.

To say that the West Grand Pré Dyke had been off duty since 1806 is probably not true. If it had not been upgraded periodically, then after some 120

Day	March *Tides	March a - m - h, Day	April Tides	April a - m - h, Day	June Tides	June a - m - h, Day
1			26.4	16 - 22 - 4, Wed.	26.9	
2						
3	(spring)		(spring)			
4	27	1 - 1 - 0, Wed.	27.7	2 - 2 - 0, Sat.		
5	27.4	1 - 2 - 0, Thurs.	27.5	1 - 1 - 0, Sun.		
6	27.1					
7	27.1		25.9	4 - 6 - 3, Tues.		
8						
9			(neap)			
10	24.3	1 - 2 - 0, Tues.	21.9	25 - 28 - 10, Fri.		
11	(neap)		21.7	38 - 42 - 11, Sat.		
12	22.1		(neap)	Sun.		
13	22		22.6	67 - 62 - 19, Mon.		
14	22.4		23.2	60 - 53 - 16		
15			23.8	75 - 68 - 22		
16			24	81 - 76 - 26		
17			24.3	1 - 1 - 0, Fri.		
18					25.6	
19			(spring)		25.7	
20	(spring)				25.4	
21					(neap)	
22					24.2	46 - 50 - 16, Mon.
23		(preparation for	23.7	1 - 1 - 0, Thurs.	23.8	77 - 76 - 26
24		April tides)	23.1		24	47 - 50 - 17
25	22.9	5 - 8 - 3, Wed.	22.7	84 - 81 - 30, Sat.	24.7	32 - 31 - 8
26	22.2	9- 11 - 7	22.4	Sun.	25.2	49 - 51 - 15, Fri.
27	21.8	15 - 17 - 7	23.1	71 - 75 - 24, Mon.	25.7	Sat.
28	21.8	Sat.		49 - 53 - 18	25.9	Sun.
29	(neap)	Sun.			25.8	
30	23.8	8 - 11 - 4	27		(spring)	
31	25.2	16 - 18 - 6	(spring)			

*High neap tides are near 22 feet, based on Tide Tables for Saint John, NB. High spring tides are near 27 feet. For Minas Basin tidal heights add 19–22 feet.

a: number of separate accounts entered in time book; m: number of men working that day; h: number of horses in use.

March 4 and 5 – Wickwire dyke destroyed. April 4 – tide overtops Grand Pré West dyke.

years (1806–1929) it would have been at least 3 ft lower, relative to rising sea levels. The Grand Pré farmers may well have been assiduously increasing its height on a regular basis under the impetus of the many breaches and floodings and retreats of the so-called "protective" Wickwire Dyke. The Saxby Gale breached every dyke in the area, and after that scare they may have taken the opportunity during the 1870s repairs to add a few extra feet in height and thickness. All of which may be why they seem to have had a reasonable dyke wall even though it was rarely called into use. Prior to the 1928 break the Grand Pré Proprietors officially dispatched inspectors to examine the condition of the Wickwire Dyke and to report back. The report was so chilling that they immediately voted to contribute $100 to the Wickwire proprietors. But alas, too late.

The Time Book's records through the rest of April are very revealing. Extreme tides were again predicted for Saturday and Sunday, near midnight. This must have been considered an emergency situation, because Palmeter and M.R. Eagles patrolled the vulnerable West Dyke for eight nocturnal hours on the Saturday night. From 12:45 to 1:00 A.M. they nervously witnessed tidal water overtopping their west wall. Only fifteen minutes of flooding occurred, and then the tide dropped quickly and would not have posed such a threat for another twenty-eight days – factors that Palmeter understood and worked to his advantage. Mr Eagles was paid $2.40 and Mr Palmeter $4. The next night, even though it was a Sunday, Palmeter spent six hours inspecting both the East and West Grand Pré dyke walls, and paid himself $3.

By Tuesday, he had organized some emergency repair efforts with six men and three horses, and then on Friday, April 10, he began upgrading the old wall in earnest, taking advantage of the low neap tides. The crews worked for six days, took only Sunday off, and finished the following Thursday evening. On that final day, seventy-six men and twenty-six horses were at the walls. They did not work again for a week because of high spring tides, but after a one-man inspection on Thursday, 23 April, Palmeter organized what appears to be an emergency effort on a Saturday, using eighty-one men and thirty horses. The next day they rested, dutifully observing the Sabbath, but were back in the sod trenches on Monday and Tuesday. These major bouts of repairs must have been adequate for the time being, for nothing was recorded in the Time Book for May. Not until the neap tides of late June did crews work on the walls again, this time from Monday through Friday of June 22–26, with shifts of fifty to seventy men. And there, disappointingly, the book ends.

We tend to imagine that when a dyke wall broke panic must have spread throughout the community, every activity must have ceased, and every able-bodied man must have rushed to the walls where sods flew all about and chaos reigned. The enlightened vision gained from Robert Palmeter's little Time Book is one of calmness and control, of highly organized procedures, of the availability of a large and competent workforce, and of detailed daily book-keeping. No panic, just professionalism.

9.6 Locality 6: Wolfville Harbour Area

Wolfville Harbour and the surrounding area has an unusual assemblage of dykeland structures, artifacts, and dykeland history: an Acadian dyke; a Planter dyke; hundreds of marsh-hay staddle posts; an unrecorded old sewer line; a riverbank wharf now 40 ft (12.2 m) below high water; a 750-year-old clam bed; a roadway buried beneath 30 inches (0.76 m) of marsh turf; and a newly discovered nineteenth-century shipwreck in the harbour muds.

Even more relicts would remain if some past proposals had come to fruition. In 1865 plans were drawn up by the Windsor and Annapolis Railway Company for a spur line from Wolfville to the riverbank just west of the harbour entrance, thereby creating a "deep water rail port." In 1907 a railway causeway across the Cornwallis River to Starr's Point was seriously discussed, with the same positive arguments (Bishop, 1907). In 1940 the War Office had plans to convert the Grand Pré and Wickwire Dykelands into an artillery range and munitions testing site (appendix 10). With hindsight, we can be thankful these particular plans went astray.

Acadians settled the area in the 1680s and 1690s, and often built small dykeland enclosures adjacent to their upland holdings. These dykes formed a loop from the upland that encircled a small plot of marsh between drainage creeks, thereby avoiding the need for constructing aboiteaux dams. Aerial photos and historical evidence (J. Fowler, in correspondence) point to one such dyke east of Wolfville Harbour (Fig. 7.2). It is in the same position as an isolated loop dyke plotted on the 1808 survey map compiled by Oliver Lyman. Oblique aerial photos from 1931 show it protruding from the hayfields within the Wickwire Dyke, and although it is now beneath ground surface, its landscape signature shows up as a difference in soil colour even in the 1992 aerial photos (Fig. 7.2).

The rest of Lyman's map is nearly aerial-photo accurate, with the creek configurations nicely overlapping the photos. However, the overlap only coincides for each of the two areas northeast and southwest of the Great

Figure 9.6.1 Hand-tinted 1910 postcard showing the government wharf and lighthouse on the bank of the Cornwallis River at Wolfville; note the breached and abandoned dyke wall in the foreground.

Discharge Creek, if they are treated as separate units. The two areas are not perfectly aligned with one another. This is because Lyman surveyed each area separately and even penned his legends differently. All his writing to the northeast of the Great Discharge is written "upside down" to that in the Wolfville area, indicating that he surveyed and drafted that northern half from a baseline on Long Island.

By the year 2000 nearly all of the original three-mile-long 1806 dyke wall had been removed by riverbank erosion. The exception is a short section that runs from the bank of the Cornwallis River along the east side of the channel entrance to Wolfville Harbour. Its location is indicated by a crest of woody Marsh Elder shrubs. The old dyke protrudes about 2 ft (0.6 m) above the present marsh surface, but beneath is another 5 ft (1.5 m) of wall still intact, having been buried by rising sea and marsh levels (Figs 7.4 and 7.5). The original wall with its brush base, sod wall, and board face, now nearly 200 years old, can be viewed in cross-section at the riverbank (Fig. 7.1).

In the early 1900s, Wolfville had not only a commercial international harbour (at one time, the smallest registered shipping harbour in the world) but also a wharf on the bank of the Cornwallis River with a freight shed, a lighthouse, and a roadway to it crossing the marsh. In a 1910 hand-tinted postcard (Fig. 9.6.1), all of the above are evident, as well as a broken dyke wall in the foreground. However, in a 1920s photo, the outer wharf is

undercut riverbank at government wharf

Figure 9.6.2   The same wharf as in Fig. 9.6.1, circa the 1920s. Note the derelict base of the wharf and the mere catwalk bridge connection instead of the previous substantial foundation with its lighthouse. By 1946 the wharf had slid down the bank, and by 1963 it was an island shoal of pilings and rocks in the middle of the Cornwallis River channel. (Jeff Wilson Collection, Lawrencetown, NS; E. Graham photo)

undercut and collapsing, and there is only a makeshift catwalk ramp from marsh to docking area (Fig. 9.6.2). The old wharf pilings, cribwork, and rockfill had begun to slide down the steep eroding slope into the river channel where it sits today, visible at extreme low spring tides. Its resting place is recorded on the 1967 topographic map as a small island shoal in the centre of the river channel.

The original wharf facility constructed in 1901 was, in today's parlance, a learning experience, for it came to a prophetic river-bottom fate in 1904. The subsequent replacement was more carefully executed, but eventually it too succumbed. The 1906 Annual Report of the Chief Engineer, Federal Government, Department of Transport, contains a marvellous description of the saga of the first five years in the life of this riverbank wharf. I quote it in full because it so concisely describes the size of the wharf, its construction, its costs, and precisely how and why it was lost to riverbank erosion and severe winter weather.

In 1900–01, the department, at a cost of $6,360.50, built by contract a public wharf on the right bank of the river, near its mouth, at a distance of about half a mile from the town. The approach consists of an earthwork embankment, 144 feet long, 25 feet wide and of an average height of 5 feet. The wharf itself which was substantially built of pile-work was 152 feet long, 36 feet wide, including an inclined slip on the south side 10 feet wide. It has an "L" on the outer end 82 feet long, giving a total face length on the river channel of 116 feet, the "L" is 40 feet wide and is from 28 to 29 1/2 feet in height along the face, giving a depth of water at HWOST, of about 46 feet. At LWOST, the river channel carries a depth of from 4 to 6 feet of mostly fresh water.

In 1902–03, the channel of the river moved shoreward owing to erosion, a distance of some 20 or 30 feet causing the two outer rows of piles of the wharf to lose more than half their hold in the mud and sand. In consequence of this it became necessary to build cribwork in the spaces between the two outer rows of piles at the end of the "L", and on the opposite end of the wharf, alongside the inclined slip. This mode of treatment being insufficient and the scour continuing, it was decided to remove the outer 20 feet in width for the whole 118 feet in length of the wharf, and rebuild it on the inner side of the "L". The work was begun on October 1, 1903, and vigorously carried on until December 24, when owing to the severity of the weather and the rapidly accumulating ice, operations were suspended.

The winter of 1903–04, was the severest known for a great many years. Ice formed in and around the piles of the wharf to a greater weight and thickness than had been known since the wharf was built. The floating power of the ice, added to the reduced hold of the piles in the bottom, from the erosion of the channel, caused the whole "L" to be lifted up by an exceptionally high tide of the third March, 1904, to a height of from 5 to 8 feet. A few days later the whole outer portion of the wharf, including the "L" was carried away and destroyed.

In 1903–04, the sum of $1,768.89, was expended in the above alterations and improvements and after the destruction of the wharf, in saving such of the timber as possible.

In 1904–05, the sum of $78.80, was expended in saving and booming old timber from the destroyed pile-wharf and the sum of $2,565.11 in beginning the construction of a substantial cribwork wharf in its place. At the close of the fiscal year the work was about one-third completed.

Spring tides rise 48 feet, neaps 40 feet.

After reading this account, one wonders how they had the courage, or temerity, to persist at this site for another twenty years. The gravel-surfaced road that led to the wharf can now be seen in section at the riverbank, where it is 8 to 9 ft (2.4–2.7 m) wide and buried 30 inches (0.76 m) beneath the marsh surface. Its previous course across the marsh is now indicated by the only straight-line drainage "creek" on the marsh (Fig. 7.2). A metal probe thrust into the marsh or into the bottom of this "creek" anywhere along this line elicits a crunching sound when it contacts the gravel layer. It became a

salt hay staddles

riverside wharf
and lighthouse

sewer access
tower

flooded pastures

Wolfville
Harbour

Figure 9.6.3   An extreme high tide on 30 October 1913 breached dykes but they were
quickly repaired. Note sewer line access towers. On the tidal marsh across the river
channel are staddles stacked with salt hay that was retrieved during the winter. (Jeff
Wilson Collection, Lawrencetown, NS; E. Graham photo)

drainage ditch by default, following the 1931 destruction of the adjacent
dykes, because the marsh grasses were slow to establish on the compacted
gravel roadbed, thereby creating a straight drainage trench across the marsh.

Between the 1806 dyke wall and the harbour entrance channel, a line of
dark pits shows up on the aerial photos (Fig. 7.2). The smaller ones are cave-
ins and the larger are where shafts gave access to the town's original sewer
line. The line appears to be a tunnel constructed of bricks and timbers, but
the Town Office has no archival information, so the story of its construction
and abandonment has yet to be told. By the late 1930s it was considered
inadequate and in need of replacement, particularly because "the surplus
sewage backed up each day when the tides are in" (*The Acadian*, 11 March
1937). This sewage backup is a further example of the consequences of those
rising sea levels. The elevated service shaft towers are detectable on old aerial
photographs, and the two near the railway are still intact. The other shafts
have been reduced to large pits, but in an October 1913 photo of dykes
breached at high tide, they conspicuously project above the high water level
(Fig. 9.6.3). The breached walls were reported in *The Acadian* (7 November
1913) to have been easily repaired before the next set of high tides.

At the far left and across the river beehive-shaped hay mows are perched
on staddle platforms. These were clusters of posts driven into a tidal marsh,

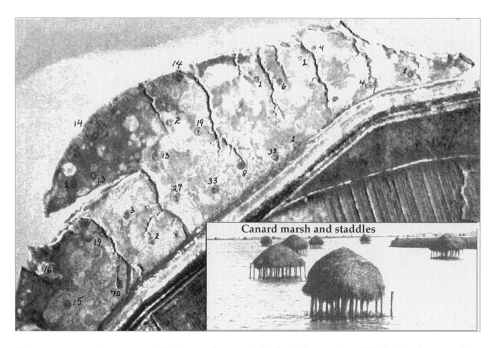

Figure 9.6.4   A 1967 aerial photo of an undyked tidal marsh at Wolfville. A ground-check in 1997 located twenty-four staddle sites with a total of 320 posts. The extracted posts measured 7 ft in length, only 2 ft of which had protruded above the turf, indicating a 3 ft rise in marsh level from the time of construction. (National Air Photo Library A 19985-166; Cleven, André/Library and Archives Canada/PA-021537)

to which a pole deck was added. Newly cut salt hay was stored on these platforms (small inset photo, Fig. 9.6.4), and through the winter months, whenever the ground became firmly frozen, wagons were used to transport this hay to the barns. The inset photo confirms that the harvesting of salt marsh hay was certainly not a minor activity – projecting staddles loaded with hay are parading all along the horizon. This aspect of dykeland agriculture became redundant by the 1940s, but in spite of drifting winter ice blocks and rising marsh levels, the clusters of posts persist. Fig. 9.6.4 is an August 1967 aerial photo of a riverbank marsh west of Wolfville Harbour; when I examined it in October 1997 I located twenty-four staddle clusters and counted 320 posts.

   In June 2001 David Herbin and I excavated several of these posts, and discovered they were 7 ft (2.1 m) long and had been driven 2 ft (0.6 m) into the marsh when first installed. The sharpened tips and original bark are perfectly preserved on those first 2 ft, but above that line the effect of weathering has removed the bark and eaten away at the wood itself. Originally, they would have projected 5 ft above the marsh surface, ensuring that the stored hay would be kept above the higher Minas Basin tides and the waters of minor storms. They now project only 2 ft, indicating a 3 ft (0.9 m) rise in marsh level. At an elevation increase of 3 ft/century, these posts would have to be close to 100 years old. Staddles were used for centuries in Nova Scotia, so how did the farmers maintain the necessary 4 to 5 ft elevation of their hay mows above marsh meadow level to protect the hay from high tides? Did they remove and relocate the old posts every thirty or forty years? Does anyone know the answer to this question?

For a fascinating detailed account of the art and science of harvesting salt hay, accompanied by drawings, photographs, and a vocabulary list of French and English terms, read *Festival de la Barge: The Rebirth of an Acadian Tradition* by Peter Crowell and Austin Saulnier, 1998. Salt hay was harvested in this Acadian area into the 1950s, so a few persons were available in the 1990s who knew exactly how it had been done, and they supervised a re-enactment of the entire process, from staddle construction to completed hay mow, and documented it with interviews, photographs, and videos.

The layer of 750-year-old paired valves of the edible Soft-Shelled Clam (*Mya arenaria*) at Wolfville, exposed halfway down the riverbank, is discussed in chapter 7 in connection with changing sea levels. First recorded in 1983, this band of shells is still a prominent feature in 2001, after nearly two decades of severe annual erosion along the riverbank. It must have been an extensive clam bed in its day, readily accessible to the Native peoples.

A recent shift in tidal currents within Wolfville Harbour itself, possibly the result of the new waterfront park construction, has revealed an unsuspected item: the ribbed hull of an old ship is now protruding from the harbour sediments. It was first noticed in July 2000, and was soon investigated by a team under the supervision of marine historian Dan Conlin of the Maritime Museum of the Atlantic, Halifax. Their report (Conlin, 2001) indicates that the vessel was about 62 ft (19 m) long, probably built in the mid to late nineteenth century; it has an interesting construction with variations from the norm. The various woods used to construct this hull included beech, larch, birch, balsam fir, and spruce.

In the 1884–1950 Minute Book of the Proprietors of Grand Pré Dykelands, I discovered several loose sheets – the printed announcements of an emergency meeting. I searched through *The Acadian* and found that the events had been followed closely and were reported in detail (appendix 10). Surprisingly, none of the local historians I consulted was aware that the Federal Government War Office planned to convert the valuable Acadian and Planter dykelands into an artillery range, displacing fifteen farming families in order to use Long Island and Boot Island as targets. The ensuing political twists and turns are detailed in appendix 10 and were published as an article in *Kings County Vignettes*.

In 1865, in spite of the known instability and vulnerability of the riverbank at Wolfville, a major proposal was drafted by the Windsor and Annapolis Railway for construction of a railway spur to a major loading wharf, just west of the harbour entrance channel. The railway purchased a block of land from farmers, as depicted in the site plans at Kentville Deeds Office, (B, P-2588). Nothing came of it, probably because of the 1869 Saxby Tide, which broke dykes and washed away sections of railbeds in the Wolfville and Grand Pré areas, railbeds that were far from the riverbank. Such a storm undoubtedly had a chilling effect on potential investors in wharf developments.

In the 12 July 1907 edition of *The Acadian*, an article by G.E. Bishop discusses the never-ending problem of the undercutting of the riverbank and its dyke walls. He notes that over the past 100 years the Wickwire Dykeland farmers had lost some 100 acres to the river. His proposed solution was to block off the entire Cornwallis River with a roadway and railway causeway crossing the river from Wolfville to Starr's Point. This would provide a deepwater port and rail access to the rich farmlands north of the Cornwallis River, and would eliminate the need for maintenance of all the small original Acadian dykes on either side of the river from Wolfville to Kentville. It was assumed that this scheme would also prevent future erosion of the riverbank at Wolfville, because tidal waters would simply reach that point and stop. However, judging from the unpredicted erosional consequences of the more recent Windsor road and rail causeway project, his plan could have created a huge silt bar at the causeway, with active erosional channels at either side. That would have silted up their intended deep water port and actually increased erosion along Wolfville's dyke front. Funding for this project never materialized.

I have been emphasizing the erosional aspects of the river channel, but the historical picture is not complete without mention of shore sites where there is but little shoreline loss. Where Wolfville sandstone bedrock formations are exposed, erosion is minimal. In Figs 3.4 and 5.5 that straight shoreline at Town Plot, Starr's Point, is not a curved meandering line because it is a terraced rock wall, unlike most of the river channel. These firm terraces were discovered by the Acadians and became a major docking site, and then deportation site, and thereafter a Planter town site. To the east and west of this landing, the river channel is curved because it is cutting into softer depositional layers of old marsh and river silt bars, possibly 3,000 to 4,000 years

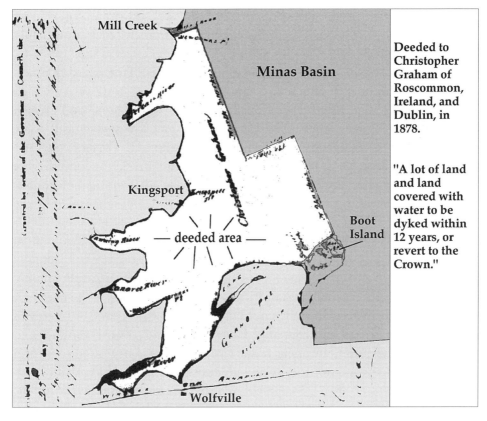

Figure 9.6.5 An example of an 1878 scheme to sell shares in a project to dyke the Minas Basin from Boot Island to Mill Cove in order to farm the "rich marsh soil" that would be enclosed within the central white area on this labelled reproduction of the original deed map. (Nova Scotia Registry of Deeds Office, Kings Co. 1878, no.1273)

old. At Wolfville a steep 40 ft bank is exposed by river erosion, but on the opposite shore conspicuous new layers are accumulating and building eastward into the river channel.

Between Starr's Point and Long Island it is possible to do a walkabout on the sea floor at spring low tides. It is that same Town Plot sandstone formation, for it continues eastward beneath Long Island and Little Island and Boot Island. The sandstone bedrock at the west end of Long Island slopes gradually, grading from a coating of grassy marsh, beyond which is soft ooze, and then gently sloping bare bedrock. A comparison of the 1760 shoreline at west Long Island with the 1963 aerial photos shows relatively minor changes, because of that bedrock substrate. When scouting these river channels on foot at a low tide, a diagnostic feature in identifying outcrops of bedrock from a distance is the presence of fully exposed stones, rocks, and boulders sitting suspiciously high on what, from that distance, mistakenly appears to be mud.

In the Minas Basin, strong tidal currents scour these large river channels and remove the finer sediments, leaving a firm ripple sand, or gravel, or bedrock surface. On these it is possible to explore, drive a horse and wagon, walk your dog, or even land a small plane. At extreme low spring tides, there is enough time to walk from Long Island to Starr's Point to Porters Point and possibly on to Kingsport. If you did accomplish that stroll, you would agree that these lower river slopes and bottoms, unlike the adjacent tidal meadows, are not prime farmland, yet they have been sold as such in what must be the ultimate of marshland scam operations.

The Acadians left such an anecdotal legacy of the amazing richness of tidal marshlands, that one Christopher Graham of Roscommon, Ireland, actually obtained a deed from an eager provincial government in 1878, mainly because of the jobs it would certainly have created. Fig. 9.6.5 is the map plot of his proposed dyke wall that would create tens of thousands of acres of rich marshland. It ran, unimaginably, from Boot Island towards Blomidon to connect at Newcomb Point, near today's Mill Cove. He neglected to inform shareholders that much of the dyke wall construction would have to be in the order of 30 to 60 ft (9–18 m) high, and that the land reclaimed would be an undulating sea-bottom terrain of rocks, gravel, bedrock, and saline sand, not the misleadingly promoted fertile marsh meadows.

CHAPTER TEN

Recent Exposures of Entombed Shorelines

Minas Basin

Into thy cup the ocean pours and fills
Thy great marsh-rivers where the ruddy stains
Mix with the waters of a hundred hills;
And then with eager quaffing lip he drains...
Once to the day, once to the night that reigns.
On thy broad rim the great Designer's wand
Has wrought the fairest things of earth and sky
And made a wonder of thy mighty tides.

J.F. Herbin, 1909, 107

One final special aspect of Grand Pré bears directly on the Acadians' successes in dyking those thousands of acres. It has to do with the availability of suitable sod pits. Several seniors who had repaired dykes informed me that, prior to conducting those repairs, someone with the special knowledge and experience was sent scouting for likely sod pit areas. He would search for large patches of single species of marsh grasses, with at least two feet of root depth, as nothing was more frustrating than to get a pit established and into production, and then run into a layer of sand. The sods would consequently be too short and the men would have to start a new pit somewhere else. Robert Palmeter was noted for his ability to find the best sites for sod cutting.

The eroding shores of Minas Basin often present vertical sections of sequential shorelines laid down centuries ago. I believe that these exposed ancient shorelines in the Grand Pré area fit into three categories. At the western end of Long Island, which is exposed to prevailing westerly winds, the old shore deposits form an exposed sea cliff about 10 ft (3 m) in thickness, made up of strikingly different layers (Fig. 10.1). The dominant content

Cape Blomidon

Figure 10.1 West end of Long Island, Grand Pré, where erosion has exposed shore deposits from former beach levels. Note protruding storm-tossed trees buried beneath successive layers of silts or plant-root turf.

of any one layer may be grasses, grey clay, the "black onions" of Salt Marsh Bulrush, sand, logs and branches, or ice-rafted stones, all of which would render it difficult to develop a highly productive sod pit. This category I term *storm-generated shore deposits*, as everything seems to get tossed onto this type of marsh. Because the effects of storms are discontinuous along a shoreline, the deposits seen in section form a patchwork that varies both vertically and horizontally. These storm-tossed layers may be interspersed with a thick layer of marsh grass roots from a successful period of tidal meadows or more usually with a layer of "black onion" corms of Salt Marsh Bulrush, representing an interlude of sandy beach.

A second category is the tidal meadow fronted by a *persistent sandy beach shore*; several lie at the northeast corner of Grand Pré (Fig. 9.3.4, p. xxxii). Extraneous items such as logs, rocks, or stones occur sparsely. Viewed in eroded section, it has layers of sand-loving Salt Marsh Bulrush that form prominent "black onion" bands, some thicker that others (Figs 10.2 and 7.11), and these alternate with thick layers of marsh-grass turf. When thick enough, the pure marsh-grass layers were mined for sods.

The third category of shore deposits, much preferred by dyke builders, is the *pure accumulation of marsh-grass turf* with entangled root systems unadulterated by sand, tree limbs, or "black onion" layers (Fig. 4.7). This

Figure 10.2   North shore of east Grand Pré, where sand accumulates now and has in the past, as indicated by the black bands of roots of Salt Marsh Bulrush. Most of these layers are of marsh grass root entanglements, potential building blocks for dyke walls.

could only happen in protected backwaters such as the marsh meadows behind that chain of Grand Pré islands: Long, Little, and Boot. When north shore erosion finally cut through between Long and Little Islands (about 1860; the cut is named Soldier's Creek on some maps) and into the large drainage creek flowing south into the Gaspereau River, it initiated the formation and progressive excavation of the Guzzle channel. Those ancient marsh-grass deposits became exposed to that north-shore erosion, and thus were being cut into from behind, from the side that had been their protective upland – an unusual situation. Today, just to the west of the Guzzle's north entrance, those grass deposits present a vertical face of about 8 ft (2.4 m) of pure root matrix sitting on buried upland soil with its many well-preserved rhizomes of wild roses from hundreds of years ago. This natural preservation process of plant material entombed in local dykelands deserves further investigation and explanation. It is startling to find, when examining dykes over one hundred years old, brush bearing green birch leaves, or spruce branches with needles that are green and firm and sharp

Without this plant preservation phenomenon, the Acadians would not have had those essential root-reinforced construction sods. In 1680 much of the sheltered Grand Pré tidal marshland consisted of a uniform deposit of such marsh-grass turf, and the Acadians would have realized the value of this feature.

Which brings us full circle to "Sods, Soils, and Spades," and perchance to a broader appreciation of this marine aspect of Acadian culture. Those ideal conditions for procurement of marsh-grass sods made it feasible for the Acadians to create their dykes and, in doing so, to develop their distinct cultural identity.

Perhaps, as they watched nutrient-rich tides swell into river estuaries, and flood in behind a protective chain of three islands, and then sweep across thousands of acres of potentially fertile saline meadows, they may have dreamed of extensive dykeland enclosures, of homes and barns on the adjacent hill slopes, of cultural independence and the possibility of economic prosperity. Their dreams gradually unfolded to a utopian reality, only to be swept away by the more powerful tides of political expediency.

SUMMARY AND CONCLUSIONS

The origin of the Bay of Fundy and its unique tidal regimes form the explanatory backdrop for the theme of this book, namely, that the Acadian people were as much a product of Bay of Fundy and Minas Basin intertidal meadows as was their agrarian produce.

This book describes special features of the tidal marshland meadows of Minas Basin, and how it was that the Acadians would become the only pioneer culture in North America to focus their community agriculture on intertidal landscapes.

Minas Basin tidal marsh soils were derived from sedimentary rocks first formed 500,000 years ago near the South Pole, later folded into mountains of North Africa, and then transported by continental drift to become Nova Scotia.

Over the past 3,000 years, rising sea levels and increasing tidal amplitudes in the Bay of Fundy generated ever deeper deposits of marshland meadow turf, an unusual configuration of nutrients and silts entrapped in entanglements of fine roots of marsh grasses.

Only two species of marsh grass had small diameter roots capable of forming a dense uniform matrix, compact enough to be sliced into uniformly shaped building blocks. These marine "clay bricks" were stacked to form living, waterproof walls that resisted the world's greatest tides. The enclosed fields of once tidal meadows were then plowed to release trapped nutrients and hasten decomposition of old root systems. Farm fertilizers were not required, there were neither rocks nor stumps to clear away, and there was the outright gift of the established system of natural tidal drainage ditches throughout the marshes, ditches that carried away salts leached by rain from the new fields.

Construction of dyke walls and their aboiteau log sluices, the latter preventing influx of sea water as well as accommodating outflow of surface runoff, was organized and efficient. To extract construction sods from marshes, the Acadians used a special, short, narrow, knife-edged spade, a technology imported from Europe. Employing work unit teams of six men equipped with spades, pitch forks, and oxen, an assemblage of 120 men could construct more than a mile of dyke wall in just twenty days.

Utilizing the natural tidal creek drainage patterns, the Acadians gradually dyked off successive blocks of tidal marshland at Grand Pré. Evidence suggests that by 1755 they had constructed walls around twelve major enclosures, and in doing so they honeycombed the Grand Pré meadows with a network of 17.5 miles (28 km) of walls, containing possibly as many as thirty-three aboiteaux.

At the final construction stages they had shut out the sea from about 2,900 acres of marshland, by means of an east wall connecting Long Island to Horton Landing, and a west wall to lower Wolfville. These two north-south barriers totalled a mere four miles (6.4 km) of wall, with only three aboiteaux in each wall, a truly elegant conclusion to a major engineering challenge.

Plowing and crowning patterns established by the Acadians defined the boundaries of their fields, and these were carefully mapped by the Planters in 1760. Most of these fields have remained unaltered since the Deportation and Expulsion began in 1755, and their distinct shapes are easily recognizable in 1963 aerial photos and in 1999 satellite images.

Throughout the period of Acadian dyke construction, relative sea level continued its inexorable rise and continues to this day. Tidal marsh meadows rise in conjunction and consequently old abandoned dykes become buried, whereas functional walls must be raised ever higher over time, thereby entombing earlier walls. Therefore, considerable archaeological material lies beneath the fields and marshes, waiting to be located and described.

Few maps produced after 1760 depict dyke walls accurately, if at all. However, many, if not most, original Acadian dykes produce distinct landscape ridge patterns on aerial photos of the 1930s through 1960s. Colour aerial photos of the 1970s through the 1990s often record differences in plant cover that also form linear patterns, ones that match those of old dykes in the black and white aerial photos of the 1940s.

On the one hand, there are documents and maps yet to be discovered, extant Acadian settlement sites and roads to be recorded and investigated, and dykelands to be explored, mapped, and excavated. On the other hand, the very tides that created the Acadian culture are, day by day, eroding shorelines at an astonishing rate, and thereby removing forever marsh-entombed artifacts that bear witness to those unusual dykeland communities of 300 years ago.

Chronology of Various Events Pertaining to Dykelands

1.0 GEOLOGICAL ASPECTS

1.1   500–400 million years ago, Silurian-Devonian Periods.

Near the South Pole, future Minas Basin rocks are formed from deposition of marine sediments from erosion of the mountains of what will become West Africa. These southern continental plates drift northwards, and their layered rocks are folded during collisions with other continental plates. This is the Acadian Orogeny of major mountain building and erosion.

1.2   340 million years ago, Carboniferous Period.

Formation of blue/black fossiliferous Horton Group of shales, one intertidal outcrop of which created the first landing site at Grand Pré used by the Acadians. Less that a century later it became the site of their Deportation and diaspora.

1.3   280 million years ago, Permian Period.

The original North American Plate presses against and retains a piece of Europe and a piece of West Africa, which it carries away with it when the new Atlantic Ocean is formed. The final conjunction of these two blocks form the northern and southern halves of Nova Scotia, with the Minas Basin enclosed at their boundary. This accidental configuration would subsequently generate the world's highest tides and attract vast concentrations of migratory fish to the area.

1.4   240 million years ago, Triassic Period.

Continental plates of Pangaea are now rifting apart and the Atlantic Ocean widening. A mountainous Nova Scotia is eroded and deposited as Wolfville Sandstones and Blomidon Shales, which will contribute to the rich soils of Grand Pré marshlands.

1.5 200 million years ago, late Triassic Period.

Sheets of lava flow from fissures in the Bay of Fundy and their layers form the substantial eighty-mile-long North Mountain, protecting the Minas Basin and fertile Annapolis Valley from the cold air of the Bay of Fundy, thus modifying the micro-climate to such a degree that even fruit trees, grapes vines, and tobacco can be grown.

2.0 TIDAL ASPECTS

More recently, only 4–5,000 years ago, the Minas Basin was a quiet lagoon with tides of probably less than 1 m. As glaciers melted worldwide, sea levels rose and the natural resonance period of the Bay of Fundy gradually became synchronous with the daily passage of the moon; tidal amplitudes increased from 1–2 m to the 15–16 m of today. These new macrotides transported suspended sediments, derived from shore erosion, onto developing marshlands such as Grand Pré. Forests became submerged and entombed in sediments, as would much of the original Acadian dyke-wall construction.

3.0 FRENCH HISTORY

3.1 1605 – Champlain established a settlement at Port-Royal, which was destroyed by the British in 1613, after which most of the French returned to France. In 1621 the British renamed it Annapolis Royal and named the land Nova Scotia (New Scotland).

3.2 1632 – British returned the land to the French, who then, in an effort to consolidate their position, imported hundreds of French settlers between 1632–36. They came to Port-Royal from the Saint Onge and Poitou districts of west-central France. Within a century, at least within their hearts, they became a nation – Les Acadiens.

3.3 1636 – Saltmakers [sauniers] were imported from the Vendée coast of France. They built dykes at Port-Royal for evaporation of sea water to produce salt for the fisheries. The enterprise failed and dyked lands became rich crop and pasture lands instead (Cormier, 1990).

3.4 1670 – French settlers began to spread into Minas Basin (Bay of Mines) and the upper Bay of Fundy (Baie Française). A small looped dyke east of Wolfville harbour may have been constructed about this time.

3.5 circa 1680 – The Acadians in Kings County began dyking Grand Pré, as well as along the banks of nearly all the major and minor tidal rivers flowing into Minas Basin.

3.6   1713 – First account of the French dykers referring to themselves as Les Acadiens (Clive Doucet, 1999, 29).

3.7   1732 – An account in Herbin's 1911 history (60–1) states that all suitable marshlands had been dyked. According to Brasseau (1987) by 1750 they had dyked 13,000 acres (or should this be arpents?) of marshlands, but only 500 acres of forest had been cleared.

3.8   1748 – British lay siege to the Fortress of Louisbourg and sink ships in the harbour; these were discovered and surveyed by an underwater team from Acadia University in 1961.

3.9   1755–63 – The expulsion of possibly 12,000 Acadians from their lands; this included the deportation by sea of perhaps 8,000. Exact figures are difficult to determine.

3.10   1755–59 – Dykelands lie fallow and dyke walls neglected. A storm in November 1859 broke the dykes in many places, flooding much of the Grand Pré farmlands.

3.11   1759 – General Wolfe captures Quebec City.

3.12   June 1760 – The New England Planters arrive to a partially flooded Grand Pré. They survey the uplands and the marshes and produce maps of exceptional quality, depicting the drainage creeks with near aerial photo exactness. These maps constitute a unique baseline source for deciphering agricultural and geomorphic changes over the past 250 years.

3.13   1763 – British win the war in the colonies and, with the Treaty of Paris, gain legal control of the land. They stop displacing the Acadians and in 1764 allow them to return and own property, but not near their previous farms and dykelands.

3.14   1763–70 – In an effort to repair the dyke walls, the New England Planters now have the Acadians teach them dyking technology. Jonathan Crane, of Windsor (Piziquid), watches these procedures in 1764, and is later appointed supervisor of dyke reconstruction and maintenance from 1777 to 1820. He described his methods in fascinating detail in an article in 1819.

3.15   1775 – The United Empire Loyalists flee the American War of Independence of 1775–83 and arrive in eastern Canada between 1776 and 1784. In New Brunswick they force the Acadians out of their newly established settlements and into northern areas of that province.

3.16   1789 – In Europe, the French Revolution and destruction of their monarchy.

4.0   NEW ENGLAND PLANTERS AND UNITED EMPIRE LOYALISTS

4.1   1805–06 – Farmers build a dyke from Wolfville to Long Island, three miles long with six large aboiteaux. This, the most ambitious dyking project ever attempted in Atlantic Canada, was completed in two years.

4.2   1817–25 – Farmers build a dyke across the Canard River entrance, one mile long with one major aboiteau.

4.3   1869 – Saxby Tide and Gale of October 5–6 destroys many dykes, wharves, bridges, railways, roads, barns, and ships, with loss of many lives and livestock.

4.4   1890–1910 – Collapse of the lucrative shad fisheries due to escalation of river pollution and construction of many small power-generating dams on rivers of the east coast of United States and Canada, all of which effectively prevented access to upper-stream spawning grounds.

4.5   1928 and 1931 – The Wolfville to Long Island dyke of 1806 is destroyed by storms, in two stages, and not rebuilt until 1959–60.

4.6   1939–40 – At the east side of Grand Pré dykelands, Robert Palmeter becomes the first person to construct a dyke using heavy machinery. Drag lines and bulldozers soon became the norm, and this innovative development was a major factor in convincing governments that assuming responsibility for dyke-wall maintenance was a practical proposition.

5.0   RECENT EVENTS AND GOVERNMENT RESPONSIBILITIES

5.1   1940 – In late October the War Department in Ottawa announced plans for an expropriation of Grand Pré farmland for use as a munitions testing ground and artillery training range. Most farmers agreed to accept if adequately compensated, but in early November an alternative site in Quebec was announced.

5.2   1943 – The dykes had long been neglected because of low demand and low prices for hay, the effects of the 1930s Great Depression, and the manpower short-ages during World War II. To assist the dykeland farmers, the federal and provincial governments entered into a fifty/fifty cost-sharing agreement, and set up the Maritime Dykeland Rehabilitation Committee (MDRC). It administered funds for emergency repairs only.

5.3   1943–47 – In Nova Scotia, eighty emergency repair projects were undertaken during this period, totalling 44.4 km of dyke walls. Much of this refurbishing involved machines that simply made old dykes wider and higher than previously possible. Thus, beneath many of the modern dyke walls are the original Acadian dykes and the Planter modifications of those.

5.4   1948 – The federal government passed the Maritime Marshlands Rehabilitation Act; in 1949 the three Maritime provinces signed the fifty/fifty cost arrangement. From that time, construction and maintenance of dyke walls and aboiteau sluice boxes has been the responsibility of governments. Farmers had been financing, building, and maintaining those marshlands for 250 years.

5.5   1968 – The federal government announces that it will pull out of the 1948 agreement in 1970. In that year, each maritime provincial government took over its own dykeland expenses within its department of agriculture.

6.0   BABY BOOMERS AND FRUSTRATED FARMERS

6.1   1980s – The miles of dirt roadways atop dyke walls are "discovered" by joggers, cyclists, nature lovers, dog walkers, drivers, ATVs, 4WDs, and snowmobiles. The consequent amount of abrasion alarms government and farmers, and gates are installed to exclude power vehicles.

6.2   1990s – Farmers become annoyed by the increase in car traffic and parking on their network of private roads that access their fields, and they post restrictive signs. Then the expansion onto dykeland fields by university athletic fields, the development of a business park, and proposals for dykeland nature trails create further frictions, as yet unresolved.

6.3 Millennium 2000 and beyond – Dyke walls have to be periodically elevated with fill to compensate for rising sea levels, but there is now so much recreational traffic with concomitant abrasion and soil compaction on the raised crests of those walls that the government is experimenting at Wolfville with a resistant, or at least resilient, rubber top coating made of chips from car tires.

This new rubber coating is, at the molecular level, not so new. Its petroleum origins in the organic deposits of the Carboniferous Period, some 300 million years ago, are actually younger than the tiny West African inorganic rock particles in the marsh soils that make up that dyke wall. Pause for a few moments and consider all this when next jogging along above an eighteenth-century Acadian dyke entombed just beneath your feet.

APPENDIX TWO

Minas Basin Tidal Marsh Flora
(major large species)

GRAMINEAE grasses
   Spartina alterniflora – cord grass
   Spartina patens – salt meadow hay
   Spartina pectinata – ditch grass (spray zone)
   Distichlis spicata – spike grass, salt grass

JUNCACEAE rush family
   Juncus gerardi – black grass, black rush

CYPERACEAE sedge family
   Scirpus maritimus – salt marsh bulrush (black corms)
   Scirpus americanus – bulrush (wet sand, upper beach)
   Carex paleacea – marsh sedge

COMPOSITAE composite family
   Iva frutescens – marsh elder (woody shrub)

PLUMBAGINACEAE leadwort family
   Limonium Nashii – sea lavender

PLANTAGINACEAE plantain family
   Plantago juncoides – seaside plantain

CHENOPODIACEAE goosefoot family
   Salicornia europaea – glasswort, goosefoot, samphire

ROSACEAE rose family
Rosa virginiana – common wild rose

JUNCAGINACEA arrowgrass family
Triglochin maritima – arrow grass

Persons Contacted for Information on Dyking, 1999 through 2003

No.	Name	Home Town
1	Allen, Jack	Grand Pré
2	Armstrong, Richard	Falmouth
3	Bishop, Avard	Greenwich
4	Bishop, Glenda	New Minas
5	Borden, James	Lower Canard
6	Bremner, James	Upper Falmouth
7	Brown, Irving S.	Chipman Corner
8	Curry, Frederick	Grand Pré
9	Eaton, Earnest	Upper Canard
10	Eaton, Malcolm	Jawbone Corner
11	Eldridge, James	Falmouth
12	Forsyth, Bradford	Aylesford
13	Frail, George	Centerville
14	Frail, Malcolm	Centerville
15	Fuller, Barbara	Grand Pré
16	Fuller, Burpee	Avonport
17	Fuller, Harlan	Grand Pré
18	Gertridge, Dean	Gaspereau
19	Gertridge, Ellis	Gaspereau
20	Gertridge, Randolph	Gaspereau
21	Hanson, Arnold	Canning
22	Harvey, Donald	Wolfville
23	Hennigar, Dean	Sheffield Mills
24	Herbin, John F.	Wolfville
25	Hovell, Charles	Kentville

No.	Name	Home Town
26	Kelly, Walter	Grand Pré
27	Knowles, David	Avondale
28	Knowles, Gordon	Avondale
29	Kolstee, Hank	Truro
30	Lawrence, Robert	Upper Falmouth
31	MacKinnon, Colin	Sackville, NB
32	Marchand, Jocelyne	Grand Pré
33	Millet, Lewis	New Minas
34	Muttart, Geoff	Kentville
35	O'Leary, Charles	White Rock
36	Palmeter, Jean	Grand Pré
37	Palmeter, Robert	Grand Pré
38	Peck, Ronald	Wolfville
39	Rand, Howard	Hillaton
40	Rand, Jon	Wellington Dyke
41	Rand, Marshall	Delhaven
42	Rogers, Basil	Hantsport
43	Russell, Miles	New Ross
44	Smith, Bernard	Greenwich
45	Van Buskirk, Charles	Wolfville
46	Van Buskirk, Roy	Greenwich
47	Walsh, Victor	New Minas
48	Weagle, Kenneth	Hantsport
49	Wood, Kevin	Kentville
50	Wylie, Robin	East LaHave

APPENDIX FOUR

Data Sheet: Tidal Marsh Sod-Cutting Spade

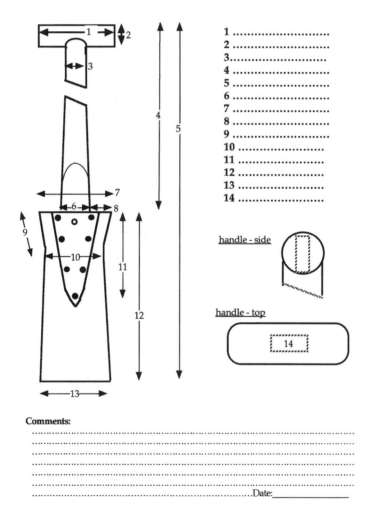

1 ....
2 ....
3...........................
4 ....
5 ....
6 ....
7 ....
8 ....
9 ....
10 ....
11 ....
12 ....
13 ....
14 ....

handle - side

handle - top

14

Comments:

....
....
....
....
....
....
....Date:_____

J. Crane's 1819 Article on Dyke Construction

ON DIKING
JONATHAN CRANE, *ACADIAN RECORDER*, 27 FEBRUARY 1819
(ANNOTATED, EDITED, AND INTERPRETED IN ITALICS)

Crane's Qualifications

I have attended the making of Dikes and Aboiteaus (A term used by the original French settlers, for a great Dam, in Diking) since the year 1764. *I was present when the first Aboiteau of any consequence was made here, by the English – which was superintended by two Frenchmen, and observed their proceedings.* I was appointed a Commissioner of Sewers in the year 1777, and having continued in that office ever since [1777–1819 – 42 years] it has given me an opportunity of improving a little, and I have been so fortunate as not to lose but very little *of my* labours. [Crane died in 1820.]

Construction of Access Roads, the Aboiteau, and Positioning of Sluices

Before an Aboiteau is commenced, if the Marsh is not dry and hard, it ought to be drained and made so. Roads *need to be* well causewayed to the place the Aboiteau is to be erected, and a clay bottom is the best foundation. *It* is proper to cut one or more broad ditches *up* on each side of the creek, where the Aboiteau is to be erected, from near the top of the bank to the *bottom* of the creek, *and thus expose any subterraneous veins of water that might undermine it. These lateral creek-bank ditches* should be ten feet wide and three feet deep, filled with brush, and sods being drove hard together. *This* will cause a strong adhesion of the Aboiteau to the bottom, and prevent the dike from slipping up or down the creek. If the creek is 100 feet over, and the tide rises 25 feet, to the top of the bank, the foundation of the

Aboiteau ought to be about 50 feet wide, and 30 feet wide at the top of the bank, before the running Dike is made,– if otherwise to be in that proportion; the sluice ought to be full as long as the Aboiteau is wide, although the work may be raised six feet before it is laid, as the end of the sluice ought to extend outside of the Dike a small distance – otherwise the discharge of the water may injure the Aboiteau; the higher the sluice is laid, the narrower the Aboiteau may be made, – for as high as the water lies, the upper side of the Aboiteau, it will be a counter-balance against the flood, to the same height. The Aboiteau ought to be built up about 10 feet over the sluice at each end, nearly perpendicular, to prevent the sluices from bending or breaking. From the laying of the Aboiteau, 'till it is raised about 5 feet, pickets ought to be drove plentifully through it, to prevent it from slipping, and to keep it firm to the bottom. But do not conceive pickets will do much good if they do not reach the foundation, for I never saw an Aboiteau slip up or down a creek, except at the foundation, even if it was much narrower than the *following* proportions. If the creek is 100 feet *wide at marsh level,* and the tide rises 25 feet, to the top of *that* bank, the foundation of the Aboiteau ought to be about 50 feet wide, and 30 feet wide at the top of the bank, before *any* running Dike is *built on top of it (about another 4 to 5 ft). If the measurements are other than the above, they should be at least in those* proportions.

The sluice ought to be full as long as the Aboiteau is wide, although the *base of the Aboiteau should be built up* six feet before *the sluice* is laid, as the end of the sluice ought to extend outside of the Dike a small distance, otherwise the discharge of the water may *undermine* the Aboiteau. [see p. 187 re need for a Sluice Apron]. The higher the sluice is laid *in the Aboiteau wall,* the narrower the Aboiteau may be made, *because* as high as the *impounded* water lies *on* the upper side of the Aboiteau, it will *serve as* a counter-balance against the *pressure of the* flood *tide,* to the same height. [These freshwater ponds served to water cattle in summer and as a source of ice blocks in winter.] The *inner and outer* Aboiteau *faces* ought to be built up *for* about 10 feet over the *end of each* sluice at each end, nearly perpendicular, to prevent the sluices from bending or breaking *during storms or from ice block scouring.*

Sluice Construction

The bigness of the sluice ought to be in proportion to the freshwater that is to pass through it, and ought to be made of large hewn timber joined well together, covered at the top and bottom with plank *set* into the timber *and* then sheathed with boards, for if it leaks but a little, it may in time be the means of ruining the Aboiteau. I have known several to be rebuilt on account of their leaking, particularly about the sluice. *The sluice* ought to be laid in a level bed of sods, with fine brush, from end to end, *as well as* bundles of fascines [faggots, sticks] under the end pointing *to* the sea) *so* that it may settle straight. *There* ought to be two gates [hanging clapper valves] put in near the end of the sluice, fronting the sea, *but* braced open until the Aboiteau is finished. The rollers [rods] *by* which they hang, ought to be *set well into* the plank or timber *so* that any thing passing through the sluice may not strike them, otherwise the gates may be carried away. There ought also to be *an additional* temporary gate hung at the *very* end of the sluice, next *to* the sea, so reversed to *the* others, that it may let in the water on the flood, and retain it on the ebb. *This should be maintained until* the Aboiteau is finished, except there should be occasion to draw off the water before that time. *Thus* the creek *will have, or could have,* water *trapped* in it as high as the *height of the* Aboiteau *at each stage of construction. Thus, on each tide,* there will be no greater *volume* to fill than *the elevation added to* the Aboiteau each *day.* Whereas, if the water is let out of the creek *during each ebb,* there may not be enough *volume running* through the sluice on *each* flood to fill the creek *at the same rate that the sea level is rising up the sea face of the aboiteau. If, for this reason,* much water runs over the *top of the incomplete* Aboiteau *from the sea side,* it may be damaged and *then* endangered.

Temporary Securing of Construction in Progress

The Aboiteau *construction* ought to be carried up nearly in the *same* shape *as that* of the creek, or *in other words,* lowest in the centre *above the creek bed.* It will then require but little securing, *for* when the water is retained above *by the reversed sluice gate,* then on the flood tide enough *additional water* will soon run in *via the sluice,* that it will be as high inside as outside, *and* the danger is then over for that tide. Before securing, [for overnight, before storms, during days of very high monthly or biweekly spring tides] particular care should be taken that the *top face of the* Aboiteau should be highest in the middle or *at the upstream* side, at least 3 feet higher than the outside [seaside face; but Crane does not indicate the degree of the slope from that height]. *This slope is necessary because if heavy waves on the* flood *tide* break at the outside *edge of the Aboiteau wall, they* will be very apt to lift both brush and sods, and injure the Aboiteau. *However,* if the water breaks *on a slope* at the centre *of a wide Aboiteau,* or upper side of *a narrow* Aboiteau, the water may rather press down the front part [recall the long sloping sea walls of Holland that are used to dissipate storms waves]. Before securing, the sods ought to be levelled and pressed well together. *The* securing ought to be of spruce brush, beginning at the upper part of the Aboiteau, laying the tops of the brush over the side close together, to protect the sods from *the scouring of* running of the water. *For* the next course [row], the top ends of the brush ought to be put over the butt ends of the first course, and so continued (like the laying of shingles) to the side fronting the sea. *Each course of* brush is then crossed *with a* long pole, then cross-staked well drove in, and withed [bound] together. *As well,* several long poles or spars ought to be put over the front part adjoining the sea, fastening the butt ends with chains or ropes to some large spruce logs, that may be covered at least 6 or 7 feet with sods [surely not 7 ft deep with sods! Perhaps 6 or 7 ft of the length of the log was buried by sods]. The *upward projecting* small ends of the spars to be *bent down* over the Aboiteau, and then fastened with cross-stakes and *bound*. This is the most speedy and efficient security *procedure to protect the construction* at the front of the Aboiteau.

Incorporation of Brush During Construction

*When secured, t*he work at the centre, or upper part of the Aboiteau, should never be more than a foot higher than the upper edge of *the Aboiteau because* when the tide goes out, the Teams ought to commence working near the upper edge, to stop the *flow of impounded* water, otherwise the whole *top surface of the Aboiteau* may be wet for hours. *To prevent the teams from miring when first driving over where the water runs across the aboiteau, a* considerable quantity of salt hay or spruce brush limbs ought to be mixed with sods.

Too much wood or brush is ruinous to Aboiteaus, yet they cannot be made without a considerable quantity, which principally answers two purposes, the one to keep the work from spreading *and collapsing* [this happened in August 1929 at the nearly completed Alison aboiteau on the Wickwire Dyke], the other is, that the butts of the brush being placed toward the sea defends the Aboiteau from the sea and ice. *They must be laid their full length, such* that if the ice freezes to any part of them, they may not be drawn out of the Aboiteau. Should short poles be laid in front without limbs, the ice may not only pull them out, but a part of the aboiteau may follow. It requires much more brush at front side than the inner side of the Aboiteau.

Begin New Dikes by Building Largest Aboiteau First

If there is a large quantity of Marsh to Dike *and* there are many Aboiteaus to be built, and it is not probable *that* the largest one can be finished between two high tides [does he mean two weeks or two days?] be sure *to* make the large before the small ones. The bad effects of pursuing the opposite mode have been recently experienced here. [He may be referring to the Wickwire Great Discharge aboiteau of 1806 that was put in last and washed away on spring tides before it reached full height]. The small Aboiteaus and running Dikes were principally first made *and* the large one was not finished before a very high tide. *The rising waters topped the Aboiteau and the tidal* vacuity was so great on the inside of the Aboiteau, that *with each successive high tide* the water *ran* over with great force until the marsh was *filled* as high inside as outside, *which occurred only after a considerable period of ebb. During the remainder of the ebb, water ran over the Aboiteau from off* the marsh, until the next flood tide, *when the same destructive sequences were repeated,* and the Aboiteau *was* carried away. *These cascading waters created* a large chasm below, the size of about half an acre, which cost thousands of pounds to fill up, *and* to plaister up the Aboiteau. *The Aboiteau had been* made with so much timber and brush, laid in all directions, without a sufficiency of sods. *It* leaked in sundry places, nearly enough to turn a mill. Whereas if the large aboiteau had been made properly at first, *even though it was* not finished before a course of high tides, the water that came over the marsh at other places *that were devoid of running dykes* would have gone out the same way, and there would have been no such continued *concentrated* torrent *over the top of* the great Aboiteau.

In summary, if an Aboiteau cannot be raised within three feet as high as the marsh before a high tide *series (full or new moon)*, it is best to have it secured, and not attempt to carry up a running Dike on it, as much has been lost by *attempting just that.*

Work Teams and Organization

Three men and a boy, to drive a Team [of oxen or horses?] is a proper number for each *sledge or cart* that carries a ton of sod. All the men working at the Aboiteau, *should* put by their tools, etc., and carry brush when required. Each man to place their respective loads where directed, as generally the Teams and all other work stops while a course of brush is laying. Much judgment and dexterity is required in making Aboiteaus, in keeping the loaded and empty teams in a regular train, and *ensuring* other labour *is* advantageously performed; *it is* as *demanding as it is* to arrange and discipline a battalion of men, or *to supervise* men attending a fire engine.

Apron to Receive Sluice Discharge

The apron *built* to receive the discharge of water from a sluice ought to be made of bundles of fascines [faggots, poles, sticks] and stones, well *constructed* under the mouth of the sluice, *and* adjoining the Aboiteau.

Construction of Running Dike

A running Dike ought to be made 12 or 14 feet *wide* at the bottom. If the Dike is made 4 feet high and 3 feet broad at the top, it ought to slope at least 10 degrees *less steeply* in the front than *on* the inner side. *A longer slope* will cause the Dike to settle better *from the* weight of water lying on it, and if sods *do* wash out of the Dike, it *will* not fall down *from the undermining*, and the salt grass will be more apt to grow on it well. *A lesser* slope will do *on the* inside of the Dike and, not being much exposed, the frost grass will soon grow on it. *All* sods ought to be drove well together in the middle of the Dike, otherwise it will leak, and not stand its shape, and may be all carried away – which was the fate of Dikes lately made here [where and when?]. Care should be taken in cutting and laying the front sods, to suit the shape of the Dike, *and* the sods ought to be laid so as to break joints, like laying of bricks – the Dike ought not to be laid within two feet of the *borrow* Ditches on each side of it.

Repairs, Blocking Sluices, Creek-to-Creek Connecting Canals

The repairing of old Aboiteaus and old Sluices, stopping up Sluices, and carrying the water from one Aboiteau through another *via canals* have been performed about the Grand Prairie [where and when?], to great advantage, and *have avoided* the enormous expense of making new ones.

JONATHAN CRANE, Horton, Feb. 4, 1819.

SUMMARY OF CRANE'S ARTICLE

Crane, Jonathan. 1819. "On Diking" This long article dated Horton, Feb. 4, 1819, and published in the *Acadian Recorder* of 27 Feb 1819, contains detailed construction information. The author had been in charge of local dyking since 1777 as Commissioner of Sewers. As a youth he watched dykes being constructed by the English and Acadians in 1764 when repairs were made to the 1759 breachings.

Crane's descriptions of how dykes and aboiteaux were constructed
Abstract and sketches by S. Bleakney, April 1997.

Aboiteau Wall Construction (see following sketches)
  1. A trench, termed a "key" is dug on the slope of the creek from the top of the bank down to the centre of the creek, from each side. Each trench is about 10 ft wide and 3 ft deep and packed with brush and sods.
  2. Posts are driven into this "key" to project 5 ft above it and the aboiteau dyke wall built up and over them. This anchors the wall so that it will not slide up or down the creek bed when water saturated or when pressured by either rainwater backup from one side or high tides on the sea side.
  3. The key trenches also serve to expose any hidden underground veins (water channels) that might eventually undermine the aboiteau wall.
  4. The aboiteau is built up nearly in the shape of the cross-section of the creek bed, in other words in a V-pattern, not as a flat wall.
  5. The aboiteau is built first, then the running dyke wall, otherwise all the waters from higher tides must pass through the unfinished aboiteau gap, and that rush of cascading water can tear the construction apart. It is best to allow the waters to flood in over the marsh and fill in behind any still under-construction aboiteaux. To enhance this back-filling technique, the permanent sea-excluding sluice-box valves are propped open and a reversed clapper valve is installed in the sluice box during construction to capture and retain sea water and thereby maintain a head pond behind the rising aboiteau wall.

Aboiteau Sluice Box Location (see sketches)

1. The higher the sluice box is located in the wall, the narrower the wall base and top can be. This is because any freshwater pond behind the wall counterbalances the thrust from sea water on the outside of the wall.

2. Sluice boxes were set on a brush and clay base, built up to about 6 ft above the creek bed so that the outflow would shoot away from the wall base and not undermine it. This vulnerable area was also well reinforced with posts, brush, and rocks.

3. The exposed ends of the sluice boxes were kept short so as not to get bent or broken, and were further protected by building up the wall above them nearly perpendicular for a height of up to 10 ft (says Crane, but that seems a rather considerable height) before stepping the construction back to establish the final width and slope of the remaining seawall construction.

4. A 30 ft wide road on top of an aboiteau wall was about maximum, where a creek was 25 ft deep and 160 ft from bank top to bank top.

Securing an Aboiteau Under Construction Against Flood Tides and Spring Tides

1. As construction of an aboiteau barrier progressed, it could be flooded during high tides at night and especially during monthly spring tides. The unfinished top of the dyke was vulnerable to storm action and appropriate preventative action was taken.

2. Daily construction proceeded such that the upstream top side of the barrier was as much as 3 ft higher than the sea-side lip. Applied to this was a protective shingle-type, back-to-front, layering of brush or small trees and sods (see sketch); thus wave action breaking at the face of the wall could not peel off the top layers of fill and sod.

3. For longer than overnight security, such as during week-long extreme spring-tide phases, poles were laid parallel to the wall axis and thus across the lines of trees (brush) and then staked down to stabilize the open surface of the top of the wall (see sketch). All this was removed prior to continuing the construction.

4. At certain tidal times, and probably on the more exposed shore lines, additional measures were taken to secure what had been accomplished. Long spar poles were laid vertically up against the faces of the wall, and then anchored to logs at the front base of the wall. The slender ends of the spar poles extended up beyond the top of the wall, and these ends were then hauled down with ropes and staked/anchored into the top or back of the dyke wall. All this had to be removed before the next construction bout.

Running Dyke Construction

1. Dyke walls on the high marsh could be built rather low, as this was an elevation affected only by the higher tides. Such walls were typically 12–14 ft wide at the base, about 4 to 5 ft high and a 2 to 3 ft wide top with a narrow foot path.

1. Aspects of aboiteau construction

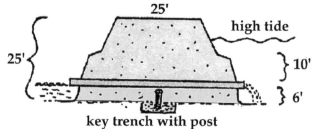

25'

high tide

25'

10'

6'

key trench with post

30'

15'

high tide

heights of
head ponds

B

A

sluices were as
long as base of
aboiteau, but often
placed higher up

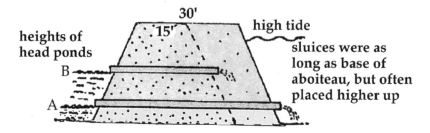

2. Securing unfinished construction against tidal action

anti-erosion tree brush layer
with poles
staked
down

exposed
sea side
of wall

sod facing, land side

poles
staked
down

tree brush
"shingles"

sod facing, sea side

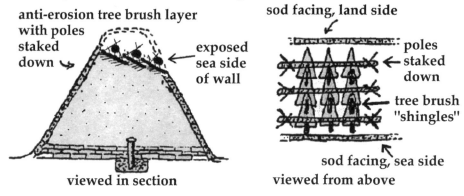

viewed in section

viewed from above

3. Crane's recommended slopes for dyke walls that lessens forces of breaking waves, helps compact sods, is not easily undercut, and the lesser slope encourages growth of the sod grasses

solid line is section of Crane's
Acadian type wall

3'

dotted line is of a
symmetrical dyke wall

borrow pit
trench

4'

sea
level

12'

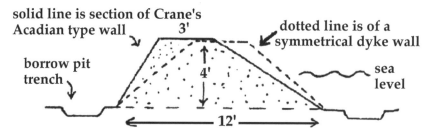

2. Sods were laid across the width of the wall, at least near the base, and pounded in firmly to create a solid interlocking foundation. The sod bricks were laid in the bricklayer's alternating pattern, so as to break joints.

3. Trenches were dug on both sides of the wall, as sources for sods and rough fill. These were termed "borrow trenches" and were never nearer than 2 ft to the base of the dyke wall.

4. The front slope of the wall was some 10 degrees less on the sea side. That longer gentler slope had important functions: the sod binding chord grasses grew poorly on steep slopes; the tidal water pressed down on the wall, packing it more firmly; and if storms did tear out sods, the wall would tend not to undermine and collapse.

A steeper slope on the inner sides of the dyke wall was acceptable because upland species of field grasses readily grew on it, forming new turf and root systems.

APPENDIX SIX

J.F. Herbin's 1911 Notes Concerning the West Marsh

This is a transcript of hand-written notes found in a school scribbler in a box of original material belonging to John Frederic Herbin. It is part of a major donation by the family, housed in the Acadia University Esther Clark Wright Archives.

Fifteen pages pertain to the planning and execution of the first dyke wall extending from Wolfville to Long Island, an area usually referred to as the Wickwire Dyke. His information must have come from the original Minute Book of Proprietors of the West Marsh, a ledger now lost. Because Herbin tended to confuse numbers, I have annotated in italics parts of the text, but I have not changed his original spellings, which can vary from page to page, and are often phonetic. Words that are difficult to decipher are in italics and followed by a question mark. The crossed-out words are as they appear in his notes. His notes are in a Yarmouth Old Home Week Scribbler, dated July 1911, which has on the cover a photograph of Yarmouth Academy and the words "A Bright Spot in The Future." Children's drawings appear on the first two pages, but three pages at the front and back have been torn out.

Herbin wrote his notes starting at the back of the scribbler with it upside down. His first page is numbered 4, so presumably the torn-out pages contained information leading up to the planning of the dyke in 1804.

Beginning on page 4:
On October 20th 1904 *(should be 1804)* the propretors of the West Marsh (~~now known as Wickwire Dike~~) *(this is his crossing out)* agreed to dike in their marsh. The parties to this agreement and the acres owned were as follows –

Wm Eagles	9 acres
Abizah Scott	6
George Johnsong	6

Israil Harding	11 ½
Joseph Allen	4
Elijah Fowler	4 ½
Jason Forsyth	10
Davis Harris	40
Abel Benjamin	3 ½
John DeWolf	20
Jacob Benjamin	17
Jeremy Kinne	6
James Duncanson	4

Page 5

John Moss *[or Noss?]*	5 ½ acres
John Davis	5
Tainl *[?]* Reed	1 ¾
Perez Martin	17
John Coldwell	15
Eliphalet Coldwell	17
Stephn Benjamin	12
~~Abram Benjamin~~	~~12~~
Abram Duncarsly	8 ½
Elisha DeWolf	10
Elijah Forsyth	2 ½
Daniel DeWolf	20
Theodore Harding	½
Jonathan Crane	12
Samuel Avery	4 ½
Robert Crow	6
Robert Laird	33
John Coldwell	24
John Coldwell	22
Mary Hill	30
Benjamin Cleavland	6

Page 6 (the back of which has math calculations)

Cyprian Davison	2
Robert Lowrie	6
John Palmator	16
Caleb Forsyth	30
~~Wm~~ Marsh	————
Wm Muhall Wallace	20
	460 ¾

On Feb 5th 1805 Israel Harding was appointed clerk Elijah Fowler moderator and George Johnson, David Harris and Caleb Forsyth Commissioners of Sewers. The last three to receive not more than six shillings a day for their services. Several meetings of the proprietors of the ~~dik~~ West Marsh were held during the year 1805. Tenders had been made by most of the Marsh owners for the supply of brush, stakes and *binders [?]* for building the sluices.

Page 7

On the 9th of April 1805 at a meeting at Forsyth's corner at the N. E. corner of the marsh near the Grand-Pré the work of building the dike was let to the lowest bidders in sections, ~~as follows each sections to be~~ of 12 rods or 8 rods in length, ~~to be~~ 15 ½ feet on the bottom and 3 feet wide on top, and to be completed by Oct. 1st then to settle for three months and to be made "full measure" before taken over by the commissioners. The running dike was let out in 26 lots of 12 rods each and 28 lots of 8 rods each in length. The bids ran from eleven ~~pounds shillings per rod to~~ to 21 shillings per rod. Extra work of filling up ditches and leveling up low places and building & setting of small sluices ran as high as forty shillings per rod.

Page 10 [there is no evidence of pages 8 and 9 having been torn out]

At this meeting a dispute was aroused in regard to the location of the aboiteau across the Great Discharge Creek, some favoring a point opposite the island, over the *sogor [?]* or false channel of the island. Others favored the site at the shad wier higher up. The majority approved the proposal to build at the island so called. Mr George Johnson thereupon declined to act as Commissioner.

   At a meeting on July 1st, 1805, ~~at the Coldwell in Horton house Daniel~~ (Elisha DeWolf, Moderator, Daniel DeWolf, Clerk) Timothy Bishop was appointed to act with the commissioners, and it was decided that the "abatoe" across the Rogers Creek be build before haying season.

Page 11

On Sep. 3, 1805 *[the 5 is written over a 6]* the place of the arboteau across the Great Discharge was again voted upon and decided as before.

   Brush, pickets, & binders were tendered for.

   Finally on Dec. 27 1805 *[again the 5 is over a 6]* the transactions of the meeting of Nov. 8th being declared recinded, the matter was ~~finally~~ definitely settled as to the various parts of the work yet to be done; Jason Forsyth acting as Moderator Daniel DeWolf Clerk.

   James Graham Jr. bid off the Great Discharge sluice work. This was to be 60 feet long with a partition forming two water courses 3 ½ x 2 feet built of 10 inch timber with two gates of oak, to cost in all £45.15 –

Page 12

The Palmeter Creek sluice with single water course, and 45 feet long was let to ~~James Graham Jr for £45.15~~ Daniel DeWolf for £12.10.

Forsyth Creek sluice, 35 feet long, went to Benjamin Davison for £2:5.

Allison Creek sluice 345 feet long was bid off by Danl DeWolf £12:2.6.

Lowrey Creek sluice went to Abizah Scott at £2:0 to be 35 feet long.

Seven more pages in the Yarmouth Scribbler follow. The first page, in pencil and not numbered, consists of scraps of information, most of which have a bracketed page reference that starts at p.43 and skips along to p.168. They may refer to a dykeland tax rates/accounting book. One note is "rates begin 1911," but this must be 1811, for he mentions 1816 as well as Oliver Lyman, the surveyor who produced the 1808 map of the newly dyked West Marsh.

Three pages numbered 1 to 3 follow. They are the start of a history of the Wickwire Dike, but the writing stops in mid-sentence. Did he ever finish this? Are there any ms pages in boxes or even excerpts published?

The final three pages are a list of dykeland owners and their acreages, and the acreage of the Commons on the dyke.

New page re history   ~~History of a~~   (1)

The Wickwire Dike

On Nov. 15, 1803 *[1808 on the original map]* Oliver Lyman, deputy surveyer, ~~had~~ completed a survey of the West Marsh, for the propretors, who were about to build a dike to enclose their land, in all about 637 acres *[687 on map]*. The plan he made shows the lots, roads, and creeks; gives the names of the owners, and states the number of acres owned by each proprietor.

The marsh, extending from Mud Creek to the division dike of the Grand Pré at Long Island, was known as the West Marsh. After the dike was built

Page 2 of history   (2)

It was known as the New Dike; and is now called the Wickwire Dike.

The account of the building of this new dike begun in 1805 is interesting, ~~showing the names~~ because of the names of the men ~~the~~ who owned the land ~~and built the dike~~ over a century ago. Also because of the details the dike records give of the cost and labor entailed in an undertaking of this kind. The length of the dike built to protect 637 acres was roughly, 3168 yards *[in fact it was 5168]* exclusive of the width of five large creeks ~~diked across. The total length of the dike built was almost two miles.~~ which added made almost two miles.

Page 3 of history

~~From time~~   (3)

During a century the Wickwire Dike has lost a hundred acres of land because of the encroachin action of the tide in cutting down the marshes and undermining the dikes

~~There are today 5~~

On the back of this page are detailed calculations for the numbers on the following page with the page number 12 used for the second time.
~~258~~

Secondary page 12

It was estimated that ~~for~~ the material for the arboiteaux would cost £540: 13: 12 to consist of 2600 loads of brush; 23000 12-feet pickets; and 600 binders over 25 ft. long. This cost added to the total amount of bids for building the dikes made up ~~about~~ over

~~12~~ £1200. This estimate did not include ~~the pur~~ construction of the arboiteaux which ~~was no doubt a costly to~~ added considerably to the whole cost.

The final three pages are in pencil and list forty-five names with acreages. They are obviously copied directly from the 1808 map prepared by Oliver Lyman, but because Herbin's writing and spelling has so many mistakes and omissions, I copied the names directly from the same map. Thus, the following is the only page not *an exact textual replication of Herbin's notes, but uses the spelling recorded on Lyman's map.*

	acres/	10ths/	rods
Robert Leard	30.	4.	8
Samuel Leard	11.	8.	11
Davison	2.	3.	8
Joseph Allen	4.	6.	8
William Hill	25.	13.	14
Samuel Avery	5.	8.	8
Josiah Bennet	5.	6.	2
Doctor Webster	9.	2.	11
James Minor	7.	6.	3
Common Land	24.	19.	6
George Bishop	21.	1.	8
Jason Forsyth	12.	1.	14
Abel Harris	8.	2.	0
Minors Davis & Phelps	19.	2.	0
Robert Lowrie	5.	3.	3
Amos Rathbun	14.	7.	7
Jesall Harding &	18.	0.	6
Joseph Johnson			
Charles Brown	19.	5.	10
[Herbin missed "Brown"]			
John Coldwell	22.	8.	6

David Harris	57.	7.	0
William Wallace	20.	3.	10
John Turner	6.	5.	9
Thomas Solme	14.	6.	5
Eliphalet Coldwell	18.	19.	15
George Johnson	23.	2.	7
James Duncanson	3.	1.	2
John Davis	11.	16.	15
Aaron Cleaveland	14.	10.	0
John Moss	6.	7.	0
Abraham Duncasley	3.	1.	2
John DeWolf	19.	6.	11
Daniel DeWolf	6.	14.	18
Caleb Forsyth	31.	7.	3
Jason & Caleb Forsyth	21.	9.	8
William Eagles	7.	6.	15
Jeramiah Harris	7.	7.	5
Elijah Fowler	4.	6.	8
Jacob Benjamin	10.	9.	11
Diah Wickwire	11.	9.	8
Perez Martin	20.	7.	8
Zebediah Wickwire	21.	0.	4
Round Rogers Dyke	5.	0.	0
Stephon DeWolf	13.	7.	12
Benjamin Cleaveland	16.	0.	11.
John Coldwell	14.	9.	8
small lots	44.	15.	0
small lots	7	7	9 [???]

Plowing Patterns for Crowning Dykelands
Evident in 1940 and 1960 Aerial Photos of Grand Pré Dykelands

Aerial survey photos that include dykeland areas originally plowed by means of horses or oxen show a pattern of parallel lines spaced apart by thirty or more feet. The visual effect from the photos is one of plowed fields with gigantic furrows. In cases where dyke walls have been moved back or where they have simply been abandoned and the sea has been flooding the area for decades, the original parallel plowing pattern is still evident from the air, even though at ground level they may be obscured by tall tidal marsh grasses.

The reason for these widely spaced lines is the plowing technique used by farmers for low wet land. To enhance runoff and drainage, they plowed narrow sections of fields such that the furrow sods of the right and left halves were thrown towards the middle and away from the outer boundary of each section. This gradually raised, or crowned, the field along its central axis and at the same time created a drainage ditch between each section. These ditches are the parallel lines in the aerial photos.

Today, crowning of dykeland fields is done on a mega scale using heavy machinery. In well-drained upland fields, the plowing pattern differs, the goal being to create flat fields with few ditches, to retain as much moisture as possible.

The following diagram is not to scale, but it does illustrate the furrow sequence pattern involved at these adjacent field sections, as first described to me by Avard Bishop of Greenwich, Kings County, Nova Scotia.

How plowing proceeds on flat fields to create a higher central ridge, the crown, and the lower ditch area between each unit, the dale ditch. The cultivated area is the dale.

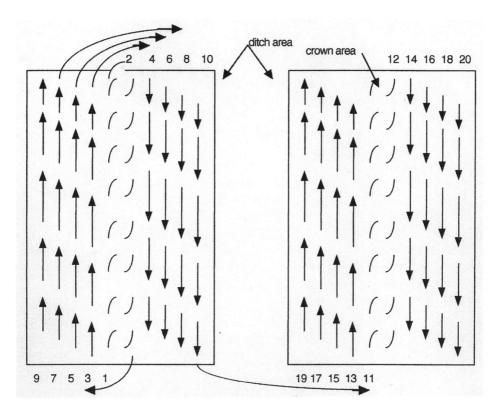

Plowing of field starts off-centre at row 1 and furrows turn sod over to the right.

APPENDIX EIGHT

"Deportation Creek" and the Iron Cross Memorial:
Fact or Fiction

1. As the aboiteau at Horton Landing was completed prior to 1755, then the deportation must have been from the Gaspereau River bank, not from a wharf far up the historically recognized "Deportation Creek."

Undoubtedly, that wide, deep creek was at one time an important and well-used navigational and economic component of the Acadian settlement. But was it functional in 1755?

J.F. Herbin (1911, 4th ed.) contains the following references:

page 40, a reference to a November 1710 landing party that came up the creek;

page 53, a reference that in 1720 trading vessels of 40–50 tons ran up the creek to the village;

page 60–1, a reference from 1732 stating that "nearly all available marsh land has been dyked."

Any areas not yet dyked could have been either the west end (the future Wickwire marsh) or the southeast corner (the future Dead Dyke marsh). Regardless of which one, there is a time frame of 23 years (1732–55) in which to build an aboiteau at Horton Landing.

It is evident in Figure 9.1.2 that the aboiteau was functioning in 1755, which means that deportation of Acadians from the head of that historic creek was an impossibility.

2. A map of 1760 by Charles Morris, of the plot of Horton Township, has the old dyke walls indicated, but at the mouth of the creek in question is the notation "Broken Boit de Eau" (Fig. 9.1.2). The broken aboiteau could have been destroyed in the November storm of 1759 that breached many other sites in the Grand Pré area.

3. If the Acadians built dykes according to the methods recorded in J. Crane's detailed account of 1819 – and there is no reason to doubt his sagacity after forty-two years of experience as a Commissioner of Sewers – then the aboiteau was built first and the lateral running dyke walls were constructed afterwards.

Thus, if the dyke walls were there, as depicted on all the circa 1760 maps, then the aboiteau must have been functioning in 1755, and therefore the Iron Cross is not located at the true site of deportation.

4. If we assume that the Dead Dyke Marsh area had been reclaimed by the Acadians by the 1740s, then that straight road into the marsh and the plots to each side of it are not such a landscape anomaly after all – they were farmed fields.

But why so many small lots (in the order of one acre) in an area that we had been considering undisturbed tidal marsh? The lot sizes in other salt-hay areas tend to be much larger. Jonathan Fowler suggested to me that the plots in this area are a Planter administrative expediency used to top up share acreages to the official total per settler.

5. Can we assume that most of the lots on those 1760 maps were simply copies of field margins long established by the Acadians? Probably yes, because the plowing patterns (crowning-drainage) are confined by the patterns of the original tidal creeks. Supporting this hypothesis is the fact that the shapes of fields on the 1760 map match those on the 1963 aerial photos, so they must have had considerable integrity since first dyked. After all, once plowed and crowned, it would be pointless for the Planters to rearrange all that soil in a contrary direction.

6. In 1760 or 1761 a map was prepared by John Bishop Jr, consisting of nine small survey sketches of all the parcels of land owned by Theofilus Sutherland of Horton Township. These map items precisely match the fields plotted on the large 1760 Grand Pré map and are particularly valuable for the unusual information included. The lot boundaries are often labelled as to whether they are a road, dyke wall, or creek.

7. The name Dead Dyke appears on the Theo. Sutherland map as "A plan of one acre in the Dead Dyke as Sizeing." So this name was not, as I have often suggested, first used about 100 years later, in the 1850s, when the aboiteau was finally "completed," thus creating a long, curved Dead Dyke wall on the west side of the marsh. On some old E. Graham photographic postcards, that dyke wall is referred to as the French Dyke, but H. Cameron labelled it Dead Dyke on his 1956 map.

Possibly, in 1760, the dyke wall along the riverbank was considered "dead" by the Planters because it was non-functional, since it lacked an aboiteau, and thus the enclosed area behind it became the Dead Dyke tidal marsh. Or perhaps the Planters saw that the southeast enclosure had recently been farmed, but was now dead from salt-water incursions, and they named the area appropriately.

With the advent of a new aboiteau (circa 1814 or 1850), its builders organized themselves as the Proprietors of Dead Dyke Marsh, an association separate from the Proprietors of Grand Pré Marsh; this arrangement seems not to have been generally realized, but it is evident in the records of the old Minute Books. It lasted into the late 1890s, at which time it was finally absorbed by the Grand Pré regional marsh body association.

It seems reasonable to assume that the newly reclaimed marsh would be named Dead Dyke Marsh precisely because that local name was already long established. Otherwise, why was it not named Horton Landing Marsh or some similar appropriate designation?

8. Have historians been misled by the fact that for many years the Acadians did use the so-called "Deportation Creek" and had built wharves there? If the storm of 1759 removed the aboiteau, then the topographic configuration would have reverted to that of earlier historical accounts and subsequent narratives possibly fitted to it.

I had been thoroughly influenced by H. Cameron's annotated map of 1956, by the consensus that dyke construction was a long slow process, and by the assumption that the Acadians were only in the process of completing their new dyke and aboiteau at Horton Landing, and were deported just before the final stage of inserting an aboiteau. I now believe that dyking proceeded rapidly and was more extensive than depicted on the 1760 Planter map, which I had naturally assumed was the outer limit of Acadian dyking. However, the accumulating new geographic evidence (Horton shale at the site of Black Landing, and the original location of the narrow Gaspereau River channel), coupled with the aboiteau-built-first concept, and further support from recent analysis of historical documents by Jonathan Fowler, lead easily to the conclusion that the Acadians had completed the Horton Landing dyke and aboiteau years before the deportation, and had even built an access road to the farmed fields in the central block of that marsh (Fig. 9.1.3).

9. If the riverbank is the site of the Deportation, and if some of the artifacts found there are their abandoned goods, then should not this area be obtained as a further adjunct of the Grand Pré National Historic Park? Preliminary work indicates the likelihood of forts and other types of dwellings just beneath the surface at this general site.

10. The following research may lead to definitive answers to the above:

• Reexamine historical accounts of the 1730–70 era in particular, searching for any references to wharves, creeks, riverbanks, and aboiteaux.

- Core the soil of Dead Dyke marshland. Plant material and foram shells will differentiate marine habitat from crop land in the vertical sequences. From today's surface to the 1814 or 1850s level there will be evidence of crop land. If everything beneath that level is marine, then the aboiteau was never completed by the Acadians. However, if there is a narrow crop-land layer representing perhaps 1735–59, then the Iron Cross Memorial is (barring some other explanation) quite definitely misplaced.

Source List for Early Aerial Photos, 1931–1967
Eastern Kings Co., Nova Scotia: Wolfville and Grand Pré Districts

Index	Frame Nos.	Year	Day/ Month	Scale	Altitude	Comments
A-3619	-4-3-	1931	5 July	1:16,000	10500	These do not include
A-3624	-12-20-	1931	5 July	1:16,000	10400	areas east of Wolfville
A-3624	-86-91	1931	5 July	1:16,000	10400	
A-3625	-38-41	1931	5, 6, 7 July	1:16,000	10500	Wolfville
A-3625	-44-42	1931	5, 6, 7 July	1:16,000	10500	
A-3620	80-91	1931	7 July	1:16,000	10600	
A-4368	-37-42-	1931	30 Sept.	1:16,000	10300	
A-8719	98-	1945	27 July	1:17,000	11745	Kingsport
A-8645	-50-56-	1945	24 July	1:17,000	11200	Oak Island – Wolfville
A-8646	-40-50-	1945	24 July	1:17,000	11200	Wolfville – Blue Beach
A-8646	89-90-91	1945	24 July	1:17,000	11200	
A-8647	-5-1	1945	24 July	1:17,000	11200	
A-10178	1-10-	1946	6 July	1:17,000	11200	Boot Is. – Evangeline Beach
A-13949	25-40	1953	16 Oct.	1:30,000	16100	
A-15150	65-68	1955	9 Dec.	1:30,000	16000	
A-14661	82-88	1955	19 June	1:16,000	8300	Grand Pré – Oak Island
A-14668	13	1955	27 June	1:16,000	8300	Boot Island
RR 942-38	Wolfville dykes	1956	14 Nov.	1:40,000	19000	*Spartina patens* patches
A-16318	177-181	1958	16 Aug.	1:6,000	3625	

Index	Frame Nos.	Year	Day/ Month	Scale	Altitude	Comments
A-16535	-32-30-	1959	12 June	1:40,000	20000	
A-16759	-35-	1959	9 Sept.	1:40,000	20000	
A-17554	69-70-8	1962	6, 7 May	1:25,000	12100	Wolfville
A-18060	-59-61-	1963	25 May	1:36,000	18000	Extreme low tide 8–9 A.M.
A-18059	118	1963	25 May	1:36,000	18000	Blomidon
A-18261	30-37	1963	1 Oct.	1:36,000	18000	Blomidon – Cape Split
A-19985	90-190	1967	28 June	1:16,000	8200	
A-19986	80	1967	29 June	1:16,000	8200	Hantsport
A-19982	9-34	1967	14 June	1:16,000	8200	
A-19985	-166-170	1967	15 Aug.	1:16,000	8200	
A-20234	-16-	1967	3 Oct.	1:16,000	8200	Kingsport

National Air Photo Library, 615 Booth Street, Ottawa, Ont., K1A 0E9

N.S. Dept. Lands and Forests – Infrared Series, Sept. 1975, Line 7–8, Roll 75551-2. 1"= 1 mile.

Pulsifer Brothers Aerial Photos (out of Windsor, NS in 1950s). Dozens of photos at Geology Dept, Acadia University, deduced to be 1952. Special low-level series flown for Professor Harcourt Cameron. Stamped on back "N.S. Research Foundation Aerial Photograph Library, Halifax, N.S." Negatives ended up, years ago, at Atlantic Air Survey, Dartmouth; probably no longer extant.

World War II and Grand Pré, October–November 1940
The 1940 Near Miss as a Target Range

The following is a condensed version of the astounding series of events of a three-week period in the autumn of 1940. An overwhelming majority of proprietors of Grand Pré dykelands voted in favour of selling Grand Pré, Long Island, and Boot Island to the War Department in Ottawa, if the price was right.

My personal interpretation is that short-term financial gain blinded a greedy majority, who actually promoted an event that would have displaced fifteen farm families and would have saturated the Grand Pré terrain with unexploded munitions rendering any future plowing extremely hazardous.

1. *The Wolfville Acadian* headline, Thursday 24 October 1940
    Grand Pré Farmers Oppose Taking Dykelands for Military Purposes
    It was learned over the weekend that:
    1.1 The federal government wanted to use Grand Pré for military purposes and that they already had detailed procedural plans formulated.
    1.2 Two British technical experts had selected Grand Pré as an ideal site for an artillery range as it had no trees to clear, was flat, had an adjacent railway line, and was backed by open ocean.
    1.3 An artillery range would be set up as a training and munitions proving ground.
    1.4 Heavy gun emplacements would be built on the Wickwire Dyke east of Wolfville.
    1.5 The dykelands and Long Island and Boot Island would become target areas.
    1.6 All fifteen families within the area north of the railway line would be removed.
    1.7 The practice range would be one mile wide at Wolfville, three miles wide at the west end, and extend outwards for ten miles.

2. Special Meeting held on Monday 21 October, chaired by Dr M.R. Elliot

   2.1 The farmers considered the land more valuable as wartime food and fodder acreage, and would strongly prefer that the Government find another site.

   2.2 If there were no alternative, they would not thwart wartime plans, but they would *expect adequate compensation* for shutting down their farms for several years.

3. It is learned that an engineer is to visit the site on October 24 and reassess the original plans.

4. Leslie Harvey, Secretary/Clerk of the Proprietors of the Grand Pré Dyke, calls an emergency meeting for Thursday, October 31, at 8 P.M., "at the written request of certain proprietors … to consider what action, if any, should be taken concerning the proposal of the government to take over the dyke lands."

5. *The Wolfville Acadian* Editorial, 24 October 1940

   5.1 "of course anything that is absolutely necessary in order to win a victory must be gladly sacrificed" and "on Monday evening … a strong resolution in protest against taking the land for the purpose proposed." However, the editorial then outlines the areas of compensation beyond the farms, namely the taxation loss from private to public ownership would be near $100,000, and would create a large reduction in taxation to the school sections. "All this would have to be taken into generous consideration in making up an equitable compensation."

6. *The Wolfville Acadian* headline, 31 October 1940

   Says Dykelands Not Satisfactory for Artillery Shell Testing Range

   6.1 Engineer reports to Premier A.S. MacMillan that the proposed range is too short, as at least five land miles are required. A further consideration is that the dyke walls themselves might be destroyed and the reclaimed lands inundated with sea water.

   6.2 Nevertheless, an emergency meeting has been called by those proprietors who wish to have the government take over their lands.

7. *The Wolfville Acadian* headline, 7 November 1940

   Owners of Dyke Willing To Sell

   Military Authorities May Have Grand Pré Dykelands

   Providing Owners Are Justly Remunerated

   7.1 At the 31 October meeting, L.H. Curry chaired. A resolution was introduced by F.C. Dennison and seconded by Earl Duncanson: that if the farmers were "justly and fairly remunerated" they would willingly sell their lands. After much discussion, the owners put the motion to a vote, weighing the votes on the basis of the number of acres owned by each voter at that meeting. About fifty proprietors were present and they finally voted 668 acres in favour and 7¼ acres against.

7.2 They drafted a five-paragraph resolution, the last paragraph of which reads: "Further, that we request the government, if these properties are taken, and as soon as circumstances permit, to make these lands available again for agricultural purposes, and the present owners or their heirs be given the first chance to repossess these lands or the crops therefrom in ration to their present holdings."

7.3 In the Grand Pré Dykeland Minutes ledger, sometime after Leslie Harvey had recorded the minutes of that October 31 meeting, he added a note beneath his signature stating that "Sometime after this meeting, information was received that" the federal government no longer needed the Grand Pré dykelands for military purposes.

8. *The Wolfville Acadian* headline, 14 November 1940
Will Not Use Dykes For Artillery Range
8.1 A letter from Col. L.M. Scott of the United Kingdom Technical Mission in Canada to Hon. John A. MacDonald, Minister of Agriculture, states that after further consideration, none of the sites in Nova Scotia fulfills all our requirements at present, but as munitions production develops we may return to Nova Scotia. At present, facilities available in Quebec have been found sufficient.

Thus ended the brief wartime saga of the Farmers of "Midas" Basin. However, government archival correspondence and memos on this topic must abound, because three other Nova Scotia sites were on the short list, yet all were suddenly rejected. Who instigated all this, who terminated it, and who is Col. Scott?

List of Seventy-Three Newspaper Articles Pertaining to Grand Pré Dykelands

The seventy-three articles were found in *The Acadian* (which became *The Wolfville Acadian* in 1935), a weekly newspaper begun in 1883. I have searched through the years 1907, 1913, and all of 1929–1947. A thorough search of 1883 to 1929 would produce even more information.

1907	July 12, 26
	September 13
1913	November 7
1929	January 3
	February 28
	March 29
	September 5, 19
1930	March 27
	August 7
	October 30
	November 27
1931	April 2, 9, 16, 23, 30
	March 5, 12, 19, 26
	June 25
	September 3, 10, 17
	December 3, 17
1932	April 28
	May 12, 19
	June 16
	September 22

1934	June 7
	August 23, 30
	September 6
1935	February 14
	August 8
	October 3
	December 19
1936	October 8, 15
	November 5, 12
	December 10
1937	January 14
	March 11
	April 8, 22, 29
1939	July 30
	August 17
	November 16
1940	October 24, 31
	November 7, 14, 28
1942	April 23
	July 30
1943	April 8, 29
	May 6
	June 17
	August 5, 12, 26
	September 16, 23, 30
	October 7
1944	February 10

Acadian Farming 1605–1755

1605   Samuel de Champlain planted a garden at Granville, Annapolis Co., NS

1606   Acadians were making charcoal under a turf cover of tidal marsh sods.
        Sieur de Poutricourt planted wheat, beans, oats, peas, rye, herbs, and
        barley.

1607   First water-powered grist mill, first plows, first fruit trees; also cattle,
        oxen, sheep, horses, and hogs.
        Acadian farms grew wheat, corn, beets, shallots, rye, oats, flax, carrots,
        herbs, chives, barley, hemp, parsnips, salad greens, cabbage, onions,
        peas, turnips.

1610–35 Fruit trees established: apples (Calville, Rambours, Reinettes, Bellefleur,
        Epicé), pears (Russet), cherries (Bigarreau), and plums.
        The new shoots of spruce were brewed with yeast and molasses to make
        spruce beer.
        Acadian livestock: Cattle were small and were used for milk not butter.
                            Sheep were large and used for wool.
                            Hogs
        Acadian poultry: hens, ducks, geese, and pigeons.
        Acadian farm implements:

        hoes   sickles   scythes
        spades   mattocks   rakes
        forks   axes   harrows
        wheel plows used on flat dykeland
        swing plows used on irregular upland.

REFERENCES

Anonymous. 1881. Papers relating to the Acadian French. Collection of Nova Scotia Historical Society, II

Clark, Andrew Hill. 1968. *Acadia: The Geography of Early Nova Scotia to 1760*. Madison: University Wisconsin Press

Diereville, Sieur de. 1708. *Relation of the Voyage to Port Royal in Acadia or New France*. Translation by Mrs C. Webster; ed. with notes by J.C. Webster. Champlain Society. Publ. 20, 1933

Hale, Robert. 1731. *Journal of an Expedition to Nova Scotia*. Provincial Archives Nova Scotia, Appendix B, 1968

Martin, J. Lynton. (nd; approx. 1970s). "Acadian Farming 1604–1755." In *A History of Everyday Things in Nova Scotia #3*. Halifax: Nova Scotia Museum of Natural History Library

Sequin, R.L. 1959. *L'équipment de la ferme Canadienne aux XVII et XVIII siècles*. Montreal: np

Webster, J.C. 1934. *Acadia at the end of the Seventeenth Century*. New Brunswick Museum Monograph Series 1

REFERENCES

A New Map of Nova Scotia and Cape Britain with the adjacent parts of New England and Canada (composed from many surveys: 1649, 1700, 1751). 1755. London: Thomas Jefferys

Acadia University Archives. *Dykes and Common Fields Collection*: Accession 1900.018

– *John Frederic Herbin fonds*: Accession 1996.002

Amos, Carl L. 1978. "The postglacial evolution of the Minas Basin, Nova Scotia: a sedimentological interpretation." *Journal of Sedimentary Petrology* 48: 965–82

Atlantic Geoscience Society. 2001. *The Last Billion Years: A Geological History of the Maritime Provinces of Canada*, AGS Special Publication no.15. Halifax: Nimbus Publishing Ltd

Baird, William W. 1953. *Report of Dykeland Reclamation, 1913–1952*. Nappan, NS: Experimental Farm Service, Canada Department Agriculture

Beke, G.J. 1990. "Soil development in a 100-year-old Dike near Grand Pré, Nova Scotia." *Canadian Journal of Soil Science* 70:683–92

Bishop Family Association. 1990. *Tangled Roots (Descendants of John Bishop, a New England Planter, 1709–1785)*. Greenwich, NS: Genealogical Committee of Bishop Family Association

Bishop, G.E. 1907. "The proposed aboiteau over the Cornwallis." *The Acadian*, 12 July. Wolfville, NS

– "Town Plot vs. Port Williams as site for proposed aboiteau." *The Acadian*, 26 July. Wolfville, NS

– "The aboiteau again – and always." *The Acadian*, 13 September. Wolfville, NS

Bleakney, J.S. 1986. "A sea-level scenario for Minas Basin." In "Effects of Changes in Sea Level and Tidal Range on Gulf of Maine-Bay of Fundy System." *Proceed-*

ings of Conference on Fundy Environmental Studies Committee and New England Estuarine Research Society. October 1985. Wolfville, NS: Acadia Centre for Estuarine Research

Bleakney, Sherman. 2000. "Grand Pré Dykelands: The 1940 Near Miss as a Target Range." *Kings County Vignettes*, vol. 10:10–13. Kentville, NS: Community History Committee of The Kings Historical Society

Bleakney, J.S., and K. Bailey Meyer. 1979. "Observations on salt-marsh pools, Minas Basin, Nova Scotia, 1965–1977." *Proceedings of Nova Scotia Institute of Science* 29(4):353–71

Bleakney, J.S. and Derek Davis. 1983. "Discovery of an undisturbed bed of 3800 year old oysters (*Crassostrea virginica*) in Minas Basin, Nova Scotia." *Proceedings of Nova Scotia Institute of Science* 33: 1–6

Boutin, Émile, and Marc Guiteny. 1987. *Breton Salt*. Monaco: Éditions Vieux Chouan

Brasseaux, Carl A. 1987. *The founding of New Acadia: the beginnings of Acadian life in Louisiana, 1765–1803*. Baton Rouge: Louisiana State University Press

Brown, John F.S. 1983. "The Ecology of *Fundulus heteroclitus* at Kingsport salt marsh, Nova Scotia." MSc thesis. Biology Department, Acadia University, Wolfville, NS

Butler, William Robert. 1894. "Petition 19376, Province of Nova Scotia, for Water Lot in Minas Basin, that was deed/granted on 12 April 1894." Provincial Archives of Nova Scotia, Halifax, NS

Butzer, Karl W. 2002. "French Wetland Agriculture in Atlantic Canada and Its European Roots: Different Avenues of Historical Diffusion." *Annals of the Association of American Geographers* 92(3):451–70

Cameron, Harcourt L. 1956. "Nova Scotia Historic Sites." *Transactions of the Royal Society Canada*, vol. L, 3rd series, section II, June 1956

Census Records of 17th and 18th Centuries for Nova Scotia and New France. Ottawa, National Archives of Canada, G1-466

Chief Engineer. 1906. "Re government wharf on bank of Cornwallis River at Wolfville" in *Federal Government, Department of Transport, iv, Report of Chief Engineer, Sessional Paper* no. 19, 5–6, Edward VIII, A.1906. 78–9

Clark, Andrew H. 1968. *Acadia: The Geography of Early Nova Scotia to 1760*. Madison: University of Wisconsin Press

Conlin, Dan. 2001. *Report on possible 19th century wreck in Wolfville Harbour*. Heritage Research Permit A2001-NS43 and Report 2001-45-12. Halifax, NS: Maritime Museum of the Atlantic

Conrad, Margaret, ed. 1988. *They Planted Well*. Fredericton: Acadiensis Press

Cormier, Yves. 1990. *Les Aboiteaux en Acadie: hier et aujourd'hui*. Moncton, NB: Chaire d'études acadiennes

Crane, Jonathan. 1819. "On Diking." *The Acadian Recorder*, 27 February 1819. Halifax: Provincial Archives of Nova Scotia

Crowell, Peter, and Austin Saulnier. 1998. "Festival de la Barge: The Rebirth of an Acadian Tradition." *The Argus, Newsletter of Argyle Municipality Historical and Genealogical Society* 10(4): winter 1998

Cuthbertson, Brian. 1996. *Wolfville and Grand Pré, Past and Present.* Halifax: Formac Publications

Daborn, G.R., and C. Pennachetti. 1979. "Physical Oceanographic and Sedimentological Studies in the Southern Bight of Minas Basin." *Proceedings, Nova Scotia Institute of Science* 29:315–33

Dalrymple, R.W., Carl L. Amos, and Gary Yeo. 1992. "Nature and Evolution of Tidal Sedimentation in Minas Basin-Cobequid Bay Area, Bay of Fundy." *Guidebook.* Field Excursion A-8. Geological Association of Canada and Mineralogical Association of Canada, Joint Annual Meeting, Wolfville, NS, 25–7 May 1992

Davies, Blodwen. 1927. "Wanted: A Literary Executor." (With quotes from Archibald Lampman about J.F. Herbin). *The New Outlook*, Nov. 30

Deschamps, Isaac (born 1722, died 1785). Undated manuscript describing Acadian agriculture and dyke construction. Provincial Archives of Nova Scotia, WIM COLL Acadiensia Nova, 35

Desplanque, Con. 1977. *Ranges and Other Characteristics of the Tides Along the Eastern Canadian Seaboard.* Amherst: Maritime Resource Management Service (and in correspondence)

Desplanque, Con, and David J. Mossman. 2000. "Fundamentals of Fundy Tides." In Abstracts of Papers presented at Coastal Zone Canada 2000 International Conference, Saint John, NB, 17–22 September 2000

Dohler, G. 1989. *Tides in Canadian Waters.* Ottawa: Canadian Hydrographic Service, Department of Fisheries and Oceans

Donohue, H.V. Jr, and Grantham, R.G. 1989. *Geological Highway Map of Nova Scotia.* 2nd ed. AGS Special Publication no.1. Halifax: Atlantic Geoscience Society

Doucet, Clive. 1999. *Notes from Exile: On Being Acadian.* Toronto: McClelland and Stewart

Dunn, Brenda. 1990. *The Acadians of Minas.* Revised ed. Ottawa: Environment Canada

Eagles, Douglas E. 1975. *A History of Horton Township, Kings County, Nova Scotia, Through Maps and Documents.* Privately mimeographed. Wolfville: Acadia University Archives

Eaton, A.W.H. 1910. *History of Kings County Nova Scotia: Heart of the Acadian Land.* Salem, Mass.: Salem Press

Fowler, Jonathan. In correspondence and conversation, 2001–04. Halifax, NS (fowler@ns.sympatico.ca)

Gallant, Melvin. 1986. *The Country of Acadia.* Toronto: Simon & Pierre (translated from the 1980 French edition by Elliot Shek)

Graham, Christopher. 1878. "Petition 14203, Province of Nova Scotia, for Water Lot in Minas Basin, that was deed/granted on 25 May 1878." Provincial Archives of Nova Scotia, Halifax, NS

Grant, D.R. 1975. "Recent coastal submergence of the Maritime Provinces." *Proceedings and Transactions of the Nova Scotia Institute of Science* 27(3):83–102

Haliburton, T.C. 1829. *An Historical and Statistical Account of Nova Scotia.* Halifax: Joseph Howe

Herbin, John Frederic. 1909. *The Marshlands.* 3rd ed. and *The Trail of the Tide.* Toronto: William Briggs

– 1911 (ed). *The History of Grand Pré.* Saint John, New Brunswick: Barnes & Co.

– 1911. School scribbler with transcribed notes from Minute Book of 1804 to 1806 concerning the planning and construction of the first of the "Wickwire" dykes extending from Wolfville to Long Island. Acadia University Archives: John Frederic Herbin fonds, Accession 1996.002

Hilchey, J.D. 1956. "A Comparison of Marshland and Upland Soils." Unpublished report, 8 June 1956. Truro, NS: Nova Scotia Department of Agriculture and Marketing

Hilchey, J.D., and D.B. Cann. nd. *Report of Marshland Survey, 1950–51.* Truro, NS: Nova Scotia Department of Agriculture and Marketing

Johnson Scrapbook. 1800s. Nova Scotia Archives and Records Management. MG9, vol. 18. 115

Keppie, J. Duncan. 1979. *Geological Map of Nova Scotia.* Halifax, NS: Nova Scotia Department of Mines and Energy

Leonard, Kevin. 1991. "Origin and Dispersal of Dykeland Technology." *Les Cahiers de la Société Historique Acadienne* 22(1):1–13

Lescarbot, Marc. 1911 ed. *The History of New France, vol. II.* Translated by W.L. Grant. Toronto: The Champlain Society

Little, Otis. 1748. *The State of Trade in the Northern Colonies Considered with an Account of Their Produce and a Particular Description of Nova Scotia.* London: np

Longfellow, Henry Wadsworth. 1962 (reprint of 1847 ed.). *Evangeline: A Tale of Acadie.* Halifax: Nimbus Publishing Ltd

– 1908 (reprint of 1847 ed.). *Evangeline: A Tale of Acadie.* Introduction by John Frederic Herbin. Toronto: William Briggs

Macfarlane, Andrew. 2000. *Shore Erosion at Boot Island National Wildlife Area 1900–2000.* Sackville, NB: Canadian Wildlife Service

Macmillan, D.H. 1966. *Tides.* London: CR Books Ltd

Map of 1711–1712. *Part of North America: A Description of the Bay of Fundy.* London: Thomas Bowles

Map of 1891. MacKinlay coloured map, *Nova Scotia & Island of Cape Breton.* Acadia University Archives, John Frederic Herbin fonds, Accession 1996.002

Martin, J. Lynton. (nd; possibly 1970s) "Acadian Farming: 1604–1755." In *A History of Everyday Things in Nova Scotia.* Halifax: Nova Scotia Museum Library

– 1982. *Hay and Grain on the Small Pioneer Farm in Nova Scotia.* Halifax: Nova Scotia Museum Library

Milligan, David C. 1987. *Maritime Dykelands: The 350 Year Struggle*. Truro: Nova Scotia Department of Agriculture and Marketing

Minute Book 1882–1936. Meetings of Proprietors of Wickwire Dyke. Acadia University Archives, Wolfville, NS

Minute Book 1884–1950. Meetings of Proprietors of Grand Pré Dykelands. Kings County Heritage Museum Archives, Kentville, NS

Moody, Barry. 1981. *The Acadians*. Toronto: Grolier Ltd

Moore, R.G., S.A. Ferguson, R.C. Boehner, and C.M. Kennedy. 2000. *Geological Map of Wolfville-Windsor Area*. Halifax, NS: Nova Scotia Department of Natural Resources, Minerals and Energy Branch. OFM ME 2000-3

Paratte, Henri-Dominique. 1998. Revised 1991 ed. *Acadians*. Halifax: Nimbus Publishing Ltd

van Proosdij, Danika, Jeff Ollerhead, and Robin G.D. Davidson-Arnott. 2000. "Annual and Seasonal Variations in Erosion and Accretion in a Macro-Tidal Salt-marsh, Bay of Fundy." In Abstracts of Papers presented at Coastal Zone Canada 2000 International Conference, Saint John, NB, 17–22 September 2000

Rippon, Stephen. 2000. *The Transformation of Coastal Wetlands: Exploitation and Management of Marshland Landscapes in North West Europe during the Roman and Medieval Periods*. Oxford: Oxford University Press, for The British Academy

Roland, Albert E. 1982. *Geological Background and Physiography of Nova Scotia*. Halifax: Nova Scotia Institute of Science

Ross, Sally, and Alphonse Deveau. 1992. *The Acadians of Nova Scotia, Past and Present*. Halifax: Nimbus Publishing Ltd

Sequin, R.L. 1959. "L'équipment de la ferme Canadienne aux XVII et XVIII siècles. *Revue d'Histoire de l'Amérique Française* 1959/60 13(4):492–508

Soil Survey Maps for Kings County. 1966. Nova Scotia Soil Survey. Report no.15. Truro, NS: Canada Department Agriculture

Starr, R.W. 1891. "The French in Kings County." In *Transactions and Reports of the Fruit Growers Association of Nova Scotia*. Kentville, NS: *The Advertiser*

Sutherland, Theofilus. 1760. *A Plan of the Several Lots and Divisions Laid Out to a Right Formerly Draughted in the Name of Theofilus Sutherland in Horton*. John Bishop Jr, District Surveyor. Halifax: Provincial Archives of Nova Scotia

Whitelaw, Marjory. 1997. *The Wellington Dyke*. Halifax: Nimbus Publishing Ltd and Nova Scotia Museum

Wolfville Breaching of Dyke. 1913. "Destruction to dykes." Editorial, *The Acadian*, 7 November. Wolfville, NS

Wolfville Harbour Sewer. 1937. "Wolfville's proposed new asset." Editor's Mail Box, *The Acadian*, 11 March. Wolfville, NS

Wynn, Graeme. 1979. "Late Eighteenth-Century Agriculture on the Bay of Fundy Marshlands." *Acadiensis*, viii (2): Spring 1979

INDEX

Acadians, 3–7

Acadian farming, 211–12

aboiteau: clappet valve, 50, 58, Fig. 5.4; installation, 50, app. 5; sluice log or box, 55–7, Fig. 5.4; walls and sluice, 50–8, 84, 110, 146, Fig. 5.4

Alward, W.J., 143

Black Grass. *See* grasses

Black Landing, 119, Fig. 3.5, Fig. 9.1.1

blacksmiths: Leonard Estabrooks, 40; John B. Lyon, 40; Charles A.D. Siddall, 40

Boot Island, 90, 138–40, Fig. 9.4.1; erosion rates, Table 9.4.1; old dykes, 90; Table 6.2

borrow pits, 23, 135, Figs 5.2, 9.3.4

botany: dykeland aspects, 20–33

Boudreau Landing, 19, Fig. 3.4

breakwater posts, 137, Fig. 9.3.5

Bremner, James, 48

Cameron, Harcourt, 72

canals, 82, 85, 146, Figs 6.2, 6.5, 9.5.5

chronology, 173–7

clappet valve, 50–8, Fig. 5.4

continental drift, 8–10

Crane, Jonathan, 45, 57, app. 5

Dead Dyke, 89–90, 122–3, Figs 9.1.3, 9.1.5

deadman iron rods, 106, 137, Fig. 9.3.6

Deportation Creek, 73, 85, 89–90, 105, Figs 9.1.2, 9.1.6, app. 8

Deschamps, Isaac, 25

Division Dyke, 145, 148

dykes, 20–94; construction, 44–70, 61–9, Figs 4.2, 4.15, 5.2, 5.8, 5.10, Table 5.1, app. 5; destruction, 18, 50, 60, 106–8, 129–30, Figs 5.3, 7.6, 7.9, 7.10, 9.2.4, 9.5.3; Record Book of repairs to, 147–55, Tables 9.5.1–9.5.3; repairs to, 59–60, Figs 4.15, 5.10; sizes, 49–50, 59, Fig. 5.1; sods for, 47, Figs 5.6, 5.7; sod placement on wall, 47–8, Fig. 5.8; sods per rod of wall, 63–7, Figs 5.1–5.4

Eldridge, James, 39, 53, 106

enclosures, 71–94, Fig. 6.5, Table 6.1; numbers 1–12, 83–90

farm fields: shapes of, 79–80, Figs 6.8, 6.9

fish, 84

fish trap creeks, 84–6, Fig. 6.10

forests: submerged, 128, Fig. 9.2.2

Frail, George, 24, 47, 53

Gaspereau River Estuary, 128–33, Figs 1.1 9.2.1, 9.2.4

geology, geography, and tides, 8–10, Fig. 2.1

Gertridge, Ellis, 29, 48, Fig. 4.14

to wharf, 95, 99, Fig. 7.2; in Wolfville area, 95, 99, Figs 7.1–7.5

Seros Cycle, 17–18, 60, Table 3.1

shells: mollusc shells, 99, 104; mud snail shells, 87; oyster shells, 13; soft-shelled clams, 99, 161

shoreline profiles, 165–8, 87, Figs 10.1, 10.2

sluice box (or log), 55–8, Fig. 5.4. *See also* aboiteau

sod cutting, 47, Fig. 4.11

sod drags, 60, Fig. 5.9

sod fitting, 47–8

sod pits, 25, 135, Fig. 4.2. 9.3.4

sods: silts in, 29–31, Figs 4.5, 4.6

sods: structure of, 27–33, Figs 4.3, 4.4

sods: weights of, 27–9, Tables 4.1, 4.2, 5.5

Soldier's Creek, 131

South Pole, 8

spades, 33–43; blade construction, 34–6, 41–3, Fig. 4.16; data sheet, app. 4; history of, 36; how used, 22–3, 36–7, Figs 4.12, 4.14; list of, Table 4.4; shapes, 34–6, Figs 4.10, 4.13, 4.16; types, 35, Fig. 4.10; wooden shaft, 42–3, Fig. 4.14

staddles. *See* hay staddles

Starr's Point Creeks, 78, Fig. 6.7

submerged bridges, 87

submerged forests, 128, Fig. 9.2.2

surveyors: John Bishop, 110; A.E. Church, 112; Hugh Fletcher, 109; Oliver Lyman, 111, 116, 155–6; Charles Morse, 120

suspended sediments, 29, 96–7, Fig. 4.6

Sutherland, Theofilus, 109, 149–51, 169

tidal meadows, 6, Fig. 4.3; fertility of, 21–2, 31

tides, 11–19; amplitudes, 13–16, 95, Fig. 3.1; of Bay of Fundy, 13, 18, Fig. 3.2; nutrient richness, 18; resonance of, 12; riptides, 12; types, 15, Fig. 3.3

Toye Dyke, 74, 87

Tufts, Robie, 145

West Grand Pré dyke, 140–7; repairs of 1931, 148–55, Tables 9.5.1–9.5.3

whales and seals, 86–7

Wickwire Dyke, other names of, 72–3, 171

Wickwire Dyke region, 140–7, Fig. 9.0.1, 9.5.1; changes in wall location, 140–7, Fig. 9.5.2; cost of 1929 repairs, 143–4; destruction of, 143–4, Figs 5.5, 9.5.2–9.5.4; first dyking of, 62, Figs 5.5, 9.5.1; plank facing, 144, Figs 9.5.3, 9.6.1

Wolfville Harbour area, 155–64, Fig. 7.2; deepwater port proposal, 155, 162; early Acadian dyke at, 155, Fig. 7.2; old town sewer line, 159, Fig. 7.2, 9.6.3; Planter Dyke of 1806, 156, Figs 7.1–7.3, 9.6.3; river bank wharf, history of, 156–9, Figs 9.6.1–9.6.3; river bank wharf road, 158, Fig. 7.2

woodchucks, 48